Responsible Business

Responsible Business

How to Manage a CSR Strategy Successfully

Edited by
Manfred Pohl and Nick Tolhurst

A John Wiley & Sons, Ltd., Publication

Registered office
John Wiley & Sons Ltd, The Atrium, Southern Gate, Chichester, West Sussex, PO19
8SQ, United Kingdom

For details of our global editorial offices, for customer services and for information
about how to apply for permission to reuse the copyright material in this book please
see our website at www.wiley.com

Library of Congress Cataloging-in-Publication Data

Responsible business : how to manage a CSR strategy successfully / edited by
Manfred Pohl and Nick Tolhurst.
    p. cm.
  Includes bibliographical references and index.
  ISBN 978-0-470-71242-9 (cloth)
  1. Social responsibility of business. I. Pohl, Manfred, 1944- II. Tolhurst, Nick.
  HD60.R4715 2010
  658.4'08—dc22

                                                                          2009054389

A catalogue record for this book is available from the British Library.

ISBN 978-0-470-71242-9

Typeset in 9.5/14pt Bitstream by Toppan Best-set Premedia Limited
Printed in Great Britain by TJ International Ltd, Padstow, Cornwall, UK

Contents

Acknowledgements

There are many people who helped to make this book possible. First of all, we would like to place on record our profound gratitude to all those authors who contributed their valuable time to this project, without whom of course this book would not have been possible. We would also like to express our thanks to Professor Gerassamo Notaras of the National Bank of Greece as well as Sandra Silvia Huble and Aron Embaye from ICCA who backed this publication from its inception. Further, a special debt of thanks is owed to Christine Pehl, Nicola McClellan, Kerstin Petter, Katja Böhmer, Marnie Guirana, Gabriella Massaglia and Francesca Warren, as well as, on a more personal level, Davina, Daniel, Angela and Roger Tolhurst for their steadfast support. We would also like to thank our publishing team at Wiley – Claire Plimmer, Michaela Fay, Jo Golesworthy, Natalie Girach and Vivienne Wickham – for much good advice, logistical assistance and, most of all, patience.

Most importantly, though, we would like to express our deep gratitude to the members of ICCA for making this book possible and, most especially, Takis Arapoglou, for his inspiration and good advice with this, as with so many other ICCA projects.

Manfred Pohl
Nick Tolhurst
February 2010

About the editors

Professor Manfred Pohl is the founder and CEO of the Institute for Corporate Culture Affairs (ICCA). Born in Bliesransbach, Germany, in 1944, he received his PhD in history from the University of Saarbrücken, Germany, in 1972. Since then, he has been an Honorary Professor at the University of Frankfurt. He is currently the deputy chairman of the European Association for Banking History e.V and of the Frankfurter Zukunftsrat e.V. In October 2001 he received the European Award for Culture at the European Parliament in Strasbourg. From June 2002, Prof. Pohl was head of the Corporate Cultural Affairs department at Deutsche Bank in Frankfurt, responsible for corporate social responsibility strategy, all cultural activities as well as charitable donations and sponsoring within Deutsche Bank globally before retiring in May 2007. Professor Pohl has written over 100 books, articles and monographs on topics as varied as business history, culture, politics, corporate ethics and travel.

Nick Tolhurst is managing director of the ICCA, which he joined in April 2004, a fellow of the Institute for Cultural Diplomacy and a lecturer on CSR at the Steinbeis University in Berlin. Before joining ICCA, he worked for the British Foreign Ministry in Germany, advising British companies in Germany and German companies investing in the UK. Previously, he worked for the European Commission at DG II (Economics and Financial Affairs) preparing for the introduction of the euro in differing cultures and economic systems. He studied at London Metropolitan University (UK) and completed a master's degree at Osnabrück University (Germany), both in European studies specialising in economics and cultural studies. Nick Tolhurst has written and edited many publications on CSR, corporate culture and economics, including, most recently, *The A to Z of Corporate Social Responsibility* and the *ICCA Handbook of Corporate Social Responsibility*. He writes regularly in the media on CSR and related issues.

List of contributors

Andrew Cartland
Managing Director and Co-founder, Acre Resources

Isaac H. Desta
Lecturer and MBA Projects Co-ordinator, Catholic University
of Eastern Africa

Hans-Ulrich Doerig
Chairman, Credit Suisse Group

Aron Embaye
Senior Project Manager, ICCA

Ulises Flores
Universidad Autónoma de San Luis Potosí

Anselm Iwundu
Project Leader, Fairfood International

Judith Kohler
Project Manager, GTZ GmbH (German Technical Cooperation)

Oliver Laasch
Professor, Tecnológico de Monterrey (ITESM), Mexico

Jason Leadbitter
Sustainability Manager, Ineos ChlorVinyls

Irina Leibold
Consultant, Scholz & Friends Reputation

Siegmar Ley
Managing Director, Host GmbH

Jonathan S. Lux
Partner, Ince & Co International

Clemens Mulokozi
Head of Sport Sponsoring and Private Customer Marketing,
HypoVereinsbank

Marie-Louise Orre
Lawyer, Ince & Co International

Bettina Palazzo
Managing Director, Palazzo & Palazzo

Manfred Pohl
Founder and CEO, ICCA

Gerhard Prätorius
Head of CSR and Sustainability, Volkswagen AG

Chris Preist
Head of UK team of the Sustainable IT Ecosystem Lab,
Hewlett Packard

Hélène Roques
Director Sustainable Development, Accor Group

Klaus-Peter Storme
CSR Manager, HypoVereinsbank

Dr Norbert Taubken
Business Director, Scholz & Friends Reputation

Ralph Thurm
Director, Sustainability Strategies, Deloitte Enterprise Risk Services

Nick Tolhurst
Managing Director, ICCA

Volker Türk
Manager CR Reporting, E.ON AG

Dr Sam Vasehgi
Senior Manager CR&S Services, Deloitte & Touche GmbH

Martin G. Viehöver
Manager CR&S Services, Deloitte & Touche GmbH

Wayne Visser
CEO, CSR International

Kirsten B. Wenzel
Senior Consultant, Brands & Values GmbH

Introduction

Manfred Pohl & Nick Tolhurst

Over the last two decades, the subject of corporate social responsibility (CSR) has made the journey from NGOs and academia on to the front pages of the financial and business press and into the boardroom and MBA courses. Indeed, as that most hard-headed of business media – *The Economist* – announced in the opening line of its 2005 special supplement on CSR, 'The movement on corporate social responsibility has won the battle for ideas.' Yet despite this, much literature on the subject still seems to be aimed at academics, concentrating on theories rather than on practical ideas and real-life perspectives of what being in the CSR sector entails. This book is thus aimed at those who – be they at university or already in business – are looking to pursue or build upon a career in a CSR-related field and deals with the nuts and bolts of how to run a CSR strategy successfully in a company or public organisation. As such, it unashamedly steers clear of most of the theories and academic debates surrounding the subject; rather, it concentrates on setting out, in a jargon-free way, strategies for incorporating a responsible business approach within an organisation in a way that is accessible to both those new to the subject and those more established in this area.

The book is divided into chapters that deal with the building blocks of CSR and sustainability, informed, wherever possible, by practical, real-life examples. The chapters and authors fully reflect the wide responsibilities now covered under the general term CSR, with practical advice on the individual aspects of a CSR manager's role as well as industry information and perspectives from those responsible for managing CSR in specific companies.

While we make no claims that this volume is completely exhaustive in the rapidly changing world of CSR, we have attempted to cover as many topics, perspectives and responsibilities as possible. This publication has also been deliberately structured so that while each chapter should complement the others, they can all be read and referred to individually on a stand-alone basis as need dictates.

The first chapter introduces us to the role, aims and activities of a sustainability manager through the personal experience of Jason Leadbitter, sustainability manager for a large chemical company. He not only deals with the tasks of the position itself, but also examines the relationship of a sustainability manger to top management and provides clear guidelines to enable sustainability/CSR managers to realise their potential to advance sustainable business practices within their organisation. Following this, Bettina Palazzo then outlines the reasons why stakeholder dialogue is so fundamentally important to modern business. Indeed, for many CSR managers, managing expectations, communication and dialogue with their various stakeholders has become, over the last few years, the major part of their role. As well as outlining what stakeholder dialogue involves, Palazzo also provides best-practice examples from the business world and provides a step-by-step guide to successful implementation. In the third chapter, Andrew Cartland looks at the CSR employment situation and examines who works in the sector, as well as addressing some of the key questions in CSR recruitment from both the employers' and the potential employees' perspectives. The chapter also includes information how to retain CSR staff, how CSR staff are organised within a company, how much they're paid and how the positions are placed. Jonathan Lux and Marie-Louise Orre provide an insight into the fast-changing legal world of CSR management in Chapter 4. Here, they examine how the legal implications of CSR practices are rapidly shifting from being a matter of voluntary practice to a subject of legal pressure and enforcement. Real-life examples such as Nike and Chiquita are used to illustrate the enhanced legal demands companies face as well as the absorption of CSR norms into standard business law.

Moving on to an issue that has risen rapidly up the CSR management agenda over the last few years – corporate volunteering – Kirsten Wenzel looks at how to achieve the best results in this field. Wenzel outlines the advantages of strategic corporate volunteering as part of a CSR strategy and illustrates the beneficial impact of corporate volunteering on human resources, stakeholder relations and company reputation as well as providing specific guidelines on how to successfully plan and implement corporate volunteering as part of a CSR strategy. In Chapter 6, Martin Viehöver looks into what CSR verification in practice involves. As the demand for responsible business practices has grown, so has the requirement for such activity to be properly measured and verified – both inside and outside the company. The chapter continues by examining the most important aspects that a CSR manager should know about sustainability verification, and outlines the most important assurance standards for CSR managers, as well as providing a first-guidance and a best-practice checklist. Following on from auditing, Ralph Thurm from Deloitte considers the importance and benefits of sustainability and CSR reporting, and provides background on the rapid development from the first generation to the next level of 'strategic sustainability reporting'. The chapter sets down the necessary steps to be undertaken to achieve the best results, provides information on Global Reporting Initiative's sustainability reporting guidelines and finally outlines pointers to future trends in this area.

The difficult subject of how best to communicate CSR is addressed by Norbert Taubken and Irina Leibold of Scholz and Friends in Chapter 8. They outline the dos and don'ts of successful CSR communication and stress the importance of communication in two crucial areas: internally with the company's own employees, and externally with target groups. Finally, the chapter provides a practical checklist for turning the CSR of a brand into a selling point and identifies the best communication channels for this. The next chapter, by Siegmar Ley, deals with the practicalities of events (CSR, HR or volunteering) from a project management perspective, as increasingly such events are organised under the auspices of a CSR department. Here the emphasis is on the business plan and tools for developing good practice in the run-up to events in order to align such events with other corporate goals.

Chapter 10 deals with the vital role that advances in IT can play in achieving sustainability goals and reducing companies' carbon and ecological footprints. Here Chris Preist illustrates this not only by examining how existing equipment can be used more efficiently but also by using IT proactively to develop more sustainable business models.

After looking at specific activities within CSR, the emphasis then switches to how CSR managers in industries and particular sectors tackle their roles, with four articles drawn from the banking, automotive and pharmaceutical industries. In the first of these, Hélène Roques, director of sustainable development at Accor, offers a personal perspective of a CSR manager in an international hotel business, detailing the various programmes enacted, an insider's guide to why specific CSR projects were undertaken, the personal characteristics required by a CSR manager and the vital importance of CSR managers having operational experience in order to ensure success. This is followed by a chapter on sustainable banking and microfinance, which provides a background to one of the fastest-growing CSR tools in the finance sector – microfinance. The author outlines the aims, approaches and challenges of microfinance, as well as the benefits both for the recipients and for the bank itself, in this case Credit Suisse. Gerhard Prätorius then presents a personal insight into CSR in the automotive sector with a perspective on Volkswagen CSR activity, from stakeholder relations to supply chain management and the mission of the company. The author places particular emphasis on the environmental challenges facing the industry, as well as addressing challenging issues such as carbon-neutral travel. Moving from one of the major corporations to smaller and medium-sized enterprises, Nick Tolhurst interviews Horst Erhardt, one of the leading lights behind Betapharm's groundbreaking use of CSR as an innovation and marketing strategy in the pharmaceutical field. As well as exploring the possibilities for CSR in this sector, the interview also examines the often underestimated potential for CSR in smaller companies.

A more traditional aspect of CSR is given a new angle in Chapter 15, as Clemens Mulokozi & Klaus-Peter Storme from HypoVereinsbank outline the advantages of sponsorship in business terms and how it can fit in to a CSR strategy. The authors look at the new CSR dilemmas and challenges facing sponsoring – in this case sport – which can involve political and social sensitivities. As sport sponsorship is being transformed from traditional 'passive' forms to more socially proactive ones, the authors look at the role that sports sponsorship can play in terms of social responsibility, where to engage and what to avoid. In Chapter 16, Anselm Iwundu explores the increasing importance of supply chain management as a part of a company's overall commitment to responsible business and provides a five-step practical guide to ensuring that companies' supply chains are sustainable. The author provides real-life business examples from the agri-food industry sector, which has become perhaps the most crucial, and in many ways the most visible, industry in debates on supply-chain good practice. Staying with the international aspects of CSR, the next two chapters look at CSR in developing countries, firstly through Judith Köhler's article on the role, advantages and challenges of public private partnerships (PPPs). Informed by her experience with the German development agency, the author outlines the role that cross-national PPPs can play in capacity-building and environmental projects, while Isaac Desta provides a background to CSR in developing countries, with particular emphasis on the burgeoning role of local CSR initiatives as well as the supply chain and how companies can achieve staggeringly effective – and efficient – results through imaginative, well-thought-out CSR policies.

The book is rounded off with three chapters devoted to the future of CSR. First, an aspect of CSR that has rapidly shot up the agenda in recent years – carbon offsetting – is addressed, and the question of how this can become an integral part of a company's CSR strategy is explored. Then, Oliver Laasch and Ulises Flores examine emerging management tools and how companies are finding new ways and techniques to realise the full potential of CSR in business. The chapter is based on a number of interviews and surveys with business leaders from internationally recognised companies. Finally, Wayne Visser considers the future of business as he argues that CSR in its present form has only gone part of the way, and outlines how the next step – CSR 2.0 – will become less Western-orientated, less risk-averse and less of a 'nice-to-have' niche, instead evolving into a mass-market 'must have' that will become incorporated into 'companies' DNA'.

We very much hope this book proves useful for you and we welcome feedback on any issue that arises out of it.

What does a sustainability manager do?

Jason Leadbitter

In this chapter, the role, aims and activities of a sustainability manager are described, based on the personal experience of the author, who is a sustainability manager for a large chemical company – he offers a step-by-step outline of the goals that are important, how they can be achieved and the challenges that will be faced.

Company background

I wrote this chapter to provide a personal perspective of what a sustainability manager actually does – in my case, for the INEOS ChlorVinyls chemical company. INEOS is the third largest chemical company in the world, with an extensive chemical portfolio. My responsibilities relate specifically to sustainability within chlorine chemistry and, in particular, to the plastic PVC and other chlorinated products. We are the largest European manufacturer of PVC, with plants in Norway, Sweden, Germany and the UK. In February 2008 my former company, Hydro Polymers (also a PVC producer), was acquired by INEOS. Much of what I have learnt on this personal journey, to which I will refer in this chapter, relates back to my experience with Hydro Polymers, although the opportunities and challenges under new ownership provide renewed vigour and excitement in the pursuit of sustainability.

The role of a sustainability manager

The overall aim is to provide the reader with a clear insight into the practicalities involved in being a sustainability manager. In particular, precisely what does a sustainability manager do? To merely write some kind of job description is important, but this is too prescriptive. It is rather like reading the rules of chess, which is often dull and boring – it is only when you play the game that things become exciting. That said, we do need rules and principles to help guide us in the right direction and to make smart business decisions along the way, i.e. towards sustainability, or, as in the game of chess, to achieve checkmate. I also want to firmly differentiate, as I do in my mind, between two distinct roles in any organisation, namely those of the corporate social responsibility (CSR) manager and the sustainability manager. They may be one and the same person and, if that is the case, please note that there is a wealth of difference between these roles. A CSR manager's responsibility has to do with how companies engage in societal issues on a voluntary basis, usually in collaboration with stakeholders, with an emphasis on public relations. Conversely, the sustainability manager should be addressing the longer-term strategy of the organisation regarding its core business and commitment to innovation in moving the business towards sustainability. Of course, the two roles are complementary and there is a necessary degree of overlap. However, to address these issues as one individual is a tall order, both from a practicality perspective and in differentiating the roles in your mind.

Down to business

To be effective as a sustainability manager, a series of essential yet basic criteria must first be met:

► commitment from top management

► an understanding of the core business activities of the organisation

► an understanding of what is meant by sustainable development and sustainability

► an appreciation of where the company is today and where it should be heading

► the skills to influence and motivate the organisation to move in the right direction and thereby execute the right actions.

Commitment from top management

There is nothing more frustrating for sustainability managers than recycling their paper clips. The job has to be taken seriously by top management and there needs to be a mechanism whereby the sustainability strategy relates directly to short- and longer-term business plans, i.e. these must be aligned to maximise efficiency and ensure that all elements of the company are rowing in the right direction. The sustainability manager should be playing a key role in any organisation to ensure the long-term sustainability of that business. The commitment needs to go beyond just fine words. Talk is easy – it is the getting down to work that counts.

Core business and activities of the organisation

Sustainability managers need to get under the skin of their organisation. There needs to be a systemic appreciation of what the organisation does or provides. We should not underestimate the sustainability footprint of any organisation – whether social, economic or environmental – and that of its products or the processes used in their manufacture. To make improvements, there is an obvious need to know the basics – this might be related to operational processes as well as the manufactured products or to those services provided by the organisation.

What is meant by sustainable development and sustainability?

No doubt you will have heard these terms mentioned many times, but what do they really mean to you? One of the simplest explanations came from Jonathon Porritt, one of the founding directors of the sustainable development charity Forum for the Future, in the UK. Put simply, sustainability could be described as a defined *state*, i.e. the point at which you could continue indefinitely without serious erosion to mankind or the environment. Conversely, sustainable development is the *process* that drives us towards sustainability. That said, if you type sustainability into Google, you will get literally hundreds of definitions. What is important is what sustainability really means to you and the organisation you represent.

An appreciation of where the company is today and where it should be heading

An effective sustainability manager should ask three questions that logically follow on from the question in the previous section:

1. Do we have a definition of sustainability?

2. Considering this definition, what is the gap between where we are today and where we are heading?

3. What can we do to bridge this gap?

The skills to influence and motivate the organisation to move in the right direction and thereby execute the right actions

Such skills are essential to ensure that a sustainability manager is fully equipped to take on this demanding task. Being a good manager merits a whole section in its own right. There are numerous management books that articulate the essential skills of an effective manager. For me, sustainability managers must demonstrate a belief and passion that they are making a difference to the company. Often they may be working with few, if any, subordinates. Consequently, the business case for sustainability must be compelling, and also pragmatic and sufficient to win the hearts and minds of peers. The sustainability manager must also be prepared to challenge senior management constructively, with good information and clear arguments about the benefits to the business in the long term of taking a more sustainable path. This may, at times, challenge fixed assumptions and 'sacred cows', so good relationships and sound arguments are essential.

So how do we get started?

There are many theories about organisational culture that lead to logical engagement in sustainability – either through the transitional stage of companies moving from regulatory compliance to addressing eco-efficiency and then sustainability, or by benchmarking themselves against their competitors. In our case, we were pushed into it courtesy of Greenpeace. Back in the late 1990s, the PVC manufacturing industry was singled out principally because of our use of chlorine chemistry. In Greenpeace's eyes, God created all the elements but one – chlorine, which was created by the Devil. And since PVC consumed around one-third of total chlorine output, it was seen as a good single-issue target. Towards the end of the 1990s, our industry had to act to prevent potential legislation and to stem the major threat that was being created by the Greenpeace campaign. Ironically, it was environmentalists themselves who questioned Greenpeace's thinking that merely by phasing out PVC, the planet would be saved. Important questions needed to be asked, from a sustainability perspective, about what would replace PVC if its use in pipes, cables and a whole range of other applications was to be phased out (see Leadbitter (2002) for further reading on this process).

Across the industry, a major 'European voluntary commitment' was begun, known as Vinyl 2010 (see www.vinyl2010.org for details), whilst a separate, independent process initiated by an international sustainable development charity, The Natural Step, tasked the industry with answering the three questions outlined above. Firstly, did we have a definition of sustainability? This was a simple question to answer at the time: no we did not. Consequently, an investigation was completed using a sustainability model, The Natural Step Framework (see www.naturalstep.org/en/applying-framework for details), the principal outcome of which was the identification of five key sustainability challenges facing the industry if it was to become fully sustainable:

▶ the industry should move towards becoming carbon-neutral

▶ the industry should commit towards controlled-loop recycling

▶ the industry should phase out persistent organic compounds

▶ the industry should use sustainable additives in PVC

▶ the industry should engage the whole supply chain in order to address sustainability.

So, in a matter of a few months, not only had we been provided with a definition of sustainability, but we were also provided with details regarding the 'gap' between where we were and full sustainability. All that was now needed were the actions required to bridge this gap. This sounds simple, but first of all, let us review the basic criteria highlighted above.

Commitment from top management

The threat posed by Greenpeace ensured that top management of all European PVC producers were fully supportive of the actions required to address sustainability, although some serious concerns were being expressed about the cost of achieving this. Speaking of which, to become truly sustainable, the economic element of sustainability is hugely important – no company can aspire to being 'clean and green' if it means going out of business! Therefore, a profitable pathway to sustainability is a basic requirement. As we begin to bridge the gap towards sustainability, we must therefore ask ourselves a further set of questions:

▶ Is the investment that we will be making in a process or product a step towards sustainability, i.e. are we headed in the right direction?

▶ Are we creating 'flexible platforms' with such investment? (We want each step to enable another that leads to our goal, and thus avoid blind alleys.)

▶ Will the investments that we intend to make bring good enough returns? The returns here include both economic savings and environmental benefits.

An understanding of the core business and activities of the organisation the sustainability manager is representing

Having, as I do, a strong background in industry is an extremely useful qualification when it comes to taking on the role of a sustainability manager. A distinct advantage for me personally was having a professional scientific background, although, beyond any doubt, the greatest driving force is a passion and appetite for such a challenge. There are many experts in most businesses and it is a question of tapping in to this knowledge base and learning the knack of how, where and when to apply it. Clearly, the better prepared you are with a good understanding of the business, the more likely it is that you will be taken seriously by your work colleagues and the more valuable will be the support they provide you with. For example, 'green' university graduates must be savvy enough to respect the sensitivities of their more experienced work colleagues. Gaining trust and respect is a mutual process and one not to be underestimated.

Heading towards sustainability

Let us assume that we now have a definition of sustainability and we at least have some understanding of where we are today and where we need to go, no matter how daunting that gap may be. What follows needs to be a sensible, logical series of practical actions that will begin to bridge this gap. To illustrate this point, let us evaluate the first of our five key sustainability challenges – the industry should move towards becoming carbon-neutral.

Back in 2000, few companies had a good understanding of their carbon footprint. Today, it is all the rage with the debate surrounding climate change to the fore. In order to make improvements, it is essential first to accurately measure current performance. So, in 2000, we set about measuring the carbon footprint of our activities across the whole supply chain entailed in manufacturing PVC. Clearly, this required some expertise in defining the system boundary, i.e. what is within the process and what lies outside it. Only until you can reasonably estimate carbon emissions will it then be possible to measure incremental improvements in reducing such emissions.

In the case of Hydro Polymers, we identified the key personnel responsible for energy management across our major manufacturing plants in Norway, Sweden and the UK. The first task was for each site to provide details of the energy consumed during manufacture. Once this task had been completed, the process of creating ideas to reduce carbon emissions was introduced. To provide some incentive, our president at the time decided that, over and above normal capital expenditure projects, an additional 4 million per annum would be set aside for sustainability projects. This created a competitive environment and allowed out-of-the-box ideas to be generated across these sites. Through a brainstorming process, such as those undertaken in total quality management, all ideas were listed (largely from the energy managers) and brought before an internally created steering committee. This committee had the responsibility of reviewing the ideas brought forward and prioritising those that appeared most attractive. This was undertaken by assessing the likely carbon savings per unit of investment.

This process was not as easy as it sounds, since the practicalities of each project required detailed assessment of business risk. In addition, the right atmosphere had to be created to allow those energy managers to start thinking outside of the box. Facilitating such processes is the job of the sustainability manager. Consequently various sustainability training sessions were undertaken with these managers to allow their ideas to flow.

One of the most successful projects was the installation of an exhaust pipe on one of the chemical crackers in the Norwegian plant. The process, known as adiabatic volume, allowed the cracking of a chemical gas to continue outside the reaction vessel, which increased the volume of cracked gas without additional energy. I take no credit for the concept, since it was a chemical engineer who had the bright idea. That said, refining the idea, planting the seeds and gaining capital approval so the concept became a reality is a good illustration of what is possible as a sustainability manager. And to see this project progress from concept to reality was very exhilarating. The icing on the cake was a saving of around 8,000 tonnes of carbon dioxide per annum with a payback period in the investment of less than nine months. But you should always remember that you are part of a team and ensure that due recognition is provided to all contributing members of such teams.

Importantly, the sustainability manager in this example holds the vision and frames the challenges, as well as being a visible symbol of the commitment of senior management to the goal of sustainability, allowing those with specialist knowledge and expertise to innovate within that broader context.

Ultimately, the process of carbon-neutrality is only complete when there are no carbon emissions from manufacture, a tall order in any manufacturing process. Yet, in the four years of working towards this target, our company achieved an 18% reduction combined with significant financial savings. Not all projects were as exciting as this one, but the process had another, more subtle outcome of engendering cultural change and energy awareness at all levels within the organisation.

Of course, not all projects are going to be as successful. However, without a strategic vision, purpose and a sense of urgency, progress is unlikely to be as rapid. It is a key responsibility of the sustainability manager to drive this agenda.

Seeing the bigger picture

A real challenge for the sustainability manager is to see the bigger picture. Whilst it is very exciting to see carbon emissions being reduced, this must be seen in the context of the product itself. For example, focusing on carbon reductions alone is not enough to achieve full sustainability. There are other major challenges, such as resource use and waste management, to consider. In the case of PVC, over half of it is derived from salt, an abundant natural resource, whilst the remainder is from natural gas, a non-renewable hydrocarbon. Equally, we must also consider the end-of-life fate of the products manufactured by our customers, such as pipes, window frames, cables and medical devices, even though these are outside our control.

Joined-up thinking gets to the core of the creative mind of the sustainability manager. For example, taking an old PVC window frame and using it to re-manufacture a new one with the same set of sustainability challenges begins to look like a smart sustainability move. The carbon emissions from recycling old PVC are some 80% lower than those arising from the manufacture of virgin PVC, providing a giant leap in carbon reduction – far greater than what could be achieved through incremental energy improvement projects in our plants. Equally, we are solving a waste management issue by diverting the waste stream into a useful resource and, in so doing, saving on non-renewable resources compared with virgin product. Of course, the economic benefits must be attractive for such a process to occur, as well as ensuring all technical hurdles are overcome in the recycling process.

One of the key sustainability benefits of PVC is, ironically, one of the aspects seen previously as an environmental criticism: it persists in nature (i.e. it is not biodegradable). Where this persistence is observed in small and disperse molecules that can accumulate in cells or other natural systems, it can be problematic, but when the persistent material is largely inert and made of large molecules that cannot enter cells then it is expressed as durability. Products that are durable and require little maintenance during their potentially long service life, and particularly those that can ultimately be recycled, deserve serious attention with regard to their sustainability credentials. They deliver a long service life requiring little maintenance, and therefore represent an efficient delivery of services for a small initial outlay of resources.

Reviewing all these options with a wide array of technical, commercial and marketing colleagues provides the sustainability manager with immense challenges and opportunities and clearly demonstrates the need to be able to multi-tasking. Indeed, such brainstorming can often begin to take a company in a strategic direction that may differentiate it from its major competitors, even in a commodity market. Not everyone will agree with some of the extreme green marketing that occurs in the retail industry, yet, paradoxically, such moves drive the sustainability agenda. However, at times we need to take a reality check – and for that I come back to the tools and principles provided by The Natural Step Framework, discussed earlier – and ask ourselves the three key questions: is the investment a step towards sustainability; is it creating flexible platforms; and are we gaining returns for such investment?

During the core period of intensive engagement of sustainability within my former company, we chose not to widely externally communicate our achievements although internally there was a pressing need to communicate. This patience paid off since, when formally requested, we could list our achievements with a high degree of credibility and thereby prevent the 'greenwash' trap (i.e. a superficial application of sustainability that does not stand up to scientific scrutiny). Perhaps more significantly was the realisation that, no matter how well intentioned any individual company may be in addressing sustainability, to work in isolation without engaging the supply chain will not achieve complete success. Hydro Polymers was no exception to this rule.

Engaging the whole supply chain

Where do you start? For a significant number of companies and organisations, we found ourselves somewhere in the middle of a supply chain, with suppliers on one side and customers on the other. There were two key reasons why we focused on our suppliers first. We believed that we could apply more pressure on them to take action and engage with sustainability and, as a learning process for all; we felt that this carried less risk compared to our customers if we were unsuccessful with their engagement.

For a period of three years, we organised an annual supplier sustainability event at which we requested each supplier to present their sustainability challenges. This task was now so much easier since we could both set out the rules of engagement (The Natural Step Framework) and provide our suppliers with clear, practical examples of what we had achieved over the last four years, thereby leading from the front and showing examples of sustainability in action that others could follow. And there is nothing more rewarding than seeing the acceleration of progress towards sustainability now being adopted electively by a large number of these suppliers, either through their use of The Natural Step Framework or through their own initiatives.

Having gained significant experience with our suppliers, we then proceeded with the riskier prospect at the other end of the supply chain: engaging with our customers. We held various workshops in Oslo, London and Paris. I can only describe the process as a rollercoaster ride and an incredible journey. We believe that we created higher value for our customers, which appeared to strengthen business relationships, something that was backed up by a series of customer feedback questionnaires.

Unlike many other roles in an organisation, a sustainability manager's task extends well beyond the factory site's boundary. Indirect environmental impacts can sometimes go unnoticed. For example, the supply of innocuous fillers requires mining and, if not managed responsibly, could lead to devastating effects on biodiversity and human health. This may not be obvious at first, and indeed is not meant to sound daunting. Like any new challenge, you need to walk before you can run, and it is essential first to address sustainability within your own company. However, the bigger picture must be appreciated in order to maximise value and address full sustainability. This can only be achieved by understanding the full supply chain. Once the low-hanging fruits have been picked internally, there is much for the sustainability manager to do beyond the factory gate. Precisely how this is achieved and balanced with other work commitments is beyond the remit of this chapter.

Lessons learned from the process

► There is no such thing as a sustainable material; it is the management of a material (in a product) across its full life cycle that demonstrates sustainability – blacklists on the procurement side alone make no sense without proper scientific scrutiny.

► Find a sustainability model that stands up to scrutiny on which to base your strategy.

► Tools such as life cycle assessment are valuable to help perform comparisons and determine where to focus resources regarding improvements.

► Full sustainability can only be achieved through engaging the whole supply chain.

► Addressing carbon emissions is but one of a number of sustainability challenges, so don't lose sight of the bigger picture.

► Make sure that creative ideas are captured and don't be dismissive of such ideas, especially during the conceptual stage.

► Much greater success will be achieved through teamwork and ensuring that proper recognition is provided to those contributing to the success of the team.

► Most companies today are operating unsustainably, even though most don't realise it.

► Don't be too impatient – transforming your company towards sustainability is no small task.

▶ Pick the low-hanging fruits and promote success internally, but be mindful not to make claims to the outside world until real progress has been made.

▶ Don't try to swallow elephants to begin with – focus instead on projects which you feel confident you can deliver upon.

Reference

Leadbitter, J. (2002) PVC and sustainability, *Progress in Polymer Science*, **27**(10): 2197–2226.

An introduction to stakeholder dialogue

Bettina Palazzo

Responsible Business: How to Manage a CSR Strategy Successfully
Edited by Manfred Pohl and Nick Tolhurst
Copyright © 2010 Manfred Pohl and Nick Tolhurst

In this chapter, the importance of stakeholder dialogue is outlined, and, using best-practice examples from industry, the author examines what is necessary for stakeholder dialogue to work and provides a step-by-step guide to successful implementation.

The stakeholder scenario

In the 1970s the Nobel Laureate Milton Friedman bluntly stated that the only social responsibility of business is to increase the profit for its shareholders and nothing else. In reality, things have never been that simple: companies have always had to integrate the interests of stakeholders other than their shareholders into their decision-making processes.

It is impossible to increase profits for shareholders without the acceptance and co-operation of stakeholders such as employees and customers. The legal framework already forces companies to assume a certain responsibility for stakeholders, such as their employees, suppliers and business partners, customers and governments. Additionally, various economic and ethical reasons can be advanced to support a stakeholder view of the corporation. Ignoring the concerns of stakeholders might trigger serious financial or reputational disadvantages and may violate existing normative standards, such as those outlined in the UN Declaration of Human Rights. Consequently, companies cannot afford to disregard their stakeholders, for all kinds of economic, legal and ethical reasons.

Instead of concentrating on shareholders alone, companies have to live up to the challenge of managing all these different and often contradictory interests (see Figure 2.1).

Stakeholder management is no easy task since one stakeholder is not automatically more important than another. The values, fears and interests of one group might conflict with those of another, and it is clear that one can never satisfy everybody. Stakeholder management means, first and foremost, that you will have to make tough choices. There is no standard solution and no magic formula for determining the priority of stakeholders

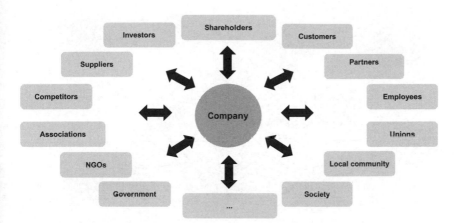

Figure 2.1 The traditional stakeholder model (NGO, non-governmental organisation).

in a given situation. We do not have shared and generally accepted standards for a dilemma such as this. Furthermore, we are living in a global economy in which the legal framework and sanctioning mechanisms are lacking.

It is also controversial how far companies should, and can, go in their responsibility for stakeholders. Are they only responsible for their primary stakeholders, those groups and individuals without whose continuing participation the company could not survive (e.g. employees, shareholders, customers)? Or is stakeholding self-legitimised, i.e. if someone judges himself to be a stakeholder, does he become one *de facto*? For example:

▶ Is a six-year-old girl who works in gruesome conditions in the cotton fields of Uzbekistan for a third-tier supplier of Puma a stakeholder or not?

▶ Are oil corporations responsible for the lack of fossil fuels for future generations?

▶ Is McDonald's responsible for overweight children?

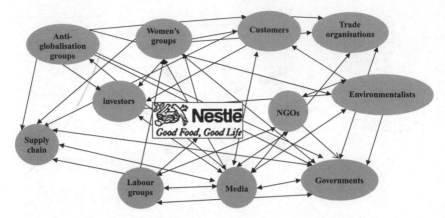

Figure 2.2 The Nestlé stakeholder model (NGO, non-governmental organisation) (from Tapscott & Ticoll, 2003).

This stakeholder scenario becomes even more complex if we realise that the traditional stakeholder model (Figure 2.1) is only a simplified one and that reality is much more complicated. A company's stakeholder relations are characterised by coalitions and interdependencies between different stakeholders. Within this stakeholder network, it is impossible to deal with just one stakeholder at a time, as the Nestlé example in Figure 2.2 illustrates.

Within this stakeholder scenario, non-governmental organisations (NGOs) play an increasingly important part. The rise of their importance becomes obvious when you look at the sheer increase in their numbers. In 1985, 20,000 international NGOs were registered by the Union of International Association, and by 2005 that number had increased to 50,000. In recent years NGOs have become more professional and internationally organised. They are highly skilled in mobilising their constituencies and – thanks to the internet, email and Skype – they can communicate and organise campaigns quickly and with low costs across the globe.

These groups monitor and criticise corporations on issues such as working conditions, environmental standards, corruption, human rights and consumer protection. NGOs request transparency and information on these issues from corporations. In cases of conflict, corporations risk boycotts, becoming the target of an NGO campaign and subsequent damage to their reputation.

In order to respond proactively to this complex and demanding stakeholder scenario, companies have to make it clear that they cannot satisfy every interest of every stakeholder, but that they are dealing responsibly with them. Companies can win the trust of their stakeholders by informing them about the choices they are confronted with. The written information found in a corporate social responsibility (CSR) report is a first step in this direction, but direct and reciprocal communication with stakeholders is a more effective approach.

What are stakeholder dialogues and why are they important?

A stakeholder dialogue is a structured discussion between representatives of a company and representatives of one or several stakeholder groups. Since NGOs play an important part in the stakeholder scenario, and since they form the most demanding and challenging group of stakeholders, this chapter will focus on stakeholder dialogues between a company and NGOs.

It is the aim of this dialogue to investigate constellations of interests and issues concerning the company and the stakeholders, exchange opinions, clarify expectations, enhance mutual understanding and, if possible, find new and better solutions. Depending on the issue, the company and its industry, the country and the goal of the dialogue, there are many different forms of stakeholder dialogues.

One way to differentiate stakeholder dialogues is to distinguish between different levels of participation. A first level of dialogue is purely *informative* communication. It cannot even be considered a true dialogue since information flows only one way. Stakeholders receive information and the company is in full control of the content and the way in which the information is communicated. The second level is *consultative*. Here stakeholders are asked for their opinions and the results of the consultation are transmitted to corporate decision-makers. The stakeholders' input can, to a limited extent, influence corporate decisions and strategies. Corresponding tools for this level of stakeholder involvement include opinion polls, surveys, interviews, workshops, focus groups, online dialogues and *ad hoc* dialogues on specific issues.

The final level is *decisional*. Since stakeholders are getting involved in corporate decision-making, this form of dialogue requires the most commitment and openness on the corporate side. It might be more risky, but, if managed properly, their long-term effectiveness can be more innovative and sustainable. The methods and forms of communication corresponding to this level of stakeholder involvement include continuous dialogue processes, partnerships and joint projects, and stakeholder panels.

Stakeholder panels are the most decisional form of dialogue so far. In this case, companies institutionalise the dialogue into their corporate decision-making process. This group of independent external experts and NGOs challenges a corporation's activities in CSR, critically reviews the CSR report and turns its attention to upcoming issues. Box 2.1 gives an example of such a stakeholder panel.

Beyond the mere exchange of ideas and opinions, stakeholder panels can also be useful to develop or implement corporate CSR activities, such as (ORSE, 2006):

▶ help in defining a company's policy

▶ help in drawing up a code of conduct

▶ employee awareness and training in CSR

▶ assistance in policy implementation

▶ help in drawing up progress indicators

▶ support with expertise on the local environment

▶ monitoring existing indicators and standards

Box 2.1   The Lafarge stakeholder panel

▶ Active since 2003, this group of 10 people representing the group's main categories of stakeholders meets twice a year.

▶ They challenge Lafarge's approach to CSR, suggest improvements and form an annual opinion on Lafarge's performance and account ability in this field.

▶ The panel makes a collective statement on Lafarge's sustainability report. Lafarge publishes this statement without censorship.

▶ Almost all of the members of the executive board participate in one of the two meetings.

Source: http://www.lafarge.fr/03062008-sustainable_development-term_of_reference-uk.pdf

▶ involvement in the design and implementation of a project

▶ social audit.

Box 2.2 sketches the stakeholder consultations process conducted by ABB in order to collect feedback on the draft of their corporate social policy.

Other variations of stakeholder dialogues are stakeholder partnerships or multi-stakeholder partnerships. In the former, companies and a stakeholder develop and implement a joint project in order to solve a problem or conduct a project they could not tackle alone. An example of this is the partnership, established in 1999, between Starbucks Coffee, TransFair USA, the Fairtrade Labelling Organisation (FLO) and Conservation International in order to promote the production of fairtrade coffee. Starbucks and these NGOs joined forces to conduct the verification process and help to improve farmers' environmental and agricultural practices.

In multi-stakeholder dialogues, as the name implies, representatives from the corporate world, civil society, government and international organisations join forces to work on an issue that affects all of them and that

Box 2.2   Consultations process conducted by ABB in order to collect feedback on the draft of their corporate social policy

In 2001 ABB published the first version of its corporate social policy. In order to 'road test' the policy and collect ideas for its implementation, the firm conducted stakeholder dialogues in 34 countries and involved national and international NGOs, trade unions, central and local government, academics, the media, religious groups and business partners. In these stakeholder dialogues the following questions were discussed:

► Does the social policy cover all the issues it should? What should be added and which issues are most important?

► How do we put the social policy into practice? How can we measure compliance and progress?

► Which of the principles should receive the highest priority in implementation?

► Which of the principles are the ones that leave ABB most vulnerable to criticism?

Source: http://www.abb.com/cawp/seitp255/74168f7a72d50e7ec1256c6a00487101. aspx

has to be approached through co-operation. Here a corporation that is involved in the dialogue is no longer the focal organisation, but becomes a stakeholder of the initiative. In this case the company enters a network to solve a problem (inside-out approach) rather than bringing stakeholders into its organisation (outside-in approach). Prominent examples of multi-stakeholder initiatives are the UN Global Compact and the Fair Labor Association.

All these different forms of stakeholder dialogue can have their justifications. It is not always possible and desirable to engage with all stakeholders in a consultative or decisional fashion. If a company wants to gather information about the opinions of large stakeholder groups, such as customers or most of the stakeholders in one country, surveys might be an adequate method. Box 2.3 describes the process adopted for Vodafone's stakeholder survey in Greece.

Box 2.3   Vodafone's stakeholder survey in Greece

"Vodafone Greece conducted a survey of 150 stakeholders during 2005. The aim was to assess stakeholder needs and expectations as well as to get detailed feedback on Vodafone's performance and future actions.

Participants were selected from 11 key stakeholder groups: academia, business customers, employees, Vodafone shops franchise, third parties' associates, government, institutions, business community, journalists, NGOs and suppliers.

The survey was organised by Vodafone Greece's CR department but all business functions were involved throughout. For example, the procurement department helped to identify and contact suppliers to take part in the survey. This contributed to the high response rate of 75%.

An independent agency carried out interviews in person using a structured discussion guide, and by phone using a specific questionnaire. Vodafone Greece provided training to ensure the agency was familiar with the company's CR programmes and understood the survey aims. Three employee focus groups were also organised.

The results were analysed in aggregate, by issue and by stakeholder group. For each issue and stakeholder group, the company was able to identify any gaps between stakeholder expectations and actual performance. After the survey, the CR team met with each business function to present the findings and define plans in response to the findings."

Source: http://www.vodafone.com/etc/medialib/attachments/cr_downloads. Par.0890.File.tmp/VF_CR_Dialogue_1_Stakeholder_engagement.pdf

In reality, these classifications of stakeholder dialogues are not always clear-cut, and the boundaries between the different forms often overlap. Consequently, this guide on how to conduct stakeholder dialogues can only describe some general principles, project stages and tools that are applicable for most stakeholder dialogues.

So why should companies get involved in stakeholder dialogues? If a company wants to become involved in or improve its CSR practices, it cannot avoid examining its stakeholder scenario and the issues and positions that are continually developing in the stakeholder network. Stakeholder dialogues are the logical step after this form of passive observation of one's stakeholder network. Consequently, stakeholder dialogues are simply part of a company's overall CSR management. And it is important that these dialogues are integrated into the general CSR strategy and the general stakeholder management. Only then can stakeholder dialogues help to create a proactive relationship between a company and NGOs that goes beyond a defensive and adversarial mindset.

Companies hope to minimise the risks to their reputation by learning about controversial issues at an early stage through stakeholder dialogues. But the opportunities of stakeholder dialogues should go beyond this merely protectionist approach. Getting involved with independent and critical opinion leaders is also a very effective way of initiating processes of learning and change within the organisation. In today's hyper-interdependent world, companies need constant contact with their external environment in order to be responsive to the needs of consumers and society. Since almost all organisations act within a global context, managers must be able to communicate effectively across cultural, social and geographic boundaries.

As with any kind of human relationship, involvement with NGOs through stakeholder dialogues brings with it risks as well as opportunities, for both parties, and Box 2.4 provides an overview of these.

Box 2.4 Risks and opportunities of stakeholder dialogues for companies and non-governmental organisations (NGOs)

	For companies	For NGOs
Opportunities	▶ To signal their willingness to become involved in corporate social responsibility (CSR) practices	▶ To be able to move their ideas forward
	▶ To improve their internal management practices	▶ To encourage companies to adopt a vision of CSR rather than managing crises one by one
	▶ To benefit from expertise on the issues of CSR and how to tackle them	▶ To encourage companies to improve the way they act in social, societal and/or environmental contexts
	▶ To improve their image within and outside of the company	▶ To be involved in determining strategy as well as in its monitoring
	▶ To be able to open up to civil society	▶ To develop relationships with other companies
	▶ To avoid or escape from crisis situations	▶ To get more visibility and therefore more people involved in the cause defended by the NGO
	▶ To create innovation	▶ To better understand how a company works and what challenges it faces
	▶ To facilitate community development	▶ To create innovation
		▶ To raise credibility in establishing real discussions, rather than having a hostile behaviour

(Continued)

	For companies	**For NGOs**
Potential risks	▶ To expose itself to potential attacks because its activities are under constant supervision – a partnership is in no way a kind of insurance against NGO campaigns ▶ To be a victim of information leaks ▶ To waste time and money if the partnership does not succeed	▶ To put its reputation on the line if it becomes involved with a company that proves unable to meet the original expectations ▶ To compromise its principles and its original intentions in the name of the partnership, and hence lose its independence and all credibility, especially when the funding is predominant ▶ To be exploited by an unscrupulous company that sees a way of destabilising one of its competitors ▶ To give rise to controversies within the NGO ▶ To replace consultants or employee representatives on some particular subjects (e.g. discrimination, human rights, respect in the workplace)

Source: http://www.csreurope.org/data/files/toolbox/Stakeholder_engagement.pdf

How to conduct a stakeholder dialogue – a four-phase process model

It is clear that many different forms and methods of stakeholder dialogue exist. Consequently, the process I will describe here is only a rough guide that has to be adapted to the specific level of participation, the goals of the dialogue and the needs, objectives and resources of the company and stakeholders involved.

The basis of this guideline is a four-phase process model (see Figure 2.3).

Phase 1: Exploration and consultation

Before entering into a stakeholder dialogue, a company has to decide what stakeholder(s) it would like to engage with, what issues it would like to

Phase 4: Follow-up
- Documentation
- Internal and (external) communication of results
- Actions
- Define learning points and modify design
- Evaluation
- Start a new cycle

Phase 3: Running the dialogue
- Self-reflection of attitudes
- Dialogue and listening skills
- Creating trust
- Taking minutes

Phase 1: Exploration and consultation
- Identifying issues
- Defining goals
- Defining levels of participation
- Identifying potential partners
- Selecting partners
- Resource planning

Phase 2: Preparation
- Approaching partners
- Selecting internal participants
- Clarifying goals and resources
- Finding neutral facilitators
- Joint definition of objectives, agenda, design, rules, roles and expectations

Figure 2.3   Four-phase process modes for stakeholder dialogues.
Adapted from: BSR Guide and the Collective Leadership Institute, http://www.collectiveleadership.com/123live-user-data/user_data/3829/public/DOKUMENTE/downloads/Phases%20in%20Stakeholder%20dialogues.pdf

discuss, what issues the potential stakeholders will want to discuss, and what the company's and the NGO's objectives for the dialogue are likely to be.

If a company pursues an instrumental approach in stakeholder management, it will start by screening the stakeholder scenario for the NGOs that have the most power and influence to threaten that company's reputation. Although this approach is understandable from a business perspective, it will never achieve a high level of credibility with stakeholders. Furthermore, it might also be a high-risk strategy to ignore less influential stakeholders, since it is always possible that these groups start new and successful campaigns that suddenly put a company under pressure.

Therefore, it is recommended that the exploration process starts with the potential issues the company has to address. There are two elements in the analysis of a company's ethical issues. Overall, companies should be aware that they are potentially responsible for all social and environmental problems that might occur along their value chain. As a consequence, corporations have to understand the chain itself and the various geopolitical contexts in which the steps of their supply chains are embedded.

First, companies analyse their ethical issues by deconstructing their value chain:

▶ How are the working and production conditions at the suppliers?

▶ What are the social and environmental impacts of the production process and the products and services?

The chart in Figure 2.4 gives an example for the analysis of the value chain in the food industry.

Secondly, a company should screen the geopolitical contexts of the countries where it is active, for example:

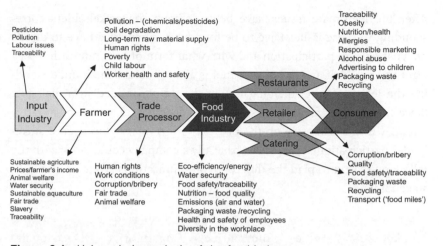

Figure 2.4 Value-chain analysis of the food industry.
Source: http://ec.europa.eu/enterprise/csr/documents/business_case/somers.pdf

▶ Is this country known for human rights violations?

▶ Do the operations involve contacts with representatives of a repressive regime?

▶ How stable is the political and economic context in this country?

In order to update the required geopolitical and supply-chain knowledge, a company should try to establish systematic communication links with stakeholders. A very promising tool to do this is a stakeholder panel. Such a supply-chain analysis dealing with geopolitical contexts can also be informed and completed by, among other things, opinion polls, press reviews and internet research.

The next step after this screening and tracking of possible hot issues is to identify the issues that are legitimate and deserve more thorough attention. One way to analyse the legitimacy of issues is to examine if the related corporate behaviour is in conflict with principles of the UN Global Compact, International Labour Organisation conventions or other corporate or industry standards to which the company is committed.

After the legitimate issues have been defined, the stakeholders corresponding to these issues have to be found and companies have to decide on what level of participation and with what form of communication they want to engage. If a stakeholder panel is already established, understanding the legitimacy of emerging issues should be decided in a dialogue. Since this chapter focuses on stakeholder dialogues, i.e. the consultative level, I will not elaborate on the process of formulating an overall stakeholder participation strategy. But basically a company could work with the following matrix to plan the different communications strategies for each stakeholder:

Stakeholder	Issue	Informative	Consultative	Decisional
Xx		Information event		
Yy			Focus group	
Zz			Stakeholder dialogues	
Ww				Partnership

Often there are several NGOs that are affected by an issue and which could be appropriate partners for a dialogue. Before selecting an NGO with which to enter into a dialogue process, companies must define the corporate goals they are aiming at with this engagement. If they know exactly what their needs and expectations are, it is much easier to select the NGO that can help the company to achieve that goal. Of course, in many cases it is the NGO that chooses the company, by criticising it. In this case, not turning this NGO into a dialogue partner and ignoring its concern would be a high-risk strategy. If they can make a choice, if they are dealing with an issue in a proactive way for instance, companies have to decide whether they want to co-operate with an international or a local NGO, or with a combination of global/local partners. This decision depends on the issue and its geographical context. International NGOs have more experience in co-operating with the private sector, whereas local NGOs have more knowledge of the local situation and may help to bridge cultural gaps. Both local and international civil society representatives can be important for a successful dialogue project.

If the company is clear about its needs, goals and expectations, it can start gathering information on potential partner NGOs. There are numerous sources of information to help find the right NGO for the issue the company wants to tackle:

▶ Various departments within the company (PR, CSR, marketing, etc.) are already in contact with NGOs.

▶ Other companies might share their experience with their stakeholder engagements.

▶ International organisations are involved with NGOs and can provide fairly neutral information.

▶ Further sources of information and advice are, among others, government agencies, unions, universities, foundations, religious organisations, the internet, media and publications, and business associations.

After an initial identification of potential dialogue partners, companies have to do their homework and conduct some due diligence on their NGO shortlist, i.e. read the NGO's publications, annual reports and website, and read media reviews of the NGO and the like. Companies have to know:

▶ What does the NGO do? In what issues are they involved? Are they an advocacy, humanitarian or development organisation?

▶ What is the NGO's vision and mission? Dialogues can only work if each party can at least respect the vision and mission of the other partner.

▶ Whom does the NGO represent?

▶ What is the NGO's reputation among stakeholders?

▶ What is the expertise of the NGO on the issue to be tackled?

▶ What is the NGO's attitude towards the corporate world?

▶ Is the NGO known for a history of dialogues with other corporations that have been conducted in good faith?

▶ Does the NGO have the internal capacity to provide the time, resources and personnel needed for a dialogue?

▶ What is the level of legitimacy and credibility of the NGO? How advanced is its financial transparency and internal governance?

It is also useful for companies to know about the selection criteria of NGOs. Some NGOs work with exclusion criteria, e.g. no dialogue with tobacco companies. The WWF has established guidelines for partnerships with companies (mutual respect, transparency, right to criticise) and only works with one company within a given sector.

Most of the time, companies already have some sort of relationship with the stakeholder group or NGO with which they want to start a dialogue. Here it is helpful to analyse the dynamics of this relationship so far. Is the relationship of the NGO and the company characterised by a gridlock of corporate moves and NGO opposition? Who is in contact with whom inside this NGO? How strong is the opposition force and how big are the chances of making the relationship more co-operative? Are there organisations that could mediate the relationship?

This process of mapping issues and potential dialogue partners is already, in itself, a very valuable exercise and is the basis of the whole stakeholder dialogue process. It provides the clarity that is needed to effectively plan the resources (staff time, travel costs, accommodation, external consultants' fees, supplies) that will be needed for the dialogue.

Phase 2: Preparation

Once the partners for the stakeholder dialogue are selected, the dialogue representatives of both sides can be identified. Corporate representatives should come from departments that relate to the issues to be discussed and there should be at least one person who is responsible for the management of the whole process. A certain level of upper management participation will be necessary to signal commitment to the partner and to sell the dialogue internally.

It is important also to verify that the NGO's representatives have the authority to make agreements on behalf of their organisation and that they match the level and the areas of expertise of the corporate participants. The careful selection of these people cannot be overestimated, as ultimately the success of stakeholder dialogue depends a lot on interpersonal dynamics.

It is therefore vital to get to know each other better before the initiation of a more serious commitment. Visiting each other's offices during the preparatory phase of the stakeholder dialogue can be very useful. In that way, both parties have entered the 'enemy's territory' and will have got a feeling for their way of working and dispelled some stereotypes. Both parties should fully understand what are the needs, interests, expectations and motives of their partners for entering in the dialogue. On this basis, both parties can jointly define the objectives, design, agenda and ground rules of the dialogue. Mutually agreed goals provide a basis for action and give guidance during the process. These goals have to be clear to all participants and as specific as possible, since lack of clarity easily leads to confusion and lack of focus of energy. Furthermore, they are necessary as a frame of reference when evaluating the dialogue.

Nevertheless, having clear objectives should not mean that the results of the dialogue are all set at the beginning. A certain openness and ambiguity are indispensable if you are to come up with creative new ideas, as well as being able to adapt to new information or changing situations.

The next logical step is the thorough preparation of the first dialogue event. The 'mantra' to keep in mind when organising such an event is: 'Will this enhance an open and creative dialogue atmosphere of trust?' Principally organisers have to decide on:

▶ *The location of the event* – it is clear that meeting at a neutral place helps to avoid a power imbalance and enhances the open-mindedness of participants as they distance themselves from their everyday working contexts. It should be obvious that it is not a good idea to meet for talks on child labour and poverty in five-star hotels.

▶ *The preparation for the participants* – should participants receive an information package, e.g. reading material for the event? Do the internal participants need extra training in facilitation, CSR or on the issue to be tackled?

▶ *The design of the event*:

 – What kind of facilitation techniques should be used (e.g. flip-charts, meta-plan, brainstorming, scenario workshops, open space)?

 – Is there enough time for informal socialising during breaks?

 – The atmosphere of dialogue is influenced by simple things like seating arrangements. If corporate representatives are seated in rows and are listening to a 'parade' of serial monologues by stakeholder representatives, for example, the development of an open and dialogical dynamic is rather unlikely. If these dialogues resemble court hearings, corporate representatives can easily feel attacked and automatically become defensive.

▶ *The selection of a neutral facilitator* – having one neutral facilitator (or several facilitators) is very important for the prevention of conflicts, misunderstandings and ineffective communication. When choosing a facilitator the following questions should be considered:

 – Does s/he enjoy the trust of all participants?

 – Will s/he be able to enhance the creativity of the group, deal with potential conflicts and avoid premature decision-making?

- Are the facilitators committed, flexible, responsive, balancing, inclusive, encouraging, respectful, neutral, problem-solving-oriented, disciplined, culturally sensitive, capable of meta-communication and comfortable with their role?

- How can the results of the dialogue be documented and measured? Reporters who will take minutes should be identified. Since they will document the meeting's outcome, these people should be acceptable to both parties (Hemmati, 2002)

▶ *Ground rules* – typically, confidentiality and costs are two key concerns that need to be covered by ground rules:

- Confidentiality and disclosure: all participants must understand that some of the information discussed during the dialogue is sensitive and has to be kept confidential. The parties have to agree beforehand when, how, to whom and by whom information about the dialogue will be disclosed.

- Costs: in order to avoid misunderstandings, the way that costs and reimbursements should be handled has to be clarified at the beginning. This is a sensitive issue since NGOs have limited resources, but at the same time they will be concerned about losing their independence if they accept corporate funds.

Phase 3: Running dialogue

It is clear that stakeholder dialogues are not supposed to be nice, comfortable meetings. Distrust on both sides is normal at the beginning and should not be taken personally. There has to be some fruitful tension and all parties should be ready to take some risks when they participate. However, the risks and opportunities should be acceptable for both parties. Both have to focus on common interests instead of polarised positions. NGOs should stay flexible and try to understand the motives and pressures of companies. On the other hand, companies should also try to expand their corporate mindsets.

Managers are often not used to talking to critical civil society representatives. Territorial fears are likely to be triggered on both sides: companies have to open up their boundaries and NGOs have to venture into the 'lion's den'.

It is crucial that corporate representatives avoid giving the impression that they are conducting the dialogue for marketing or image purposes. Therefore, the information they provide to the NGO partner should be as neutral as possible, for example, and should not be influenced by a hidden corporate agenda or spin.

There are differences in language patterns between the corporate world and civil society organisations: People in corporations operate in a mode of power language (e.g. decisions, effectiveness, interests, bargaining) whereas representatives of NGOs use a more affective and identity-driven language (concern for people, values, being on a mission, higher-order purposes). These different language patterns generate potential for profound misunderstandings. Consequently, participants should try to talk simply, avoid their own professional jargon and make their background assumptions explicit. If they express their opinions or make interpretations, it is important to explain the thinking behind their statements.

In a stakeholder dialogue, the participants' listening skills are even more important than the way in which they express their views. Only if one really listens to someone will that person be able to speak authentically. Here are some ideas for developing listening skills:

▶ Cultivate your willingness to really listen.

▶ Even if you strongly disagree with your partner's view, look for the one grain of truth that you can find.

▶ Ask your partner to outline the assumptions that have led him or her to see things in that way.

▶ While listening, always keep the question, 'What else is important?' in your mind. Ask this question, or versions of it, until everything has been said and the situation or context your partner describes is clear.

▶ Verify as best as possible that your record of the discussion corresponds with that of your partner's.

It is not always the case that participants, both corporate and NGOs, are reflective enough to be aware of their own mindsets, language patterns, assumptions and prejudices. This is one reason why skilled facilitators are so important. They must constantly be on the lookout for different and unconscious assumptions getting in the way of mutual understanding and then make these hidden assumptions clear to everybody. Only a neutral facilitator can help participants suspend the negative perceptions they have of each other. Such a facilitator helps participants to understand that their world-view is not necessarily the only one and that a different perspective can bring value. Furthermore, the facilitator has to play time-keeper and be aware of attempts to dominate by certain participants, blocked communication, intimidation, gossip, manipulation and the like.

If properly prepared and conducted, the dialogue can become a process of thinking together that collects multiple perspectives and creates an understanding for the whole.

Phase 4: Follow-up

Like in any project management, the follow-up phase is the least popular one, since it involves a lot of work and energy, when everybody is exhausted from the process. Follow-up tasks are often time-consuming, administrative and not very glamorous. Nevertheless, if the results of the dialogue are not proficiently managed, the whole process loses value, legitimacy, and thus impact.

Documentation

A first step in this follow-up process is the finalisation of the dialogue's documentation. Minutes and reporting should be completed in a neutral fashion. They should reflect the width and depth of discussions and must be acceptable to all participants.

External communication of results

There should be one person on each side responsible for the external communication of the stakeholder dialogue and its results. That way conflicting information is avoided and both organisations provide consistent information. In general, public communication about the project should be kept at a low level in order to avoid the impression of PR motives on the corporate side and of loss of independence on the side of the NGO.

Internal communication of results

More important than the external communication is the internal communication of the stakeholder dialogue. The project co-ordinators have to decide what people within the organisation need information about the dialogue and how these target groups should be informed.

Actions

Of course, to show their NGO partners that their engagement goes beyond the exchange of words, actions should follow. If the dialogue does not have any effect on corporate behaviour, the NGOs may not be motivated to enter in another cycle of talks. However, due to complex corporate decision-making procedures and time-lags, it is not always easy to make a direct link between a specific dialogue event and a company decision or action.

Here corporate dialogue managers have to keep track in order to be able to show their NGO partners how their co-operation has influenced corporate policies, strategy and practice. One adequate way to communicate these connections is the company's CSR website and the CSR report.

Evaluation

The results of the dialogue have to be weighed against the initial goals and expectations. One general performance indicator for the success of a stakeholder dialogue is its impact on the issue tackled in the dialogue. For example, a company wants to find new ways to recycle its waste and – thanks to the stakeholder dialogue – comes up with an innovative solution that reduces waste to a certain percentage. In cases like this the impact on the issue is even quantifiable.

Other performance indicators are the value and benefits that the dialogue added for the organisations involved. These results are often more qualitative than quantitative. The corporate managers involved might have improved their understanding of the issue, expanded their communication skills and enhanced their ability for 'out of the box' thinking. The NGO participants might have gained a new understanding of corporate decision-making processes and dispelled their bias against managers. The NGO–company relationship might be transformed from an adversarial one to a more co-operative one.

In order to analyse the results of the stakeholder dialogue, it is necessary to get formal feedback from all participants. Since the assessment of the dialogue as such may be different from the assessment of the actual results, both topics have to be evaluated separately. When evaluating the stakeholder dialogue in itself, it is helpful to identify learning points that can be used to modify the design for future dialogue events and processes.

Start a new cycle

A first stakeholder dialogue event should not stay a single one-off project, but should be the start of a continuous and long-term relationship. The trust built in a first dialogue has to be maintained. Here it is vital to ensure the continuity of the corporate representatives involved in the dialogue. Trust is mostly created by individuals, and if the people who interact with NGOs constantly change, this relationship is easily destroyed. Of course, staff turnover cannot be avoided, but it can be managed by appointing corporate dialogue managers who are likely to stay with the company for longer, and by overlapping replacement managers and providing new dialogue members with adequate preparatory material.

Conclusion

Conducting stakeholder dialogues is a complex and challenging task that requires diligent project management. Usually this is something companies are already good at. The deeper challenge of a stakeholder dialogue is actually that companies that open up to external dialogue cannot keep up an internal monoculture of command and control.

If companies want to truly engage in transformative stakeholder dialogues, they also have to be ready to transcend their short-term thinking, because the results of stakeholder dialogues are long-term and stakeholder management has to be conducted with a long-term attitude. Furthermore, companies have to broaden their narrow focus on the finishing line, since this inhibits true dialogue and openness to new perspectives and unfamiliar approaches.

In summary, stakeholder dialogues can help companies to stop behaving like blinkered horses in a race for profit, and to start looking around and joining forces for more sustainable success.

References

Hemmati, M. (2002) *Multi-stakeholder Processes for Governance and Sustainability*, Earthscan.

ORSE (2006) *Strategic NGO Partnerships Guide*, L'Observatoire sur la Responsabilité Sociétaled des Entreprises.

Tapscott, D. and Ticoll, D. (2003) *The Naked Corporation: How the Age of Transparency will Revolutionize Business*, Free Press.

Who works in CSR? Staffing and recruitment in CSR

Andrew Cartland

This chapter gives an overview of the most up-to-date information on working in CSR. Whether you are reading this as an employer or as a job-seeker looking to move into the sector, this chapter aims to address some of the key questions in CSR recruitment. The chapter also includes information on how to retain CSR staff, how CSR staff are organised within a company, how much is paid and how the positions are placed. The information is partly based on recruitment consultant Acre Resources' own experience as well as on the CSR Salary Survey, the only regular survey of personnel and recruitment practices in the CSR industry.

Introduction

With few exceptions, the most valuable asset of any firm is its staff, and success is driven by the quality of individuals hired and also by the ability to retain them. This is a huge challenge – identifying the best talent in the first place isn't always easy and there is always a good deal of competition when trying to recruit that talent. As such, it is essential to understand the market place in which you are hiring – from the levels of remuneration required to get people on board to what makes people tick.

Established in 2003, Acre Resources was the first recruitment firm to have a focused corporate social responsibility (CSR) recruitment division and rapidly built a global reputation by working with companies to source the most talented CSR professionals for their organisations. Over the past six years, Acre have filled over 1,000 roles and have placed staff with many of the leading proponents within the CSR sector. In 2007 we launched the first ever *CSR Salary Survey* in partnership with specialist consultancy Acona and sector newsletter *Ethical Performance*. This groundbreaking research surveyed professionals working in CSR and gained valuable insight into job function, salary levels, educational backgrounds and even job satisfaction. The results of the latest salary survey were published in February 2009 and much of the data included in this chapter are based on those results. As such I must acknowledge and give thanks to Paul Burke at Acona and Peter Mason at *Ethical Performance* for their part in compiling the research.

Acre's unique position in and understanding of the CSR job market leave us well placed to advise on recruitment in this area. This chapter aims to give an overview of the most up-to-date information on working in CSR. Whether you are reading this as an employer looking to understand the role of CSR within your organisation, or as a job-seeker looking to move into the sector, this chapter aims to address some of the key questions that we hear everyday.

Much of our research is based on the UK market. As the UK CSR and sustainability sectors are relatively advanced they are a good model by which to plot global trends.

Finding the best people

Employers need to think carefully about the methods they are using to source and attract the most talented staff. At the time of writing we are experiencing a global recession. However, many enterprises are still hiring in the green and CSR sectors and there is ferocious competition for the best staff. The first step to a successful hire is being aware of this competition and the challenge that it brings – hiring the best people is not easy and needs a highly active approach. The second step is to work out the rewards your organisation can offer that no one else can match. These won't necessarily be financial; within the unique 'green job space' they may well be the opportunity to create change or the chance to have a significant and positive impact. Alternatively it might be the opportunity to work on innovative ideas or technology. Within a rapidly developing marketplace, and one which is tipped by presidents and prime ministers to outstrip the growth of other job sectors, candidates are also likely to be wooed with the chance of personal development and personal growth.

The green job space, and CSR in particular, is unique and job-seekers are often (although not always) driven by personal values. Students are now graduating with a very clear understanding of the implications of green and ethical issues, and at the graduate level there is an overwhelming demand to become involved in the sector. It is likely that this is linked to the desire to have a positive impact on the world at large. This is quite different from the drivers to enter many other professions and it is worthwhile employers bearing this in mind when approaching the job market. Job-seekers tend to join (and are retained by) companies with shared values and it is important for employers to demonstrate this in their recruitment process.

Picking out stars is essential for any company and due to the nature of business we are in, no matter how jittery the economy, good people are needed now. For any organisation, enduring success can only come from adding the best people to their teams.

Overview of the CSR job market

Corporate social responsibility professionals work within every business sector, from corporates to consultancies, from non-governmental organisations (NGOs) to public bodies. Large companies often have teams, and small companies will often have at least an individual overseeing these obligations even if it is not the sole purpose of their role. CSR spans a broad range of industries and our 2008/09 *CSR Salary Survey* showed that the highest representation of CSR professionals was in the financial services sector. This isn't surprising, as in my experience banks and financial firms have sizeable and well-developed community and charitable programmes that need managing. Professional services and retail were also shown to employ a high number of CSR experts (see Figure 3.1).

Our research suggests that the CSR space is heavily dominated by women (comprising over 60% of the workforce) and this reflects my day-to-day experience of the sector. It is also the view that many CSR directors have shared with me over the past few years. The research and our experience also reveal a bias towards men in more senior positions and roles focusing on the more technical aspects of CSR, such as climate change and environmental roles. On the other side, there are considerably more women

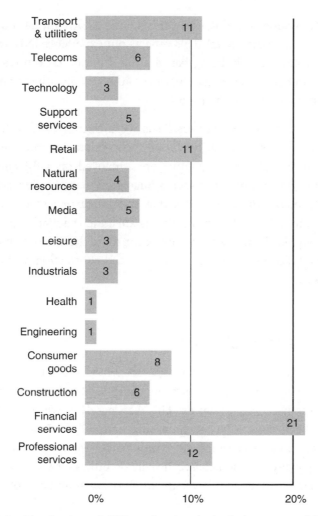

Figure 3.1 Distribution of CSR professionals by industry type (*CSR Salary Survey 2008/09*).

in the areas of community involvement and charitable giving and they are disproportionately over-represented in more junior positions. We will look at the inconsistent salary levels for men and women in detail later in this chapter.

In the UK, London is undoubtedly the hub for CSR with 64% of professionals working in the capital. This reflects our experience in Europe also, with CSR roles typically being based around industrial centres such as Geneva, Zurich and The Hague. Just over 40% of CSR professionals have an international focus to their work.

The vast majority of CSR professionals work from a fixed location and home working is a relative rarity (about 7% overall falling into this group). Currently it also appears that most are employed on a full-time basis. Indeed, until now we have not seen a huge growth in the contractor marketplace, although there are clues that this is starting to develop. It is likely that the lack of job security that is affecting the market at the time of writing will lead employers to choose the more flexible option of hiring contractors (allowing for easier expansion and contraction during uncertain periods).

Salaries and packages

Until the first *CSR Salary* Survey in 2007, Acre observed large fluctuations in pay. Companies hiring in much the same levels of experience would often pay vastly different salaries. This was largely down to the fact that there had been very little benchmarking undertaken. Fluctuations still exist but are now based much more on tangible elements – for instance, where a company's brand is based heavily on ethics, or where a company has very large social and environmental risks, remuneration is often higher.

There is often the misconception that individuals working in CSR are not heavily driven by financial factors such as salary. And while it is certainly true that the vast majority of people entering the sector do so for altruistic reasons, in my experience CSR professionals are just as demanding and negotiate just as fiercely with regard to salaries as people in any other areas of business. Whilst there has not been a huge amount of growth in salaries between 2007 and 2009, the sector has come a long way in pay over the last five years. This is possibly a reflection of the tangible value that companies now place on CSR from both risk mitigation and revenue-generating perspectives.

The *2008/9 CSR Salary Survey* analysed salaries from two perspectives: the first was for those working within corporations (also known as in-house roles) and the second was for those working in consultancy. We did see a large pay gap between these two types of organisation, with consultants generally being worse off with regards to salary, bonus and benefits. At the time of writing the median salary in CSR is between £45,000 and £50,000 (€51,000–€57,000) (see Figure 3.2). Salaries over £150,000 appear to be relatively rare, and this is backed up by our day-to-day experience. However, it is worth noting that in the first part of 2009, Acre experienced an upsurge in jobs paying in excess of £100,000 – in fact, we see a higher frequency year on year in this regard.

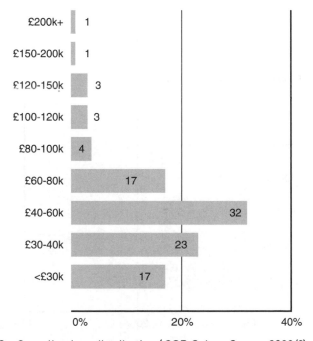

Figure 3.2 Overall salary distribution (*CSR Salary Survey 2008/9*).

Benefits and bonuses

While the median bonus for CSR professionals in our 2008/09 survey was between £1 and £5,000, it was no surprise to see that the largest companies were the most generous in terms of bonuses. In the UK almost a quarter of CSR practitioners working for FTSE-100 organisations received a bonus of £10,000 or more and, perhaps predictably, the banking and finance sector paid the most generous bonuses. By contrast, consultants received less in the way of bonuses in comparison to those working in-house, with only 6% receiving over £10,000 and nearly half receiving nothing at all (see Figure 3.3).

Corporate social responsibility practitioners in in-house roles are particularly favoured when it comes to benefits, in comparison to their counterparts in consultancy. They are more likely to have medical cover and shares

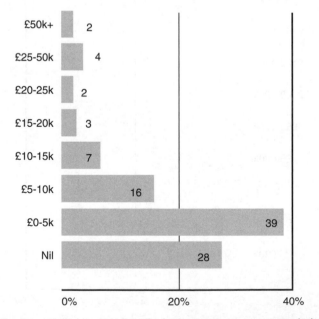

Figure 3.3 Overall bonus distribution (*CSR Salary Survey 2008/09*).

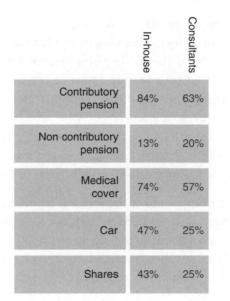

	In-house	Consultants
Contributory pension	84%	63%
Non contributory pension	13%	20%
Medical cover	74%	57%
Car	47%	25%
Shares	43%	25%

Figure 3.4 Benefits distribution (*CSR Salary Survey 2008/09*).

and almost twice as many have a car (or car allowance) as part of their benefits package (see Figure 3.4).

Job titles

In the 2008/09 *CSR Salary Survey*, in partnership with our survey partners Acona and *Ethical Performance*, we attempted to give descriptions to various job levels. The descriptions below are based on the survey data and we feel they give a good indication of the likely education and career background of professionals at each level.

In-house

Director/head

This is the most senior CSR person in the organisation. Despite the latest survey showing a dominance of women in CSR, this position is still more likely to be held by a man. They will have been in post for up to three years, work in a team of up to nine people, and have three or four employees reporting directly to them. They will control a budget of between £500,000 and £1m and have been in full-time employment (post education) for 10–15 years. They are more likely than not to have worked in CSR before their current job and, if so, will have had five to 10 years' experience in the sector. They will almost certainly have a first degree (probably in a non-CSR-related discipline) plus a postgraduate qualification and, on occasion, a professional qualification in CSR.

Depending on the exact nature of the role and reporting relationships, we believe the average salary in London and the south-east of England is around £95,000, with a bonus in the region of £20,000 (or 25% of salary). Much higher salaries are not uncommon – in some cases with higher bonus levels. We suspect these significant differences in remuneration reflect reporting relationships, the degree to which CSR has been recognised as a core issue, and the personal qualities and expertise of the individuals concerned. Team size (except where the team comprises 20+ people) appears to have little direct impact on salary, while those with control of £1m+ budgets are more likely to have salaries in excess of £100,000.

For this job level, 80% of the respondents received a car or car allowance. Everyone had access to a pension scheme and just under 90% had private medical cover.

Manager

People in this role will report to a more senior individual who has a specific and overarching responsibility for CSR. Almost certainly graduates (possibly with a postgraduate qualification) and probably female, they will control a budget of between £100,000 and £150,000, although they will not necessarily have any people reporting directly to them. They will have been in full-time employment for 10–15 years and are more likely than not to have worked in CSR for less than five years previously.

While salaries for the most senior CSR jobs have risen, the average for this level has remained fairly static at just over £50,000. Around 10% are earning in excess of £70,000 and 30% fall below the £45,000 threshold. Three-quarters of the respondents receive a bonus – typically worth less than £5,000 – and just over half receive a car or car allowance.

Advisor/analyst

Individuals in this role sit within the larger CSR team and report to the manager or director/head. Most likely to be a female graduate with no one reporting directly to them, they will have little, if any, budgetary responsibility. They will have been in their current role for three years or less and are likely to have had no prior experience of CSR, although they will have been in full-time employment for five–10 years.

While the average salary is around £35,000 in this role, those working for FTSE-100 companies can expect up to £10,000 more. The fact that an individual has direct control of a budget has no bearing on remuneration – and neither does location.

Assistant/team member

This is a junior, usually entry-level, role that provides support to others within a team across a range of CSR activities (with a possible bias towards community involvement and charitable giving). Occupants are typically female graduates who have been in full-time employment for five years or less and they are unlikely to have any previous experience of CSR.

Consultants

Director/senior partner/senior manager

This could be the owner of a smaller consultancy, its directors and senior partners, or the most senior individual within a CSR-focused team of a larger consultancy. They will be based in London and have a first as well as possibly a postgraduate degree – though neither will necessarily be in a CSR-related discipline. They will have been in full-time employment for around 15 years, the overwhelming majority of which has been spent in CSR, and will have been in their current role for around three years.

The average salary has remained at around £70,000 for this role (or possibly a shade less), although there are considerable variations, with much higher, and lower, amounts being earned. In part we believe this wide range reflects the different ownership structures within the consultancy sector and the personal motivations of the individuals concerned. Around a third receive no bonus – though whether this is due to the effect of the economic downturn on fee income is difficult to say. The average bonus was less than £5,000 but some people did a lot better. Neither the average salary nor bonus levels were affected by the size of consultancy. Most have access to a company pension scheme – less so in smaller consultancies – while hardly any receive a company car or car allowance.

Senior consultant

This role is performed by someone with either an in-depth knowledge of a particular area (e.g. the environment) or more wide-ranging knowledge of CSR. Typically a female graduate/postgraduate, they will work in London and have been in full-time employment for around 10 years, of which around half or more will have been in CSR. They will have been in their current job for less than three years.

The average salary in 2008/09 is in line with the previous year, at £40,000. Just under half of the respondents at this level receive no bonus and, of those who do, we estimate the average is less than £3,000. Again the size of consultancy appears to have no impact on average salary or bonus. Most had access to a pension scheme of one form or another and the vast majority of those working for larger consultancies were in receipt of a car or car allowance – compared with none in the smaller consultancies.

Consultant

This role is occupied by someone with limited experience of CSR who works under the guidance and supervision of more senior colleagues.

Slightly more likely to be female than male, and based in London, this graduate will have been in full-time employment for around five years, with about half of that spent in CSR.

The average salary was in line with last year at £30,000 and less than half of those who responded received a bonus. The vast majority had access to a contributory pension scheme and less than 10% received a car or car allowance as part of their package.

CSR in companies

The structure of the CSR team/department will vary a great deal between organisations, depending on their business focus and the overall size and structure of the company. The information provided below offers some general insight into how CSR teams are organised within companies.

In 2009 it appears that CSR professionals were, on average, controlling smaller budgets than in the previous year (Figure 3.5). The same is true

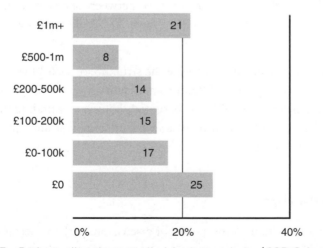

Figure 3.5 Budgets directly controlled by respondents (*CSR Salary Survey 2008/09*).

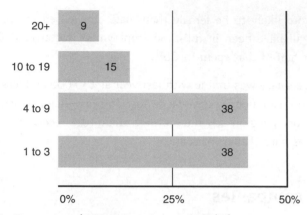

Figure 3.6 Team sizes (*CSR Salary Survey 2008/09*).

of team sizes, which appear to have slightly reduced overall. The reductions are not significant and it may be a clue that CSR is becoming further embedded into mainstream business disciplines, with more responsibilities typically associated with CSR being passed on to other business functions. The majority of CSR teams have between one to nine individuals within them whilst just under 10% have 20 people or more (see Figure 3.6).

There is no magic formula to devise the structure of a CSR team or department – every company is different and has its own staffing needs based on numerous variables. What is essential, however, is finding individuals with a high level of commitment and talent to deliver and communicate the necessary objectives.

Job function

Job function is often a topical area of discussion, perhaps because CSR as a discipline is still relatively young and therefore less defined than other business sectors. This is particularly apparent when it comes to naming the discipline and there is a good deal of contention around this point alone – 'corporate responsibility', 'corporate social responsibility', 'sustainability', 'corporate citizenship' to name a few.

In the past, some companies, particularly in the US, focused CSR strategy primarily on corporate philanthropy – the sector has certainly come a long way since then, but nevertheless there is still debate around what the core duties of the CSR professional should or should not be.

Many aspects of CSR are becoming embedded within the business at large. This includes the areas of environmental management, climate change, stakeholder dialogue, reporting and ensuring that the supply chain is operating in accordance within ethical and environmental guidelines. Broadly speaking this is a positive thing as the end-game must surely be that ethics and responsibility are not simply managed by a distinct team but shared by each and every business function.

Climate change is certainly one of the most prominent issues that businesses are currently facing and is an example of where the boundaries of the CSR professional can blur. In our current experience at Acre, some CSR professionals have an overall responsibility for climate change strategy. However, in other businesses, this function is led by a new type of employee, the climate change director, who may have some interaction with the CSR team but will sit quite separately.

Community involvement is undeniably a major activity for CSR professionals – in the 2008/09 *CSR Salary Survey*, this was identified by corporate respondents as the top activity (see Box 3.1). Reporting is also a key duty in both consultancy and corporates. This ties in with external marketing which for consultancies is a top-three activity demonstrating the importance and value that organisations place on communicating their sustainability message to stakeholders and the public at large. Environment and climate change are both high on the agenda, although this should not be taken to reflect the resources that companies put into these areas; as mentioned previously, environmental and climate change expertise often sits outside the CSR team.

Box 3.1   Top five activities for CSR professionals (*CSR Salary Survey 2008/09*)

Corporates

Community involvement

Reporting

Environment

Internal marketing

Climate change

Consultancies

Reporting

Environment

External marketing

Climate change

Community involvement

The gender gap in CSR

While we believe (and the data show) that there are more women in CSR positions, men still dominate at the higher salary levels. Considering that CSR is fundamentally based on ethics, responsibility and sometimes specifically on equality, this fact invariably raises concern. Between 2007 and 2009 the gender gap in terms of salary actually increased within the CSR space. A similar trend was reported in late 2008 in relation to the UK job market as a whole by the Office for National Statistics, so it appears that CSR is simply following the trends within the job market at large (see Figure 3.7).

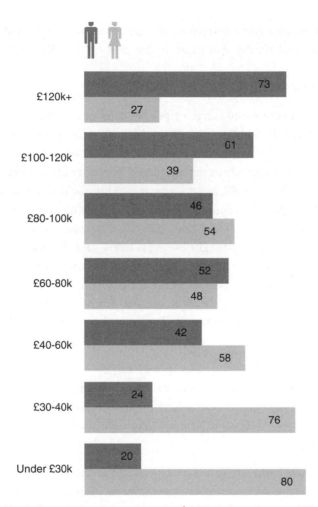

Figure 3.7 Salary according to gender (*CSR Salary Survey 2008/09*).

Getting into CSR

As more and more businesses start to integrate 'responsibility' into their core processes and communications, an increasing number of job-seekers – both fresh graduates and those experienced in other sectors – are looking to focus their careers in CSR. Before jumping headlong into the search, it's essential for anyone interested in this space to start to really understand what CSR means, and begin to see how their skills might fit.

Is a career in CSR right for me?

We've had a really broad range of people coming to Acre over the years with an interest in building a career in this area. Most people are passionate about doing 'good' in business, and to add positively to the world around them through a commercial career. There are also, however, those who mistake a job in CSR as an 'easy ride'. This couldn't be further from the truth. Corporate responsibility roles are challenging and require a great deal of commitment and drive. With increasingly advanced technical work underpinning hard-fought business cases, and the need to persuade a broad range of stakeholders – from board directors to consumers – of the merits of CSR, this isn't a sector for the faint-hearted. Having said that, it's also an extremely rewarding career for people who enjoy a challenge and who have the passion and ambition to make things happen.

How do I get into CSR?

This is a difficult question to answer, as the routes into CSR are varied. To make things simple, I'll focus here on advising both fresh graduates at the start of their professional careers and experienced individuals who'd like to change focus.

As a fresh graduate, passion and dedication are the key to securing your first job. In general, companies don't tend to recruit graduates through recruitment agencies like Acre, for the simple reason that there are a huge number of talented graduates competing for relatively few positions. Most companies can avoid paying fees to a recruitment consultant at this level and will tend to hire people who apply to them directly.

The key is to try and show in a clear CV and covering letter why you are the best candidate for their company. Try to build your experience wherever you can, either by securing some internships (prepare for these to be largely unpaid) or by highlighting work you've done at university or beyond that is relevant to CSR. Don't forget to mention what you have achieved through these experiences and why this is relevant to their business.

For 'career switchers', making the move can be slightly more complicated. Your first steps are to find out how your experience is relevant to CSR. Which elements of the CSR landscape would most benefit from your previous experience and transferable skills?

Many of the most senior CSR executives are career-switchers themselves, highlighting the most common route for people wanting to make the move. In the vast majority of cases, people will move into CSR within their organisations (rather than quitting to find a new job in this space). If you work in a large company, the chances are that CSR-related activities are going on somewhere within that corporate structure. By seeking out the decision-makers, being clear about your ambitions and focused on adding value to their work, you should find that they're open to you helping their work as a small part of your role.

By expanding your activities in CSR over time, you will then be in a position to move into it full-time. There is a large and growing workforce of highly experienced CSR professionals out there. When you apply for the more 'senior' positions without an explanation of how your background is relevant, getting through to interview stage will be a challenge. So be sure to identify parts of your former or current roles that are relevant to positions, and underline the value in those transferable skills.

Whether you're a new graduate or a career-switcher, your chances of getting that dream job will be hugely increased by two things: in-depth industry research and networking. Make sure you've done your homework – there are lots of resources where you can start to really understand the different elements of the CSR landscape and help identify where you'd best fit. It's also worth reading a number of books and publications that are readily available through bookshops and online stores.

One of the great things about CSR is that most people working in the sector are genuinely passionate about what they do, and as such they're generally keen to share their experiences with new entrants into the market. There are lots of conferences, events and online networking groups that can help you to meet people, make connections and open doors for yourself. Meeting people face-to-face is always preferable to sending off a CV, so attend as many events as you can, and use your existing contacts to find people that might be able to help.

If you're sure that a career in CSR is right for you, then perseverance and dedication will help get you where you want to be. There are lots of people who flirt with the idea of CSR without putting their all into the job search. You need to be committed and focused whilst being realistic about the timescales – you will find that your dedication will win out.

A legal perspective on CSR

Jonathan S. Lux and Marie-Louise Orre

Responsible Business: How to Manage a CSR Strategy Successfully
Edited by Manfred Pohl and Nick Tolhurst
Copyright © 2010 Manfred Pohl and Nick Tolhurst

In this chapter, we look at how CSR has shifted from being a matter of voluntary practice to a subject of legal pressure and enforcement. Real-life examples such as Nike and Chiquita are used to illustrate the enhanced legal demands companies face, as well as the absorption of CSR norms into standard business law.

Introduction

Corporate social responsibility (CSR) tends to be thought of in terms of actions that organisations can undertake on a voluntarily basis, over and above minimum legal requirements. There is no universally accepted definition of CSR but it is helpful to think about it as 'people, planet, profit'. The concept revolves around the notion that corporations should take responsibility for their activities that have an impact on the wider interests of society. The traditional focus was on financial regulation. But today there is a wider focus, embracing the environment and the community as well, and it is not far-fetched to suggest that these matters may become subject to similar audit requirements.

That organisations choose to contribute to the wider society is nothing new, and such actions are not necessarily in conflict with shareholder interests. For example, spending more than the bare necessity on staff activities may enhance staff morale, which in turn may increase the productivity – and hence the profit – of the company. CSR is sometimes presented as 'beyond mere compliance with the law' and it has often been criticised as merely being a way to create PR or 'defensive marketing' and something that cannot be legally enforced. But what has changed is that CSR has shifted from being a matter of voluntary practice to a subject of legal pressure and enforcement. These days corporations need to take CSR seriously. But why should they do so?

The power of corporations

Milton Friedman famously stated that 'the business of business is to make business', meaning that the only social responsibility of a business is to make profits. In line with this, both states and courts have traditionally been reluctant to interfere with how a company is run. But this has changed, as will be explored in this chapter, because of the growing power of corporations.

In 2000, a report called *Top 200: The Rise of Corporate Global Power* was published (Anderson & Cavanagh 2000). Some of the key findings of the report were the following:

► Of the 100 largest economies in the world, 51 were corporations and only 49 were countries (based on a comparison of corporate sales and country GDPs).

► To put this in perspective, General Motors was bigger than Denmark; DaimlerChrysler was bigger than Poland; Royal Dutch/Shell was bigger than Venezuela; IBM was bigger than Singapore; and Sony was bigger than Pakistan.

► The 1999 sales of each of the top five corporations (General Motors, Wal-Mart, ExxonMobil, Ford Motor and DaimlerChrysler) were bigger than the GDPs of 182 countries.

► And the combined sales of the top 200 corporations were bigger than the combined economies of all countries minus the biggest 10.

In other words, corporations are often more powerful than nation states and the way a company is run can have a much stronger impact on society than state actions.

In recent years we have seen an increase in litigation against multi-nationals for their involvement in, for example, human right abuses across the globe. We have also seen new legislation being passed that seeks to enforce CSR, but also some rather creative uses of old law to make corporations account for the impact of their activities around the globe.

Human rights

This is the area of CSR that has probably generated most case law. Numerous lawsuits have been filed against multinationals conducting operations in countries with questionable human rights records. The majority of these lawsuits have been brought in the USA under the Alien Tort Claims Act (ATCA). The history behind ATCA is worth mentioning because it illustrates how creatively the law can be used. ATCA dates back to 1789 and was passed by the first Congress, giving the federal courts 'original jurisdiction of any civil action by an alien for a tort only, committed in violation of the law of nations or a treaty of the United States'.

The Act has an uncertain history but it is said to have been designed to deal with piracy. It lay forgotten until the late 1970s when it was used by lawyers acting for the family of a 17-year-old tortured to death by a Paraguayan police officer. The police officer had left Paraguay and was living in New York. New York lawyers brought a claim on the basis that the police officer's actions were in 'violation of the law of nations'. In a landmark decision the US second circuit court held that: 'In the 20th century the international community has come to recognise the common danger posed by the flagrant disregard of basic human rights and particularly the right to be free of torture – for the purpose of civil liberty, the torturer has become – like the pirate and slave trader before him – the enemy of mankind. Our holding today, giving effect to a jurisdictional provision enacted by our first Congress, is a small but important step in the fulfilment of the ageless dream to free all people from brutal violence.' The family of the 17-year-old was awarded $10m.

Since the 1970s ATCA has increasingly been used against multinationals, based on activities that occurred outside of the US. That is, they impacted foreign citizens alone and had no effect whatsoever within the US. There are many cases that illustrate how ATCA can be used to enforce CSR against corporations, but the scope of this chapter does not allow for a detailed analysis of these cases. The following case summaries clarify how important it is for corporations to understand that they must not only assess the human rights records of governments in the regions in which they operate, but they must also assess and monitor the activities of the public and private contractors they might engage or who might engage them.

Unocal Corporation – US Ninth Circuit Court of Appeals, 2002

In this case, the claimants were Burmese peasants alleging that the defendants (comprising the military government of Myanmar, a Myanmar-owned oil and gas company and US oil companies, most prominently Unocal) subjected them to forced labour, forced relocation, murder, rape and torture during the construction of a gas pipeline through Myanmar. Unocal's response to the claim was to ask the court to dismiss the case, arguing that there was no theory of law that would allow Unocal to be liable for the acts occurring in connection with their projects in Myanmar. The trial judge agreed with Unocal and dismissed the claim. The judge thought that the evidence presented was not sufficient to support claims of torture. The claimants appealed and, in a landmark decision in 1997, the Federal District Court in Los Angeles agreed to hear the case against Unocal. The court concluded that corporations and their executive officers can be held legally responsible under ATCA for violations of international human rights norms in foreign countries, and that US courts have the authority to hear such claims.

Before the trial could take place, there followed three years of discovery. This is a formal pre-trial process during which each party requests relevant information and documents from the other side. The evidence that the claimants presented demonstrated that, in the court's words, 'Unocal knew that the military had a record of committing human rights abuses; that the Project hired the military to provide security for the Project, a military that forced villagers to work and entire villages to relocate for the benefit of the Project; that the military, while forcing villagers to work and relocate, committed numerous acts of violence; and that Unocal knew or should have known that the military did commit, was committing and would continue to commit these torture acts.'

In 2002, a three-judge panel of the Court of Appeals for the Ninth Circuit held that Unocal could be held liable. Two judges looked to international law and one to domestic law standards. Soon afterwards, the Ninth Circuit agreed to re-hear the case en banc (before 11 judges) to decide which standards applied. The en banc hearing was scheduled for December 13, 2004 but was cancelled because of a settlement.

Unocal agreed to compensate the claimants and provide funds for programmes in Myanmar to improve living conditions and protect the rights of people from the pipeline region, but the sum and specific terms of the settlement have not been disclosed. The only information available is that Unocal sued its insurers for failing to indemnify it beyond $15m, indicating a settlement well in excess of that amount. The Unocal litigation was the first in which it was held that ATCA actions could be brought against private corporations.

Chiquita Brands International – US District Court, 2007

A number of lawsuits were brought against Chiquita Brands International, Inc., and its subsidiaries in funding, arming and otherwise supporting terrorist organisations in Colombia, with a view to maintaining their profitable control of Colombia's banana growing regions.

The claimants were family members of trade unionists, banana workers, political organisers, social activists, and others targeted and killed by terrorists, notably the paramilitary organisation United Self-Defence Committees of Colombia (*Autodefensorias Unidas de Colombia*, or AUC), from the 1990s to 2004. In order to 'protect its employees and infrastructure' Chiquita had made regular payments to AUC and other guerrilla groups during this period.

The complaint brought under the ATCA was that Chiquita's involvement violated not only Colombian law and US law, but also international law, prohibiting crimes against humanity, extrajudicial killing, torture, war crimes and other abuses. Chiquita admitted they had they had made business with a terrorist organisation and agreed to pay a $25m fine.

Pfizer – US Second Circuit Court of Appeals, 2009

A group of Nigerian minors and their guardians sued Pfizer under ATCA, alleging that the company violated customary international law by administering the untried drug Trovan to minors in Kano during a meningitis outbreak. The claimants alleged that the drug was administered without the informed consent of the children and their parents and that this experiment led to the deaths of 11 children and serious injuries to many others. A second US lawsuit was filed against Pfizer a year later. These claimants were also a group of Nigerians injured in the Trovan drug trial under the same circumstances. Both cases were dismissed in 2005 on grounds of forum non conveniens ('inconvenient forum'). Inconvenient forum means that a court sometimes refuses to hear a case before it, if it takes the view that there is a foreign court where it would be more suitable for the case to be heard. The judge also said that the claimants had failed to show a sufficient legal source for an international prohibition of non-consensual medical treatment.

But in January 2009, the Court of Appeals reversed the lower court's dismissal of the case. By a majority the court found that the prohibition of non-consensual medical experimentation on humans is binding under customary international law. Pfizer is currently in settlement negotiations with the claimants.

The position in England and Wales

The position under English law is slightly different. A claimant can, as of right, serve proceedings on a defendant within the jurisdiction irrespective of the degree of connection with this country of the defendant or the cause of action. That is, it is possible for a claimant to bring a claim as long as the defendant has a presence, such as headquarters or offices, in the UK. A claimant can also apply to the court for permission to serve English court process on a defendant who is out of the jurisdiction (i.e. resident abroad) – for example, in circumstances where a claim is made in respect of a contract which is said to be governed by English law or, in the case of a claim in tort, where either the claimant sustained damage in England or the claimant sustained damage outside England but as a result of an act committed in England. However, if a claim is brought before an English court, a defendant can challenge the court's jurisdiction on the ground of 'forum non conveniens'. This often means that an English court will refuse to hear a claim against a defendant who has no connection with England and where the action took place in another part of the world. But there are exceptions, as the following case summary will illustrate.

Cape plc – UK House of Lords, 2002

The Cape case involved asbestos mining and the hideous asbestos-related diseases resulting from those operations. The parent company of the group was UK-registered with its office in London. Its principal subsidiaries, for the purpose of the litigation, were mining companies in South Africa.

The claim was brought by South African asbestos victims. The evidence indicated that over a period of many years Cape had suppressed information which would have revealed the acute danger of working with asbestos and which therefore substantially delayed the implementation of measures necessary to protect those working with asbestos. Additionally, Cape took advantage of the apartheid system. They employed black women, children and other workers for far lower wages than were paid to whites, with less/cheaper protective clothing and with less in the way of medical back-up and facilities in order to increase the profitability of their business. The profits were channelled back to England.

The defendants, Cape plc, challenged the English court's jurisdiction on the ground of 'forum non conveniens' and argued that the case should be tried in South Africa. The case went all the way to the House of Lords, which is the final court of appeal. The claimants argued that the legal aid in South Africa had been withdrawn for personal injury claims, that there was no reasonable likelihood of any lawyer or group of lawyers being able or willing to fund proceedings of this weight and that there was no other available source of funding open to the claimants. The House of Lords decided in favour of the claimants and allowed the case to continue in the English courts.

As the cases outlined above illustrate, companies must not only assess the human rights records of governments in the regions in which they operate, but they must also assess and monitor the activities of the public and private contractors they might engage as well as those of their subsidiaries. If this is not done, a corporation runs the risk of being taken to court, no matter where the wrongdoing took place.

New legislation

There are plenty of codes of conduct, from codes adopted by international organisations and social interest groups to codes drafted by business support groups. But while there is much talk about CSR, there are surprisingly few pieces of legislation that directly address corporations and CSR. However, there are signs of increasing responsibility being placed on company directors to have regard to more than just profit maximisation, which is often referred to as 'enhanced shareholder value'.

For example, the UK Companies Act 2006 (the Act) includes the first ever statement of directors' duties in respect of the environment and the social impacts of their company's business. The new law requires directors to pay regard to these issues, making sure there is a link between responsible business behaviour and business success. There are a number of matters that a director needs to take into account when discharging his duty to promote the success of the company, including:

▶ the likely consequences of any decision in the long term

▶ the interests of the company's employees

▶ the need to foster the company's business relationships with suppliers, customers and others

▶ the impact of the company's operations on the community and the environment

▶ the desirability of the company maintaining a reputation for high standards of business conduct

▶ the need to act fairly as between members of the company.

However, as you may have noticed, some of the matters that a director needs to take into account when making decisions are potentially in conflict with each other. Take, for example, the situation that Chiquita found themselves in and let's pretend the AUC was not listed as a terrorist organisation. How should the directors go about discharging their duty to promote the success of the company under the Act? The directors said that the decision to make the payments to the AUC was based on the fact that they thought this was the only way they could make sure that their employees would be safe. And yes, there was a real threat against Chiquita's employees in Colombia. The guerrilla groups had previously killed employees at the Colombian plant. The directors can therefore be said to have taken the 'interests of the company's employees' into account when making the decision to pay the AUC. But the decision had an adverse effect on the community, as it made an organisation that targeted and killed civilians in Colombia even stronger. That is, by taking the interests of its employees into account when making the decision to pay the AUC, they disregarded, for example, 'the impact of the company's operations on the community'.

There appears to be no hierarchy among the matters a director needs to take into account under the Act and the list is not exclusive. English courts have usually refused to make value judgments and interfere with business decisions. So how does a director discharge his duties?

Some critics of the Companies Act have said that it will just be a formal 'box ticking' exercise. However, the UK government has responded to that in a ministerial statement from June 2007:

The words 'have regard to' mean 'think about; they are absolutely not about ticking boxes. If 'thinking' about leads to the conclusion, as we believe it will in many cases, that the proper course is to act positively to achieve the objectives in the clause, that will be what the director's duty is – in other words 'have regard to' means 'give proper' consideration to.

While the duties imposed by the Companies Act on directors can be seen as a step forward in the CSR debate, the new legislation has not yet been the subject of any legal guidance from the courts. But it seems to suggest that CSR can no longer be ignored by directors when making business decisions and that there is at least a potential risk of litigation if they fail to pay regard to each and every one of the six matters listed in the Act.

CSR policies/statements

It has become increasingly popular among corporations to produce CSR policies. As stated in the introduction, CSR policies are often criticised as being 'defensive marketing' or 'just another way of making PR' and something that cannot be legally enforced. However, caution should be exercised when drafting CSR policies or when making public statements. If not, a corporation can find itself subject to litigation.

Kasky v Nike, US Supreme Court, 2002

In 1997, Nike found itself at the centre of a heated debate on working conditions and human rights in its supply chain. The key allegations were that the workers who made Nike products, who were mainly women under the age of 24, got paid less than the applicable local minimum wage, were subjected to physical, verbal and sexual abuse and were exposed to toxic chemicals, noise, heat and dust without adequate safety equipment, in violation of applicable local occupational health and safety regulations.

In response to the adverse publicity, Nike made statements to the public that the allegations were false and misleading. Specifically, Nike said that workers who make Nike products are protected from physical and sexual abuse, that they are paid in accordance with applicable local laws and regulations governing wages and hours, that they are paid on average double the applicable local minimum wage, that they receive a 'living wage', that they receive free meals and health care, and that their working conditions are in compliance with applicable local laws and regulations governing occupational health and safety.

Marc Kasky, a Nike critic, objected to the campaign. He sued Nike under California's unfair competition and false advertising laws, alleging that the company's claims were misleading. He wanted the court to grant an injunction requiring Nike to 'undertake a court-approved public information campaign' to correct any false or misleading statement, and to cease misrepresenting the working conditions under which Nike products are made. An injunction is an order made by a court to a party, ordering him or her to do, or refrain from doing, an act or acts.

The legal issue was whether Nike's statements were commercial or non-commercial. The distinction is important because non-commercial statements on public issues enjoy special protection and freedoms under the US constitution. Commercial speech, on the other hand, is not subject to the same protection. The case was appealed all the way to the Supreme Court, which concluded that Nike's speech was commercial and that government may entirely prohibit commercial speech that is false or misleading. However, the court did not rule whether the statements made by Nike were misleading. Instead the court sent the case down to a lower court for a decision.

Before the lower court passed judgment the case was settled out of court. Nike ended up paying $1.5m to the Fair Labor Association.

Conclusion

One of the roles of a lawyer is to advise clients on what they can do without running the risk of being subject to litigation. The case summaries above are intended to give the reader a flavour of how CSR has shifted from being a matter of voluntary practice to a subject of legal pressure and enforcement, rather than provide specific guidance on what can be done to avoid litigation. At the moment the typical defendant is usually a multinational which allegedly is in breach of human rights. But this is likely to expand and it is probably just a matter of time before we see more claims relating to the environment.

The fact that most of the cases in which corporations are alleged to be in breach of CSR norms are settled out of court also makes it difficult to provide guidance on what exactly increases/decreases the risk of litigation. The main reason why the lawsuits are settled out of court is that while the legal costs for defending a claim can be significant this might be nothing compared to the damage caused to the company's reputation.

As illustrated by Nike, corporations should also be careful not to draft CSR statements without assessing the feasibility of actually implementing them. That is, a company should avoid using CSR statements as PR. Instead, companies should be careful to make sure that the CSR statements/policies reflect the values of the firm and that they address the actual issues that come up in their specific business operations. As Nike illustrates, your CSR statement can be used against you.

What corporations need to do is to be aware of CSR and anticipate the major issues that could arise in their business operations. Corporations would be well advised to assess the concerns posed by their operations and to develop their responses to those concerns, before the lawsuits are filed and the protests begin. ATCA is an example of an old piece of legislation that has been creatively used to enforce CSR against corporations. The Companies Act 2006 is a new piece of legislation that is obviously drafted in order to make sure that company directors keep CSR in mind when making their decisions. In other words, CSR norms must become a part of the business-making process.

References

Anderson, S. and Cavanagh, J. (2000) *Top 200: The Rise of Corporate Global Power*, Institute for Policy Studies.

Corporate volunteering as a tool of strategic company development

Kirsten B. Wenzel

Responsible Business: How to Manage a CSR Strategy Successfully
Edited by Manfred Pohl and Nick Tolhurst
Copyright © 2010 Manfred Pohl and Nick Tolhurst

This chapter will help you to understand the advantages of strategic corporate volunteering as part of a CSR strategy and give you hands-on advice on how to achieve the best results. It will illustrate the beneficial impact of corporate volunteering on human resources, stakeholder relations and company reputation. Further, specific guidelines are given on how to successfully plan and implement corporate volunteering as part of a CSR strategy.

Introduction

When a company allows its employees to paint their children's schools, spend time as development aid workers or help out at a local non-profit organisation during working hours, that company supports a good cause by excusing its employees from work – this is called corporate volunteering (corporate volunteering). In other words, corporate volunteering describes a company's commitment to society expressed in its donation of employees' competencies, manpower and working time. Corporate volunteering is generally managed by a human resources department, but may also be handled by corporate responsibility or communications departments.

Most companies allow employees to volunteer for one-off projects, i.e. painting the school, on a short-term basis. In this context, corporate volunteering is often seen as a philanthropic activity rather than a strategic investment as part of a corporate social responsibility (CSR) strategy. It is only recently that companies have begun to see the positive impact of corporate volunteering on their employees, the company itself and society. Hence, there is a noticeable shift from short-term to long-term activities and from viewing corporate volunteering as a philanthropic activity to actually incorporating it into a broader strategy. Deutsche Bank, for example, has successfully implemented corporate volunteering as part of its CSR strategy (Blumberg & Scheubel 2007). In line with the company's guiding principle 'Passion to perform', its corporate volunteering principle is based upon 'Passion creates: opportunities.' Deutsche Bank distinguishes between long- and short-term corporate volunteering projects and between core and complementary expertise used by its employees. The established social days, for example, are of a short-term nature and ask for complementary expertise of employees. Groups of 10–100 people take on practical tasks, such as gardening and renovations or conversion work to accommodate handicapped persons. On these action days, employees can see the results of their work at the end of the day and often gain valuable insights into a different world. At the other end of the scale, the bank's programme 'Expert Plus' is a long-term involvement that asks employees to apply their core competencies to projects. For example, customer consultants teach finance-related topics in schools or consult non-profit organisations regarding their strategic, marketing and financial issues.

A large proportion of employees value their company's commitment and would love to engage in societal projects on their own time. By offering corporate volunteering programmes, companies obviously meet their employees' needs and desires. But what's in it for the company? The following chapter is based mainly on Blumberg & Scheubel's (2007) survey carried out in Germany and is structured as follows:

▶ benefits to the company in strategic corporate volunteering

▶ a how-to for corporate volunteering – strategy and implementation of corporate volunteering programmes

▶ 10 golden rules of successful corporate volunteering: hands-on advice.

Benefits to the company

Corporate volunteering has a lot to offer to an organisation, its employees and society. Obviously, the primary benefit goes to the cause that is supported by corporate volunteering. That might be a school that is being renovated, a non-profit organisation that money is raised for, or people who benefit from advice they would not have been able to afford themselves. But the company and its employees also benefit from the involvement. Corporate volunteering can support environmentally friendly behaviour in employees and increase their customer orientation.

The relationship with existing suppliers can be strengthened and work–life balance improved. However, corporate volunteering has a much more fundamental influence on the company and its employees when it is used to further develop a company's values and culture. This can be achieved by influencing five primary dimensions:

▶ human resources

▶ change management processes

▶ company reputation

▶ employees

▶ society.

Human resources

Human resources staff face the challenge of combining companies' and employees' interests for the good of the company. It is their duty to assure that employees have the knowledge and ability to perform in the company's best interest. There are three key competencies that are regarded as highly important for nearly all employees (Pinter 2008):

▶ methodological competence – analytical skills, organisational talent and creativity

▶ social competence – ability to communicate, team spirit, the ability to assert oneself and the ability to handle conflicts

▶ self-competence – motivation, flexibility, emotional intelligence, mobility.

All of these factors have in common the fact that they cannot be learned but have to be experienced. They are the required 'soft skills' of a person. Because corporate volunteering allows employees to experience rather than to learn, it is an innovative instrument for human resources to reinforce and expand employees' knowledge and abilities. Development projects and social placements, in particular, are effective corporate volunteering tools. Siemens Automation & Drive Division combines CSR engagement with personnel work (Pinter 2008). The 'open up doors' programme invites employees to work at a social institution (i.e. supporting the youth drug rehabilitation organisation MUDRA e.V.) for a week (social placement). These kinds of assignment sharpen awareness of social realities different from one's own. 'Open up doors', for example, enables employees to meet with the person behind the label 'alcoholic' and recognise the other person's need to be known and appreciated. That way, a new appreciation develops for one's own – usually very comfortable – situation. Furthermore, employees may appreciate their company more and see job-related problems in their proper perspective.

Change management process

Secondments and development projects are very suitable in supporting change management processes. The PricewaterhouseCoopers programme, Ulysses, demonstrates that experience gained through corporate volunteering enhances the development of defined key competencies (Pinter 2008). In the Ulysses programme, partners change their job-related surroundings as well as their social and cultural background by living and working in a foreign country for two months. They are forced to deal with their tasks and solve their problems without the familiar routines or structures for back-up. In order to find suitable solutions for development aid, they have to question approved methods and established approaches. This is exactly the time when thinking processes are initiated that challenge individual beliefs and company values. This process helps to open up employees' minds to the potential of realigning established company processes when they return home.

Company reputation

Corporate volunteering has a strong influence on company reputation, too. Corporate volunteering supports the development and anchoring of companies' values within the company culture. Employees feel pride in working for a responsible company and more closely identify with that company. For example, Henkel KG in Germany has successfully implemented its corporate volunteering programme MIT (*Miteinander im Team* – Together as a team) (Richter 2003). Originating in the mid-1990s when the German government was reducing its involvement in social projects, Henkel was flooded with thousands of petitions for social causes. The company decided to implement a strategic corporate volunteering programme. In January 1998 a team of six, which included members from personnel, PR and the works council, defined Henkel's MIT corporate volunteering criteria. Supporting employees' own initiatives was the central aspect. One employee, who volunteered in a horseback-riding project for handicapped children, sought and received funding from MIT for special equipment for one horse. Because the project was so successful, a second horse was financed by MIT a year later.

The company reports the following advantages for its business:

▶ enhanced self-confidence of employees

▶ enhanced creativity of employees

▶ older employees find new prospects before retiring

▶ strengthened corporate feeling

▶ enhanced relationship with stakeholders in the local community

▶ enhanced public trust, leading to a stronger company reputation.

As the example shows, corporate volunteering activities can strengthen a company's image and its reputation as a good corporate citizen in the local community. In return, employees are proud to work for the company and may even become so-called company brand advocates, i.e. they talk positively about their company to clients and friends. Their activity may in turn attract more excellent people who want to work for the company. If a company achieves such a high level of positive word-of-mouth, it develops its brand as a good employer.

Employees

As outlined in the introduction, Deutsche Bank has successfully incorporated a corporate volunteering programme into its overall strategy. The company aims for a more strategic focus of individual activities by strengthening long-term projects with employees who devote their core competencies to a project. Employees are, in turn, highly motivated to participate in the programmes and to work for Deutsche Bank. The bank reports the following positive aspects of its strategic corporate volunteering alignment (Blumberg & Scheubel 2007):

▶ higher employee motivation, resulting in increased loyalty

▶ consequently, reduced employee turnover rates

▶ increased overall attractiveness as an employer

▶ development of employees' professional expertise

▶ development of employees' social expertise

▶ better employee effectiveness.

Employees value corporate volunteering as a plus when choosing a company to work for. The majority of job-seekers prefer to work for a company involved in CSR activities, all other aspects being equal. More than one-third go even further and would take on a job for less money if given the opportunity to work in corporate volunteering projects. From a company perspective, corporate volunteering not only secures employee loyalty and encourages their development, but it also benefits the recruiting process in the first place.

Society

Corporate volunteering also shows to what extent companies feel responsible for their local environment. Moreover, corporate volunteering is a great opportunity to get involved with relevant stakeholder groups. In turn, society and its different stakeholder groups have rising confidence in the company and therefore greater acceptance of its economic decisions. Ideally, corporate volunteering multiplies existing CSR activities within the company's environment.

A how-to for corporate volunteering

A good corporate volunteering programme is designed bottom-up and not top-down and it is of a long-term nature. This approach ensures employee identification with the company and cause, and guarantees continuous collaboration among company, employee and societal cause. Generally, companies should allow time for employees to get involved in social/ ecological projects, reward engagement for accepted projects during employees' spare time with money, time or allowance in kind, and include corporate volunteering in each employee's goal-setting. Taking into account employees' wishes regarding their project choice also helps to ensure successful projects. It cannot be stressed enough that a successful corporate volunteering programme should be regarded as a strategic investment that benefits the company involvement as much as the cause supported. Consequently, the design of corporate volunteering programmes should be result-oriented and professional. This will minimise the danger of outsiders judging the programme merely to a philanthropic activity.

The five-step plan in Figure 5.1 is advisable for successful implementation of corporate volunteering programmes (Blumberg & Scheubel 2007). Successful implementation of such a programme is well illustrated by IBM's 'On Demand Community' (Diehl & Conrad 2008). The On Demand Community was established in 2003 as one of several corporate volunteering projects in the IBM department 'IBM and society'. For IBM it is important to have a close connection between the voluntary, non-profit commitment and IBM's core competencies in IT, consulting and project management innovations. Thus, IBM supports employees' volunteer work with relevant IBM resources for their individual social/environmental involvement.

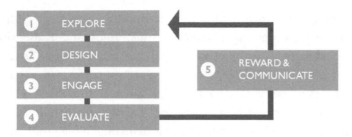

Figure 5.1 A five-step plan for successful implementation of corporate volunteering programmes (Blumberg & Scheuble 2007).

Phase 1: Explore

An essential factor for the success of corporate volunteering is balancing the needs, interests and goals of participating stakeholders (society, employee, company). The exploration stage identifies individual stakeholders' claims, defines mutual goals and determines potential topics for the corporate volunteering programme. Results of internal and external analyses are then aligned with business objectives (HR strategy, PR/marketing strategy, CSR strategy). This results in a specification for the corporate volunteering programme that also factors in the needs and interests of employees and expectations of society (needs-based matching and strategy development). IBM places great value on the use of an employee's special expertise and on a verifiable advantage for society when it collaborates with non-profit organisations. Additionally, employees initiate a project 'on demand'. In other words, a perceived need in employees' surroundings (e.g. network optimisation at a school or support of a village development programme) will be supported if the project meets IBM corporate volunteering programme criteria.

Phase 2: Design

The design phase translates results of the 'needs-based matching' into a corporate volunteering strategy while creating specific project concepts.

Precise projects are identified within conceptual workshops with previously defined partner organisations. Aims, roles and responsibilities between the partner organisation and participating employee are defined, time and training resources allocated and key performance indicators (KPIs, the importance of which will be discussed in Phase 4) for the project agreed upon. Typical KPIs for a corporate volunteering programme are the number of employees participating in the programme, the hours spent on a single project (company-supported and employees' own time), the percentage of core expertise used in the project and the price of the work carried out in monetary terms (i.e. the value of pro bono projects in financial counselling). The workshops ensure that non-profit organisations suggest projects that suit a company's overall strategy and employees' core competencies. Additionally, goals should be agreed upon that allow employees to experience the actual value of their commitment.

Phase 3: Engage

This third phase starts with employees' preparation for their specific assignment. For an effective project realisation, it is important to provide a complete project description with relevant instructions. Furthermore, the establishment of a feedback process generates a continuous exchange of experience among employees, non-profit organisations and the company. Additionally, the previously defined communication measures (e.g. intranet, employee newsletter, corporate volunteering flyer/brochure) have to be implemented. Internal communication is the main instrument for creating awareness of and motivation for the corporate volunteering programme. It is essential for the programme's success that colleagues and management reward involved volunteers with respect and also pay tribute to their commitment. IBM supports its volunteers by publishing successful stories on the IBM website. Additionally, hours spent on the cause during official working hours can be accumulated and exchanged for a monetary donation to the partner organisation. Fifty hours of voluntary activity are rewarded with an additional donation of €1,000 by IBM.

Phase 4: Evaluate

Corporate volunteering programmes should be evaluated against the same standards as all investments made by a company. It is vital that the return on investment is also made transparent for corporate volunteering programmes. Measuring and evaluating corporate volunteering allow benchmarking against set goals and serve as the basis for a continuous process of optimisation and development. Therefore it is important to define KPIs that reflect organisational goals, on the one hand, and quantify societal effects on the other. Corporate volunteering programmes are sustainable and in line with a CSR strategy only when they pursue critical business objectives. The IBM corporate volunteering programme was evaluated by the American Point of Light Foundation Institute one year after its introduction. A significant positive influence at the international level has already been reported.

Phase 5: Reward and communicate

The reporting tool is the basis for internal and external communication, i.e. a CSR report, and for the remuneration of employees' commitment by the company and society. Internal communication (storytelling) should be carried out continuously in order to attract a rising number of employees to the programme. Corporate volunteering can also be communicated externally in a discrete and authentic manner. Partner non-profit organisations, for example, are a very valuable channel for informing local and regional media about the engagement. The annual International Volunteer Day is also a good platform for presenting the company and enhancing its reputation. Increasingly, recruiting fairs are used as a communications platform, reflecting the importance of CSR involvement in choosing an employer.

In summary, strategic corporate volunteering benefits the company as much as it benefits society and those employees who are involved, through its positive impact on human resources, change management processes and company reputation. What all examples have in common is their strategic nature. They are not single philanthropic activities. Furthermore, they are in line with the company's particular CSR and overall strategy. If you follow the five-step plan described, your corporate volunteering programme will be successful over the long term. To help with the strategic task you as a manager are facing, Box 5.1 outlines 10 golden rules for successful corporate volunteering.

Box 5.1 Ten golden rules for successful corporate volunteering

1. Respect employees' self-governance
Corporate volunteering arises from people's unsolicited support of a cause. Therefore, there should be no pressure to participate in a programme.

2. Create a strategy
Offer an umbrella for corporate volunteering activities that incorporate company values and long-term goals. The umbrella should allow employees to organise their activities proactively and independently.

3. Orientate yourself according to employees' needs
It is of crucial importance for employees' motivation and initiative that a company's corporate volunteering programme is in line with employees' wants. A survey among employees can be used to identify those wants and needs and to take the first communication steps.

4. Make sure that top management supports the programme
Approval from the board of directors is vital for the programme's head-count and budget. It may be advisable to persuade a member of the board to act as an ambassador for the corporate volunteering strategy.

5. Involve human resources and communications departments from the very beginning
Arrange close collaboration with human resources for the programme implementation. Moreover, assure yourself of support of

internal communications in order to promote the programme within the company.

6. **Measure programme's success**
Think about measuring and evaluating the social impact and define relevant KPIs for your programme. Install an appropriate reporting tool (preferably on the intranet) that allows employees to communicate their accomplished activities as well as the numbers of hours spent.

7. **Be precise regarding your offer to employees**
Negotiate a time-off policy with the board of directors, i.e. how many salaried working days per year employees can be excused from work for their social/environmental engagement. Reach an agreement regarding matched funding, i.e. employees' engagement will be rewarded by a monetary contribution by the company to the cause.

8. **Create an effective information stage**
Create an intranet page for corporate volunteering, informing employees about the programme, and use a 'road show' concept to illustrate the corporate volunteering programme and attract new, interested parties.

9. **Acknowledge employees' commitment**
For example, use storytelling via internet and intranet, internal newsletters and customer magazines; reward especially committed employees' or teams.

10. **Start small and develop a flexible and rather informal programme structure**
Size and complexity of the corporate volunteering programme should be defined by employees. Develop initiatives in collaboration with employees. If you implement a decentralised programme structure with less bureaucracy, and delegate authority and responsibility to a single employee, high motivation and reduced costs are guaranteed.

Source: Blumberg & Scheubel (2007).

References

Blumberg, M. and Scheubel, V. (2007) *Hand in Hand: Corporate Volunteering als Instrument der Organisationsentwicklung in Deutschland*, Bremen: Brands & Values GmbH.

Diehl, B. and Conrad, C. (2008) Corporate volunteering – chance für das Talentmanagement, *Wirtschaftspsychologie Aktuell* **3**: 57–60.

Pinter, A. (2008) Corporate volunteering als Instrument zur strategischen Implementierung von Corporate Social Responsibility. In: Müller, M. and Schaltegger, S. (eds), *Corporate Social Responsibility Trend oder Modeerscheinung?* Oekom Verlag.

Richter, M. (2003) 'Die Teamlösung', In Schöffmann, D. (ed.), *Wenn alle Gewinnen – Bürgerschaftliches Engagement von Unternehmen*, Herausgeber: edition Körber-Stiftung.

CSR assurance in practice: measuring and auditing sustainability[1]

Martin G. Viehöver, Volker Türk and Sam Vaseghi

Responsible Business: How to Manage a CSR Strategy Successfully
Edited by Manfred Pohl and Nick Tolhurst
Copyright © 2010 Manfred Pohl and Nick Tolhurst

In this chapter, sustainability (CSR) verification in practice is explored. The authors look at what sustainability (CSR) verification is and why it is important to a company and its stakeholders, from both internal and external points of view. The authors continue by examining some prominent aspects that a CSR manager should know about sustainability verification. The chapter further outlines two of the most important assurance standards – the ISAE 3000 and the AA1000AS – and provides a first guidance and a best-practice checklist.

Introduction

The significance of extra-financial (sustainability/CSR) information to a company's stakeholders has increased over the years and is expected to continue in this way for the foreseeable future. In this respect, trust in the level of a company's commitment to being 'a part of the solution' rather than 'a part of the problem' has become a key factor to corporate success. The main goal and key benefit of CSR assurance reports is to leverage trust from a wide range of stakeholders, both externally and internally. In particular, those stakeholders who have a financial stake in the company increasingly pay attention to CSR-related information. (Readers should note that there are a number of terms used in this field, including but not limited to sustainability, corporate social responsibility (CSR), corporate responsibility (CR), and environmental, social and governance (ESG) issues. Frequently they are referred to as 'non-financial' information; however, the more commonly used term is 'extra-financial' information, as are often linked to financial performance.)

Mainstream investors, especially institutional investors such as pension or state funds, increasingly rely on the validity and reliability of information surrounding performance and management quality in the area of CSR. They do so because they understand that extra-financial information is increasingly important in determining a company's ability to meet and maintain its stakeholders' expectations.

In short, independent or third-party assurance is a process aimed at internal and external stakeholders and users of the report whereby the reporting organisation provides the criteria, and an independent assurance provider tests whether there is evidence that the information in the report meets these criteria. The verification may be applied either to the information itself or to the selection of the information, i.e. verifying whether the information is 'right' against a specific definition or whether the 'right' information has been presented. However, we believe that beyond its external role in building trust, its function as a driver for continuous improvement of internal processes and systems of an organisation is often underestimated.

As in financial audits, 'material' misstatements around extra-financial issues – incorrect or missing information – could originate from errors in the selection, collection or aggregation of information as well as from fraud. Material, in this sense, could be defined as misstated in a way that would cause stakeholders to alter their decisions. Thus, the focus and scope of CSR assurance engagements can range from testing management systems, reporting processes and the issue of identification, to testing the resulting performance and even management statements.

In addition to assurance performed by a third-party assurance provider, assurance by a stakeholder panel or by inclusion of an expert review in the report are also common practice. However, the latter two are frequently combined with an independent assurance, as they have certain limitations, especially in scope. We will focus on third-party/independent assurance, as we expect this to remain the predominant form or, at least, its underlying basis.

This chapter will provide readers with an insight into different elements of an assurance engagement and provide introductory guidance on internal decision-making, planning and management of such an engagement.

Background

As previously stated, the primary aim of an assurance engagement is to increase the level of trust of stakeholders. However, the importance and the needs of the various (internal and external) stakeholders will vary depending on, among other things, the sector, the company's size, its legal form and its position in the value chain.

Think about the needs of your company's relevant stakeholder groups when deciding on the scope and level of your external assurance. The level of assurance determines the depth of testing performed by the assurance provider (discussed later in the chapter). You might even include this topic in your stakeholder communication in order to get an understanding of the elements of your reporting (the scope) and the level of confidence they require. Table 6.1 gives examples of typical stakeholder needs that can be addressed by CSR assurance reports.

Table 6.1 Examples of typical stakeholder needs that can be addressed by CSR assurance

Internal stakeholder	Typical needs
All	Common needs: ▶ To gain confidence that the CSR measures are more than just lip service or PR ▶ To gain confidence that the material and relevant CSR issues are addressed at a reasonable level ▶ To gain confidence that the quality of the information within the assurance scope meets the reporting criteria published
Employees	▶ Inclusiveness, feeling recognised being part and playing a role from the visions values and principles to daily operations ▶ Recognise management's commitment and leadership ▶ To understand the full picture of sustainability reporting across the organisation ▶ To understand goals and objectives as well as the road map, and which areas of the company's CSR management need further improvement and how they can contribute to this

Internal stakeholder	Typical needs
Managers	*Non-CSR managers* ▶ To get an understanding of how committed management are to CSR, and thus to what extent they are expected to reinforce their department's contribution to CSR goals or activities *CSR managers* ▶ To take ownership and express commitment ▶ To ensure the quality of CSR information and management systems of CSR ▶ To understand which areas of the company's CSR management need further improvements ▶ To raise commitment towards CSR management within the organisation and 'walk the talk'
Owners	▶ To gain confidence that CSR management systems are reliable and deliver the expected outcomes ▶ To raise an understanding, at least on the level of compliance, of the stakeholders' expectations ▶ To understand which areas of the company's CSR management need further improvement

External stakeholder	Typical needs
All	Common needs: ▶ To gain confidence that, following the CSR measures and objectives, the company will 'walk the talk' ▶ To get a reasonable picture of the fulfilment of stakeholders' expectations
Suppliers	▶ To get a better understanding of the importance of supply-chain-related CSR issues for the company (client) and how they might use this to gain or maintain a competitive advantage ▶ To demonstrate influence towards suppliers to move from a 'compliance only' attitude to a 'collaborative' and 'proactive' attitude
Society	▶ To gain trust in the company, seeing its business as a legitimate source of products, services or employment embedded in the society

Table 6.1 (*Continued*)

External stakeholder	Typical needs
Government	▶ To ensure a broad understanding of the region's/country's societal, environmental and economic expectations with respect to the level of compliance as well as determination of its own agenda for regulatory actions
Creditors	▶ To gain a better understanding of the nature and extent of CSR-related risks which could interfere with the company's cash flow, and to gain confidence that the management has reduced these risks to an acceptable level
Shareholders	▶ To receive a trustworthy picture that both management systems and the reported information are robust
Customers	▶ To gain trust in the company and its brands, and thus have a clear conscience when purchasing its products or services ▶ To understand company's CSR road map and, at an early stage, become proactively involved in their needs and expectations

Benefits and risks of CSR assurance

When discussing and ultimately deciding in favour of, or against, an external assurance, the benefits and risks of potential assurance options should be understood and assessed. Even if CSR reporting and assurance are made compulsory, options regarding the scope and level are likely to remain.

You may derive various options from the mapped and weighted needs of your relevant stakeholder groups. For all options that are likely to be achievable, benefits and potential risks should be identified and assessed. However, in doing so you should consider how the relevance of assurance and the perceptions and expectations of your stakeholders may develop over time and what this would mean for your assurance journey/strategy. Remember that a successful assurance engagement is not necessarily achievable off the top of one's head, particularly when considering the option not to assure.

Assurance alternatives are roughly pre-defined through standards that are likely to be applied in the engagement (e.g. ISAE 3000 or AA1000). The focus of the assurance (e.g. data, management systems, business processes or statements) and the corresponding levels (limited/moderate, reasonable/high or full) should be narrowed down to those that seem most suitable for the desired aims.

Benefits of external assurance

There is a wide variety of motives and drivers for external assurance on CSR-related matters. Among others, they depend highly on the relevance of sustainability issues in the organisation's sector, its business and sustainability strategy and the maturity of its sustainability management. In general, the assurance should aim to achieve internal, external and integrated benefits. Table 6.2 highlights some typical benefits, both tangible and intangible, that an external assurance can bring to an organisation. A tangible benefit is one with direct financial consequences that are easily measurable, while an intangible benefit has indirect financial consequences that are either not measurable or only able to be estimated or modelled approximately.

Risks of an assurance engagement

As with most processes, there are also potential down-sides or risks. A risk describes an adverse outcome, and thus a risk of an assurance engagement describes adverse results occurring during or after a successful or unsuccessful assurance engagement. Table 6.3 gives examples of potential risks in a CSR assurance engagement, from the company's perspective.

Standards

The predominant reporting guideline in the field of CSR is set by the Global Reporting Initiative (GRI). The current version, the *G3 Guidelines*,

Table 6.2 Some typical benefits of external assurance

Internal	External[a]	Integrated
▶ Identification of errors in, or improvement points for, the internal reporting/ management system (T/I)	▶ To provide a level of confidence for stakeholders who base their decisions on the reported information (T/I)	▶ To reduce the cost of capital by improving sustainability ratings and the attraction of additional investors (T)
▶ Identification of efficiency potentials of the reporting system (T)		
▶ To emphasise to internal interrupters and 'non-believers' management's commitment to sustainability management (I)[a]	▶ To improve the ranking in sustainability ratings and rankings, or to become eligible if this is a prerequisite (T/I)	▶ To use the assurance itself or the type and/ or level of assurance as a differentiator (first-mover advantage) (I)
▶ Enhancement of employee involvement and increased motivation of employees to achieve CSR goals (I)	▶ To reduce the risk premium/ cost of capital (T)	▶ To increase sales from customers where assurance is a prerequisite (T)
▶ Facilitation of internal learning processes and feedback to reporting units (I/T)	▶ To emphasise the management's commitment to the sustainability management (I)	
▶ Identification of improvement points for internal training and information systems (I/T)		▶ Identification of non-compliance issues (T/I)
▶ Improved acknowledgement and leverage of the work of sustainability managers as their work is checked and perceived to be more important (I)	▶ Not to be identified as a laggard as it becomes common business practice for key peers (I)	▶ Systematic contribution to an enhanced understanding of company risks (T/I)

T, tangible benefit; I, intangible benefit.
[a]Depends on the scope and level of the engagement, the standards used, the type and reputation of the assurance provider and the internal/external stakeholder group.

Table 6.3 Typical risks of external assurance

Internal	External[a]	Integrated
▶ An internal audit was either not performed, poor or missed material errors (bugs) in the management/reporting system ▶ A lack of competence, knowledge or control measures lead to material errors ▶ A poorly executed assurance engagement can miss material misstatements ▶ For the staff involved, assurance engagements often require resources that come on top of the day-to-day work ▶ Performed too early or with the wrong aim, it might scare people off rather than motivate them to get involved in CSR issues ▶ You might prefer to let sleeping dogs lie. Assurance provider might discover issues that need to be addressed	▶ Lack of trust of relevant stakeholders in the competence of the assurance provider ▶ Scope of the assurance engagement is seen to be too basic for stakeholders who use this in their rankings/ratings or decision-making process ▶ The assurance is seen to be a diversionary tactic in case material issues are neglected or left aside, and by contrast the accomplished assurance is emphasised in the stakeholder communication[b] ▶ Stakeholders are likely to expect that an organisation continues and expands its assurance engagement once started	▶ Loss of reputation in case the assurance statement was rejected or contains material qualifications ▶ Loss of reputation (internally and externally) if it is obvious that material issues or units were not covered in the scope

[a]Depends on the scope and the level of the engagement, the standards used, the type and the reputation of the assurance provider as well as the internal/external stakeholder group.
[b]It should be noted that the scope of an assurance engagement can contain the question whether the organisation focuses on the 'right' things in their sustainability management and reporting.

outlines principles for external assurance (Global Reporting Initiative 2006) and allows a '+' to be added to the level of reporting (e.g. A+, B+ or C+) when this has been used. Even though the G3 is not an assurance standard itself, the application of the GRI Reporting Framework can fall within the scope of an assurance engagement.

Currently, two explicit assurance standards are applied by assurance providers: the ISAE 3000, published by the International Auditing and Assurance Standards Board; and the AA1000AS, published by AccountAbility.

About the ISAE 3000

The ISAE 3000 is the assurance standard of the International Federation of Accountants and focuses on matters other than historical financial information. Even though it is not specifically designed for CSR reports and statements, it is the predominant standard used by professional accounting firms when auditing such information. It defines two levels of assurance: the 'limited assurance engagement' and the 'reasonable assurance engagement'. Both talk about the reduction of assurance engagement risk, which is the risk that the assurer fails to notice material errors. Table 6.4 summarises the levels of assurance defined by the ISAE 3000.

Table 6.4 ISAE 3000 levels of assurance

	Reasonable assurance engagement	Limited assurance engagement
Engagement risk	'Reduction in assurance engagement risk to an acceptably low level ... as the basis for a positive form of expression of the practitioner's conclusion'	'Reduction in assurance engagement risk to a level that is acceptable ... , but where risk is greater than for a reasonable assurance engagement, as the basis for a negative form of expression of the practitioner's conclusion'
Scope	'Assurance engagements other than audits or reviews of historical financial information'	

The ISAE 3000 can be applied to any 'non-financial' information which is 'assurable', i.e. where sufficient appropriate evidence can be obtained by the assurance provider. The reporting organisation is free to define the subject matter of the assurance engagement; however, the verification should be performed against, for example, the set defined by the AA1000 standards or the GRI *G3 Guidelines*. The use of the ISAE 3000 is free.

About the AA1000

The AA1000 series is published by AccountAbility, a global non-profit network, and consists of three standards:

▶ AA1000APS (2008) AcountAbility Principles

▶ AA1000AS (2008) Assurance Standard

▶ AA1000SES (2005) Stakeholder Engagement Standard

The standards were developed in a broad-based multi-stakeholder process. The 2008 edition of the APS and the AS represent the revised version of the initial standard published in 2003. The APS contains and explains the three AccountAbility principles – inclusivity, materiality and responsiveness – and is addressed to the reporting organisation. The AS is addressed to assurance providers and describes how they should perform an assurance engagement under the standard. In doing so, the assurer evaluates and provides conclusions on:

▶ the nature and extent of adherence to the AA1000 AcountAbility principles

▶ the quality of publicly disclosed information on sustainability performance, where applicable.

The AA1000AS is compatible with the ISAE 3000 as it also covers two levels of assurance which are intended to provide the same levels of

Table 6.5 AA1000 Levels and types of assurance

	High assurance	Moderate assurance
Objective	'The assurance provider achieves high assurance where sufficient evidence has been obtained to support their statement such that the risk of their conclusion being in error is very low but not zero'	'The assurance provider achieves moderate assurance where sufficient evidence has been obtained to support their statement such that the risk of their conclusion being in error is reduced but not reduced to very low but not zero'
Type 1	All three AccountAbility principles	All three AccountAbility principles
Type 2	All three AccountAbility principles Specified performance information	All three AccountAbility principles Specified performance information

confidence ('moderate assurance' and 'high assurance'). In addition, the AA1000AS distinguishes between two types of assurance: a type 1 engagement, which covers the adherence to the AcountAbility principles, and a type 2 engagement, which covers, in addition to that, performance information. The commercial use of the standard is linked to a licensing fee of £500 for each assurance statement (£200 if the annual turnover of the reporting organisation is less than £2 m). Table 6.5 summarises levels and types of assurance defined by the AA1000AS.

Levels of assurance

Both standards, ISAE 3000 and AA1000AS, distinguish between an entry level (called 'limited' and 'moderate', respectively) and an advanced level (called 'reasonable' and 'high', respectively) of assurance in order to allow for different intensities of confidence (and effort). In addition, a 'full' assurance is also possible, which represents an audit of 100% of the underlying subject matter.

The difference between a limited and a reasonable assurance engagement has to do with the 'depth' of testing performed and ultimately in the wording of the assurance statement produced. In a limited assurance statement, the provider will conclude with a negative statement, such as the following: 'Based on our work described in this report, nothing has come to our attention that causes us to believe that the responsible party's assertion that internal control is effective, in all material respects, based on XYZ criteria, is not fairly stated' (ISAE 3000). The conclusion in a reasonable assurance statement would be positive – for example: 'In our opinion the responsible party's assertion that internal control is effective, in all material respects, based on XYZ criteria, is fairly stated' (ISAE 3000). However, the assurance provider needs to apply a significantly higher level of scrutiny to gain a higher 'level of comfort' in order to be able to come to such a conclusion. What this means in the end will depend on the subject matter, the inherent risk and the assurance provider's opinion as well as the stakeholders' expectations.

As a beginner it is recommended to start with a limited assurance engagement. The predominant level of assurance is the limited assurance, but a new trend is to combine different assurance levels. In these cases, the main part of the report is covered by a limited assurance engagement, and specific subject matter (focus themes or selected key performance indicators) under a reasonable assurance.

Typical subject matter of assurance engagements

In principle, an assurance engagement can address processes, management systems, stakeholder management, identification of material issues, data and statements by the reporting organisation. The GRI *G3 Guidelines* provide guidance on what to consider (cf. GRI *G3 Guidelines*, p. 38) and the AA1000 clearly defines the options available to comply with the standard. At a minimum it requires an evaluation of the nature and extent of the organisation's adherence to all three AA1000 AccountAbility principles. In a type 2 engagement the AA1000AS defines that specified sustainability performance information can be included in the scope which 'is selected based on the materiality determination and needs to be meaningful to the intended users of the assurance statement'.

Selection of an assurance provider

Gaining insights into and scrutinising processes and performance data are fundamental parts of an assurance provider's job. Having comfort and trust in working with the organisation should be a 'must' criterion in selecting a provider. In particular, in an organisation where CSR is still a relatively fresh issue, the assurance provider often also serves as an ambassador of the topic. The following is a list of criteria you may wish to consider in the selection process:

▶ *Competence and skills*

- Experience of the assurance provider in your sector

- CSR expertise and experience of proposed staff

- (International) network of the assurance provider

- The providers' competence on desired standards

- Language and cultural skills

▶ *Synergies*

- You might be able to realise synergies by asking your financial auditor to perform the work; this might also help to leverage the relevance of CR within your organisation

- You may even consider including a stakeholder panel in the assurance process or inviting individual stakeholder representatives/experts to comment on your report in your report.

Checklist

The following checklist summarises some elementary steps to consider in conducting an assurance engagement. It may serve as a precursor to be expanded upon and tailored for your organisation and its specific needs:

▶ Identification and weighting of your own and your stakeholders' expectations/needs

▶ Identification of material issues and thus the relevant subject matter and the level of assurance

▶ Definition of the scope (issues and topics, headquarters, business units, entities (geographies), etc.)

▶ Selection of the standards for the assurance and the assurance provider

▶ Specification or determination of the criteria which the assurance provider should use in the testing

▶ Development of an assurance journey.

Footnote

1 This information contains general information exclusively that is not suitable for addressing the particular circumstances of any individual case. It is not meant to be used as a basis for commercial decisions or decisions of any other kind. This information constitutes neither advice nor any legally binding information or offer and shall not be deemed suitable for substituting personal advice under any circumstances. Should a reader base decisions of any of the contents of this chapter or extracts therefrom, that reader acts solely at his or her own risk. The authors will not assume any guarantee or warranty and will not be liable in any other form for the content of this information. Therefore, the authors always recommend obtaining personal advice.

References

AccountAbility (2008) *AA1000 AccountAbility Principles Standard*, AccountAbility.

AccountAbility (2008) *AA1000 Assurance Standard*, AccountAbility.

International Auditing and Assurance Standards Board (2005) *ISAE3000, International Standard on Assurance Engagements 3000*, International Auditing and Assurance Standards Board.

Global Reporting Initiative (2006) *Sustainability Reporting Guidelines: G3 Guidelines*, Global Reporting Initiative.

Sustainability reporting 2.0: from 'Trojan horse' to 'value booster'

Ralph Thurm

This chapter examines the importance and benefits of sustainability and CSR reporting and provides background on the rapid development from the first generation to the next level of 'strategic sustainability reporting'. The chapter outlines the necessary steps to be undertaken to achieve the best results, provides information on Global Reporting Initiative's Sustainability Reporting Guidelines and finally outlines pointers to future trends in this area.

Introduction

The Rio+5 conference in 1997 was a major eye-opener. Five years after political, corporate and civil society leaders met in Rio de Janeiro to discuss and sign the Rio Declaration and the Agenda 21 – the first ever global set of documents that confirmed an agreed-upon state of the world and how to tackle sustainability challenges – it was barely possible to account for and present the success achieved since Rio. A lack of data, formats and benchmarking opportunities caused people to think about how to asses, streamline and discuss necessary information, and the old business saying that 'what gets measured gets attention' finally reached the sustainability community's conference circuit.

It was in this year that the idea of a global reporting scheme for sustainability, to be used by all sorts of organisations, all sizes and all regional as well as cultural backgrounds, was born. It was obvious that existing financial accounting and related annual reports were incapable of assessing forward-looking information that could give insights into a company's (long-term) plan to be a good global citizen and also how that contributes to the economic success of a company. Bob Massie of CERES and Alan White of the Tellus Institute started to frame a multi-stakeholder process and governance structure, that, five years later, took the step from being a loose network of people interested in the possibilities of sustainability reporting, funded by United Nations Environment Programme (UNEP) and some other interested foundations, to an independent institution of its own, known as the Global Reporting Initiative (GRI) Foundation, with its new headquarters in Amsterdam, in the Netherlands.

Today the Global Reporting Initiative's G3 (third generation) of *Sustainability Reporting Guidelines* (GRI 2006 – to be referred to as 'the *Guidelines*' in the rest of this chapter) form the globally accepted and globally applicable standard on which thousands of sustainability reports are based, not always as explicitly as it could be, but it is usually the most important reference document. In this chapter we reflect on how best to embed sustainability reporting into the 'genes' and 'DNA' of an organisation, using some of the 'collective wisdom' that has emerged after around a decade of experience with the GRI's *Guidelines*, and look into some of the emerging trends to ensure a link to other chapters of this book. (Readers should note that as the *Guidelines* are meant to be used by all sorts of organisations, we will not refer just to 'companies' in this chapter. However, most users of the *Guidelines* today are companies.)

We will not reproduce any of the text of the *G3 Guidelines* since they are accessible in many languages free of charge from GRI's website (www. globalreporting.org), but we will focus on the crucial enablers and important process steps, necessary milestones and additional help they offer to a successful reporting campaign.

How to approach sustainability reporting in general

After more than a decade in which we have seen the amount of sustainability reports grow from less than a hundred to several thousand every year, coming from more than 80 countries worldwide, we are still a long way from being able to say that sustainability reporting has reached its goal to be mainstream reporting practice on a global scale, compared with the amount, standardisation and rigidity of financial reports. It is estimated that there are around 60,000 multinational companies on the planet, and only a small percentage actually publish sustainability reports. However, of the 500 biggest companies worldwide – the Future 500 – more than 70% are publishing reports of this kind, meaning that, given these companies' influence with all sorts of stakeholders, they will reach a huge number of individuals. It is therefore to be expected that the number of reporting organisations will continue to grow. Pending more regulation, an even higher growth and spread seem possible, and there are indeed signs of serious thought being given to making sustainability reporting mandatory in many European countries and in other emerging markets (see 'The future of sustainability reporting' later in this chapter).

We are now also facing a development that could be called 'from sustainability 1.0 to sustainability 2.0', meaning that the way in which available tools are used in organisations can differ considerably. Sustainability 1.0 stands for the slow and burdensome process of introducing sustainability reporting like a 'Trojan horse', convincing the non-believers internally that the transparency of a set of sustainability indicators would be useful to save money and make all sorts of stakeholders feel confident that a company is compliant, has integrity and generally feels responsible for the environment and society – in essence the opposite of Milton Friedman's idea that 'the business of business is business'. Most initiatives in organisations were started in environmental management or PR or communications departments and these people had to fight against internal windmills, in particular the ignorance of top management, financial departments, investor relations and market-oriented staff, who generally feared 'reporting just for the sake of reporting' and simply couldn't believe that the proponents of sustainability reporting would eventually make their life easier. Although some of the most successful organisations needed to go through this 'school of hard knocks', finally getting the attention of their top management, and are seen as today's role models, we should avoid the path they took, not just because it was an inefficient process, but because we lack the time to do it this way. It is refreshing to note that many organisations are already leapfrogging ahead by adopting a more strategic approach.

In this sense, sustainability 2.0 is the result of a learning curve, allowing us to copy and paste some of the lessons learnt from the leaders in sustainability reporting. Many organisations embarking on sustainability reporting today already have a different attitude. The financial disasters experienced by companies like Enron and Worldcom some years ago, and recent cases such as Lehman Brothers, Hypo Real Estate, Chrysler and GM, offer very good examples of what is an 'unsustainable' business, with a wide variety of causes, from accounting fraud, naïve risk management and overestimating the power of size ('we're too big to go under'), to being 'asleep at the wheel' regarding the incorporation of macroeconomic trends and customer demands into new and innovative products. These examples clearly tell the tale that sustainability management aiming to overcome 'silo thinking', seen as a primary cause of the slow change in organisational culture, needs to start from a holistic perspective and embed the logic that it is a cross-functional discipline. This means that the old concept of having sustainability departments that merely take care of anything that 'smells like sustainability' is not good enough. This approach simply discourages other functions from taking ownership and gives senior management the wrong idea that somebody, centrally, is dealing with it.

The global economic crisis that started in 2008 is, in essence, a crisis of confidence. The companies involved have not been able to holistically assess, understand and react to the conglomeration of market conditions. The crisis has been partly due to internal 'silo thinking' and unbalanced corporate governance structures that were unable to stop greedy behaviour, but has mainly resulted from systemic malfunctioning of market pricing, tax effects, subsidies, a lack in the internalisation of external effects, and short-termism in financial market philosophy (which still exists). As a result, it has become clear that trust between market players has the highest value of all. Comparable sustainability reporting has a major role to play in this environment.

Fortunately, at the same time, it has turned out that the leaders in sustainability enjoy better reputations, are sought out by high-potential employees, and demonstrate on average higher share price results (and less volatility) than the laggards. Furthermore, the existence of standards, platforms, initiatives and new customer communities to reward leaders for having made the right moves is growing every year. It is also very revealing that many of the leading strategy advisors have recently written of their support for a strategic integration of sustainability as a centrepiece of future business (see Peter Senge's *The Necessary Revolution*, C.K. Prahalad's *The Fortune at the Bottom of the Pyramid*, Stuart Hart's *Capitalism at the Crossroads*, Daniel Goleman's *Ecological Intelligence* and Thomas Friedman's *Hot, Flat and Crowded*; Michael Porter has also published several articles on the importance of strategic integration of sustainability). To sum up: the infrastructure to allow sustainability reporting to be embedded as part of an overall strategy is much better than it was a decade ago. And that should be your starting point. Don't accept less!

Embedding sustainability reporting in a strategic context

Before we delve deeper into some of the dos and don'ts of sustainability reporting, we'd like to revisit the idea of strategic integration. As mentioned previously, the old-school sustainability 1.0 approach first focused on compliance with existing regulation and offered some response to stakeholder demands by using a combination of internal checks by corporate staff and an add-on sustainability reporting process that was mainly triggered by the communication departments. Only later, after spending a lot more time and money, did the operationalisation of sustainability issues take place. Another disadvantage of this approach was that middle and senior management did not focus much on this sort of approach and – apart from an internal audit or certification audit interview to reach a management system certificate – was not really involved. In many cases there was a top-management commitment that was not taken seriously by middle managers and therefore left many questions unanswered among those who needed the support most urgently.

We therefore advise you to take advantage of the winds of change and start the other way around, with a sustainability strategy process that leads to questions about how to operationalise, report and seek assurance accordingly, but in a much more natural and logical manner (see Figure 7.1).

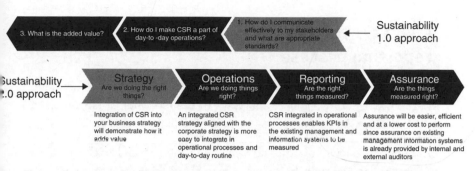

Figure 7.1 Overcoming the burdens of an add-on sustainability management process by choosing a strategic integration of sustainability into an organisation. KPI, key performance indicator.

Adopt this precondition and you will already be halfway towards a successful sustainability reporting process.

The sustainability reporting process

We will now consider sustainability reporting from a procedural perspective. The GRI (2008a,b) has already published additional learning material, in addition to the *Guidelines*, on how to approach the sustainability reporting cycle. The GRI recommends a five-phase reporting process cycle (see Box 7.1) that can be easily integrated in a plan–do–check–act management systems logic. The GRI (2008a,b) publications lay out the necessary activities of each step in detail and offer various ready-to-use templates, so we won't focus on them here. We recommend using the basic logic of the five-step approach to:

▶ plan the timeline, milestones and all related necessary activities with external parties involved (e.g. stakeholder meetings, surveys, selection of assurance provider, printing or web design, launch event)

▶ create the necessary level of ownership of involved staff at all levels (the responsibilities need to be shared between different functions to avoid silos and to respect the cross-cutting nature of sustainability)

Box 7.1 The five phases in the reporting process

1. **Prepare** – gives an overview of what your final report might contain, the process to get there, and ways to prepare your organisation to go through this process

2. **Connect** – shows how to identify your main internal and external stakeholders and discuss their concerns to help decide what to report on

3. **Define** – helps to define the report content based on stakeholder input, assessment against basic reporting principles, and an analysis of your organisation's current commitments and measurement capabilities. This step also addresses which internal modifications might be required to enable improvements, and which indicators will be added to your future reports

4. **Monitor** – describes how to collect information needed to report on the indicators, and how to ensure data quality. This step also provides ideas on how to make data collection and analysis more efficient

5. **Report** – helps understand the actual dynamics of choosing a format for the report, writing it and getting it finalised.

▶ define budgetary needs for stakeholder dialogue, internal data system creation/maintenance, publications and website, and assurance provider

▶ co-ordinate the sustainability reporting process with other corporate functions, e.g. internal audit, risk management, corporate governance, strategy development, financial department, HR, investor relations, communications and marketing

▶ co-ordinate content development with especially important players in the company's supply and production chain (most likely including product take-back function and R&D)

▶ organise a plan–do–check–act understanding that puts the sustainability reporting process in the context of the overall strategic target-setting and communication plans. That is to say, the end of one reporting process – meaning the publication of the report – is just the beginning of the next cycle.

The following additional points will address some existing stereotypes, misunderstandings and views that still pertain with regard to use of the *Guidelines*. Proper understanding of these issues is crucial to ensure a smooth reporting process and will increase the buy-in from other internal and external stakeholders. We recommend reading the text of the *Guidelines* in parallel with the information in the following sub-sections.

Use of the reporting principles

One of the biggest mistakes in using the *G3 Guidelines* is to underestimate the importance of the reporting principles, as described in Part 1 (entitled 'Defining report content, quality and boundary'). From experience we know that readers of the *Guidelines* tend to use them as a reference document, but in doing so purely look at the set of defined indicators, clustered by aspects and built around the three pillars of sustainability (economy, ecology, social matters) as described in Part 2 ('Standard disclosures'). Many readers of the *Guidelines* therefore fail to understand that an organisation does not need to report on all 79 indicators to be a high-quality GRI reporter. This misunderstanding is noted again and again when talking to organisations about their use of the *Guidelines*. The purpose of the reporting principles is to help users of the *Guidelines* to adopt logic mental steps when defining the reporting content and quality, and to remind them not to forget important decisions. The principles generally help to answer three important questions, as discussed below.

What to report on?

Every reporting organisation needs to fine-tune the report's content and obtain a balance between the principles of 'materiality' and 'completeness'.

It is therefore imperative not to be diverted by the variety of issues that could potentially be reported on, and instead to focus on understanding what is 'really important'. Of the many different possibilities, the principles of 'stakeholder inclusiveness' and 'sustainability context' are also important. They help to embed a holistic view and starting point for the discussion and they also help to ensure that there has been a thorough process of defining all relevant stakeholder groups, as well as a thorough analysis of their needs, and those of the reporting organisation, in the context of the industry, the value chain and important related matters.

How to report?

It is clear that information that is publicly available should be trustable. In financial accounting, reporting principles have long been in use, and these understandably set a benchmark of quality for all other published information of critical value. This is crucial to inspire the necessary trust, especially at a time when trust seems to be the fundamental requirement to get economies back on their feet. The six principles in the *Guidelines* – balance, comparability, accuracy, timeliness, clarity and reliability – help to frame the qualitative backbone of reporting once the question of what to report on has been settled. We believe that, without properly focusing on the report's quality principles, a serious data governance framework – ideally linked to existing data-gathering sources that allow the management information system (MIS) to support management with performance information – will not be possible. This issue should be given great attention since a lot of the ownership created for the sustainability matters will be linked to the information available and the quality of information gathered. An approach that is able to link the external reporting matters with the internal reporting needs (ideally achieved through the correct use of the 'materiality' concept in the *Guidelines* – no information should be gathered that is not important internally as well as externally) will create the necessary buy-in. You should aim to make use of the existing MIS structures and data-gathering systems (e.g. enterprise resource planning

(ERP) systems such as SAP, Oracle and JD Edwards) to maximise the overlap. Making use of the high-level performance management design, e.g. balanced scorecards, will also be beneficial.

Where to draw the line?

The question of how to define reporting boundaries is the third crucial issue that needs to be settled early in the reporting process. Many reporting organisations only include information about other organisations if they have a major stake (>50%) in them. However, there can be significant influence, and therefore impact (always with a focus on sustainability), when the stake is less than 50%, e.g. in parts of the supply and demand chain, through the use of policies that require certain standards. We therefore recommend a less rigid approach and suggest basing the decision on more than one layer of responsibility, particularly in respect of the overall enlarged value chain, product life cycle/cradle-to-cradle theory, and looking at direct and indirect impacts of what the organisation is doing. The answer to the question of where to draw the line should be seen as a crucial prompt concerning where a reporting organisation sees its responsibility beginning and ending. Hence while quantitative information that undergoes an internal and/or external assurance process should be tested by the report's quality principles, additional information reflecting a wider responsibility can also be more qualitative. The general view is that, owing to a very 'legalistic' approach to the boundary question, some stakeholders may miss important information to help them better understand the company's overall take on its responsibility in sustainability matters and the role it wants to play in the future. A less legalistic approach on matters that have specific merit is advisable, especially when the reporting organisation is increasingly trying to follow cradle-to-cradle concepts.

Stakeholder dialogue – defining stakeholders

A stakeholder is, in general terms, anyone who has a 'stake' in the company. Defining stakeholders has always been a difficult prospect, owing to the general rule that no one should be excluded (stakeholder inclusivity). But clearly an organisation cannot handle one-on-one dialogue with each and every stakeholder, so clustering stakeholder groups and defining how to approach them as a group are good ways to start the dialogue process. From a *Guidelines* perspective, it is crucial that the reporting organisation gives enough evidence on how the stakeholder groups were defined, how the actual dialogue was organised, which issues were addressed and how feedback was taken into account during decision-making inside the organisation. Essentially, the reporting organisation always has the last say, but readers of the reports want to see an explanation as to why certain decisions were made, accepting or otherwise particular stakeholder views.

There is not only one design format of how to approach stakeholders. It is not even necessary to say that a dialogue has been organised in relation to the sustainability programme. Many different forms of dialogue are possible: customer satisfaction studies (which can include questions on certain sustainability issues, e.g. product stewardship), facilitated stakeholder feedback workshops (most likely facilitated by a neutral third party), internet forums, Wikis, questionnaires, interviews, and so on. In some cases, reporting organisations may have difficulty in finding a good representative of a stakeholder group, e.g. a representative of an NGO who can give substantial answers to questions. It makes sense to do sound research and to build relationships with representatives of the major stakeholder groups who enjoy the group's trust. Some organisations choose to design a separate 'stakeholder expert panel' in addition to the report assurance process, with the aim of using the panel to focus on the materiality choice while the assurance provider focuses on the data quality aspect of the reporting process. Figure 7.2 shows additional indicators of a good stakeholder process, especially when designed to prepare a valuable sustainability report. But let's be clear: in most organisations, a high amount of stakeholder dialogue is already taking place and can be exploited for the sustainability programme – one should start with what is already in existence and take it from there.

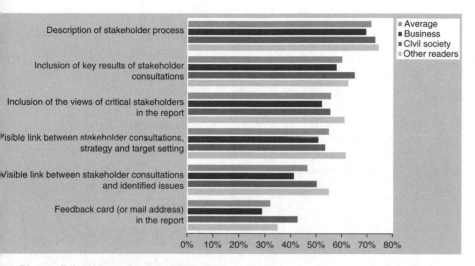

Figure 7.2 What shows appropriate stakeholder engagement for the purposes of preparing the report? (Responses from participants of the first GRI Readers' Choice Awards questionnaire – results presented at the GRI conference 2008, highlighting the views of 2,300 sustainability report readers) (KPMG International and SustainAbility Ltd 2008, p. 10).

Defining materiality

A sustainability report needs to reflect on the tension between 'completeness' and 'materiality' by making clear statements about how material issues have been chosen. The *Guidelines* recommend a matrix that shows, on the one hand, the significance of environmental, social and economic impacts (of certain themes) and, on the other, the influence of these themes on the stakeholder's assessment of and decisions about the organisation; the matrix then shows the relative importance of specific sustainability themes. The idea of such a matrix has been widely adopted (see Figure 7.3 for an example from Royal Dutch Shell's 2008 sustainability report, p. 40). An essential ingredient for the reader will be the level of transparency achieved by the reporting organisation, in order to give relevant insight into the decision-making.

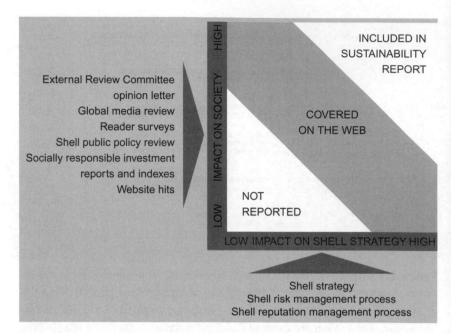

External Review Committee
opinion letter
Global media review
Reader surveys
Shell public policy review
Socially responsible investment
reports and indexes
Website hits

HIGH

IMPACT ON SOCIETY

LOW

INCLUDED IN
SUSTAINABILITY
REPORT

COVERED
ON THE WEB

NOT
REPORTED

LOW IMPACT ON SHELL STRATEGY HIGH

Shell strategy
Shell risk management process
Shell reputation management process

Figure 7.3 Royal Dutch Shell's sources of input to define the materiality of issues that should be included in the sustainability report, on the web, or ignored (for the purpose of the report) (Royal Dutch Shell 2008).

The self-assessment

The *Guidelines* offer 'tests' for all reporting principles, a sort of self-assessment based on statements, to allow the reporting organisation to see how far they understood and embedded the principles in their reporting process. These self-assessments have proven to be excellent prompters – as long as they are taken seriously and are not neglected. Companies that are used to excellence programmes, such as European Foundation for Quality Management (EFQM) or the Malcolm Baldridge Model, should recognise the similarity to those approaches. The results of the self-assessment are not required disclosure elements, so we advise a rigorous and honest use of the self-assessment opportunity. In discussions with internal stakeholders, jointly deciding how the principles were understood can be another valuable way to create the necessary glue and a higher level of ownership.

The above sub-sections have focused mainly on enabling aspects towards a good sustainability reporting process. The following sub-sections will emphasise aspects of the report disclosure.

Strategy and analysis

Another area that is still much neglected in sustainability reports, but which should be given a lot of attention, is described at the beginning of the 'Standard disclosures' chapter – namely, a clear signal from top management as to how sustainability and the reporting organisation's strategy are interlinked. In many sustainability reports, there are no clear descriptions of long-term objectives and targets. This means that the ability to backtrack from those targets and translate them into what needs to be done over the next few years to achieve them is missing. The result is to leave many readers with a 'so what' feeling, since the reference point is missing and therefore the reader hardly understands the relative substance of what has been achieved. It is important to understand that this part of the sustainability report will need to have an inside-out as well as an outside-in perspective. In other words, for the former, how are we positively or negatively contributing to certain sustainability issues through our strategy and business model(s); and, for the latter, how far is our strategy or business model(s) already affected or restricted due to sustainability issues?

By telling a good story describing the reporting organisation's role in industry, as well as upstream and downstream, and how macroeconomic trends influence performance, readers' trust can be won – and don't forget that many readers are from ranking and rating organisations and financial institutions. The current discussion about the need to create business 'at the bottom of the pyramid' will not bear fruit without a deeper understanding of the two directions described above. It is profitable to see how sustainability strategies have evolved over time – for example, starting with pollution prevention, moving on to stakeholder inclusion strategies, then clean production and product strategies, and finally to discussions on adapted strategies for developing and emerging markets, with the aim of meeting the needs of those whose needs were not previously met and, at the same time, helping to develop new market conditions for the reporting organisation. It is here that innovation meets sustainability and really gets to the core of a company's business models.

The disclosure on the management approach

Comparing reports with each other has always been problematic, but it is part of the logic of standardised sustainability reporting. Comparing figures between different organisations around the same dataset is a well-developed aspect of financial reporting, but it is something that is still in its infancy when it comes to sustainability reporting. In order to offer readers the chance to gauge the full picture of an organisation, additional qualitative disclosures are possible through the 'disclosure on management approach' part of each major indicator-related chapter of the sustainability report. We recommend taking this opportunity, as it is a chance to explain to readers how certain numbers were arrived at and, in particular, how the numbers should be interpreted.

Since companies are increasingly merging and demerging, due to ever more globalised markets, shifting strategies and technological, logistical and customer behaviour changes, it is unlikely that reporting organisations will be able to continue datastreams unchanged over many years. The *Guidelines* recommend noting key success factors, risks and opportunities, training and awareness procedures, and also awards or fines in certain aspect areas, as well as information on the monitoring process, certifications and verification processes. The disclosure on management approach builds the bridge to some extra (and needed) flexibility in the absence of a rigorous and one-size-fits-all benchmarking approach. It is expected that this will evolve slowly and is likely only to be realised by the industry sector; the GRI's approach to develop more and more sector supplements is a helpful support towards better benchmarking opportunities in the future (see later discussion).

Reporting on indicators – use of technical protocols

The *Guidelines* offer 79 indicators in total, which are classified as 'core' or 'additional' indicators. This classification is a leftover from the second generation of *GRI Guidelines*, the importance of which is somewhat diminished by the materiality search process that every reporting organisation needs to go through. In that sense, there is no direct connection, other than that hundreds of experts who worked on the development of the *G3 Guidelines* felt that this distinction still had some worth, highlighting what has been identified as priorities by developers from a wide range of constituencies all over the world.

Each of the 79 indicators is explained at length in the 'technical protocols' that are published together with the *Guidelines*. It is important to note that a reporting organisation is free to interpret or use variations of the indicators, but is advised to clearly state in the report why they have chosen a variation of the indicator, in order to enable, as much as is possible, comparability with other reports.

The GRI content index and the G3 application level check

The GRI content index is a must-have element of a good sustainability report. Not only is it easier for report readers to find the information (via page numbers, web links or references to other documents), but it also greatly helps to elevate a report to the 'A' level of the GRI application level check, helping to outline to what degree the components of a complete GRI-based sustainability report can be found (or not) in the report. In order to go from a 'C' or 'B' level report to an 'A' level report, it is not absolutely necessary to report on more than 10 or 20 indicators; it is more important to explain why the other indicators were not reported on, the so-called omissions. There are many good reasons not to comply with certain indicators (e.g. aspects of materiality for the industry sector or the stakeholders, or the availability of data), but it is important to 'comply or explain'. The use of omissions, clearly stated and laid out, will not disqualify the report from attaining an 'A' level. To achieve the extra '+' in combination with the A, B or C level, the sustainability report needs to be externally assured. It is likely that reports with level C or B will need limited assurance and that the degree of reasonable assurance will grow towards a level A.

The G3 application level check can be done by the reporting organisation itself (as a self-assessment – please don't confuse this with the self-assessment statements from the reporting principles section of the *Guidelines*, which are voluntary and not part of the required disclosure), by a third party (most likely an assurance provider) or directly through the GRI. Various 'stamps', reflecting the chosen approach and the level achieved, are available from the GRI's website. It is a helpful signal for readers and ranking and rating specialists. It is important to mention that this only assesses the level of coverage of the required reporting elements in alignment with the *Guidelines*; it does not replace or cover a professional assurance process (however, the application level check can be done in combination with an assurance engagement). While most assurance providers use the ISAE 3000 as the basis of the assurance engagement, a combination with the AA1000AS (latest version, 2008) is possible if the company wishes to combine the best of both worlds.

Sector supplements

The *Guidelines* are increasingly accompanied by sector-specific guidance, contained in sector supplements. The purpose of the supplements is to clarify industry-specific language *vis-à-vis* the *Guidelines* and to offer an additional set of indicators that help to capture more precisely the essence of sustainability issues in a specific industry. Many of these supplements are already available for download from the GRI website. In relation to the application level check mentioned in the previous section, process sector supplements play a crucial role for those industry sectors where a final version is already available. In these cases, the reporting organisation also needs to cover (meaning 'comply' or 'explain through valid omissions') the indicators of the sector supplement to achieve an 'A' level. The newest information on sector supplement availability is available on the GRI website.

The future of sustainability reporting – some trends

We'd like to close this chapter with a short discussion on the future development of sustainability reporting. A recent trend in some European countries is to make sustainability reporting mandatory for certain groups of companies. Sweden, for example, has decided to make GRI-based sustainability reporting mandatory for all 55 state-owned companies (thereby also sending a signal to other companies to follow suit), while Denmark is asking around 1,100 companies to publish information (optionally in their annual reports) on a 'comply or explain' basis. It is expected that many more countries will follow (most likely there will not be one 'best way', but a variety of approaches), among them non-European countries like China and Brazil. One can clearly see that sustainability reporting as an important means of regaining trust is picking up pace. Other issues surrounding the further of sustainability reporting are discussed below.

Standalone sustainability report or one merged with annual financial reporting?

More and more companies are trying to merge their sustainability reports with their annual reports. The reason for this development is to show that the reporting organisation is taking sustainability seriously and showcase its ability to deliver the necessary management information at the same time as the financial information. In addition, a combined assurance engagement has the potential to be less burdensome (and less costly) for the reporting organisation, and design, editing, layout, web-publishing and communication can be streamlined.

However, there are still reasons to hesitate when it comes to combining both reports. In particular, in poor economic conditions there is a tendency to cut down on content by combining the reports, which could be seen as a loss of quality by the different report readers. Another reason to hesitate is the fear by the responsible experts that, due to the dominance (and available budgets) of the financial report over the sustainability report, the communication team will simply carry out the sustainability reporting process and cause a shift in internal responsibilities. Last, but not least, the question remains as to whether the market is ready for merged reports. Will companies still perform strongly in ranking or ratings if certain components are difficult to find, or use a different vocabulary? Will the assurance statement, which may not make additional specific reference to sustainability in the case of a merged report, be accepted by the rankings? We believe it will take a while and require agreement between the reporting organisations, and especially the professional report readers, to allow a fair and balanced interpretation of merged reports.

XBRL

The development of taxonomy for standardised reporting has taken root in the last couple of years. Tagged information and its exchange in clearly defined electronic formats can drastically decrease the transaction costs of information delivery. This process will also be developed for sustainability information. An initial taxonomy for the *G3 Guidelines* was developed in 2007 and will be refined through a pilot group of users. It is to be expected that sector supplement taxonomies will be developed as well. It remains to be seen how quickly and how smoothly the further development will be.

Transparency 2.0

The internet has caused a transparency revolution the like of which we have never seen before. While huge efficiency steps have been made possible in the global delivery of information, and new business models are evolving as a result of the limitless possibilities, the internet also throws up a huge challenge for organisations that need to take these developments on board. This will also have consequences for sustainability reporting. The notion that anything in an organisation can be kept secret is naïve; as long as people are connected, whistle-blowing is increasingly likely and anything that may be seen as illegitimate (it doesn't have to be illegal) could surface outside the organisation. Clearly, stakeholders want to increase their influence, and it will remain a fine line in how far companies are opening up for this trend and could make it an asset of their business models. It is clearly a positive step to proactively address transparency, and thus not only to react honestly to the positive stories but also to balance this with honesty about what has not been achieved (see Figure 7.4).

It remains to be seen how far new developments in technology will push things. It is not unlikely that there will be companies that invite stakeholders to be actively involved in report writing. Moreover, the constant updating of reports on websites, and the addition of blogs and Wikis are adding

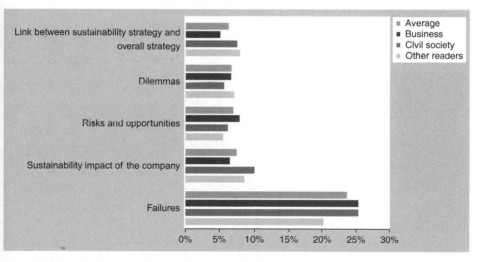

Figure 7.4 What is the most important element that is left out of reports? (Responses from participants of the first GRI Readers' Choice Awards questionnaire – results presented at the GRI conference 2008, highlighting the views of 2,300 sustainability report readers) (KPMG International and SustainAbility Ltd 2008, p. 9).

to the fluidity of information-sharing between the reporting organisation and stakeholders.

References

AccountAbility (2008) AA1000 Assurance Standard, AccountAbility.

Global Reporting Initiative (2006) *Sustainability Reporting Guidelines: G3 Guidelines*, Global Reporting Initiative.

Global Reporting Initiative (2008a) *Pathways – The GRI Sustainability Reporting Cycle: A Handbook for Small and Not So Small Organisations*, GRI.

Global Reporting Initiative (2008b) *Starting Points – GRI Sustainability Reporting: How Valuable is the Journey*, GRI.

KPMG International, SustainAbility Ltd (2008) *Count Me In – the Readers' Take on Sustainability Reporting*. KPMG International and SustainAbility Ltd, p. 10.

Royal Dutch Shell plc. *Sustainability Report 2008*, Royal Dutch Shell, p. 40.

Ten rules for successful CSR communication

Norbert Taubken and Irina Leibold

Responsible Business: How to Manage a CSR Strategy Successfully
Edited by Manfred Pohl and Nick Tolhurst
Copyright © 2010 Manfred Pohl and Nick Tolhurst

This chapter outlines the dos and don'ts of successful CSR communication. The authors summarise both the criteria for success and the pitfalls to be avoided, stressing the importance of communication in two crucial areas: internally, with the company's own employees, and externally, with target groups. Finally, a checklist is provided for turning the CSR of a brand into a selling point, including the communication channels to be used.

Introduction

The corporate social responsibility (CSR) of companies is not perceived and valued as much as committed firms would like. Indeed, it is often difficult for customers to name even one company that acts responsibly in their view, and, accordingly, as many as 93% feel that the information they have on sustainable company action is insufficient (University of Applied Sciences Wiesbaden and 2hm & Associates 2008). So why don't companies respond adequately to this need for information on CSR? The answer lies in fear of distrust and fear of disclosing shortcomings. The result is that communication of this topic has often been less than extensive. This fear is not entirely without cause, as CSR communication is as complex as the subject itself.

The economic benefit of CSR becomes apparent when it enables a company to position itself as a 'responsible brand'. In this context, CSR communication is the tool that facilitates an external evaluation of this strategy. Any communication about responsibility must consider the heterogeneity and the different interests of the most important target groups, which raises the following question: under what conditions will CSR communication be successful? This chapter provides 10 rules for successful CSR communication that help to develop a specific instrument in corporate communication and public affairs departments. These rules were developed from the know-how gained from advising and supporting companies in a wide variety of sectors and industries.

Rule #1: Act first, talk later – avoid the trap-door of greenwash

The relationship between talking and acting is essential for the evaluation of companies in relation to their responsibility to stakeholders (see Figure 8.1). The first provides the perception, the second the credibility. Initially, the path to being a 'CSR brand' for companies should always be via the action. A lot of talking and no action is a combination that makes people suspicious that a company is abusing CSR as a label. If this happens, even reasonable activities can be interpreted as part of the pretence. The trap-door of greenwash – a false claim to being socially responsible – is lurking.

Rule #2: The why and the wherefore – create a framework of interpretation for the company's actions

In order to be accepted as a CSR brand, a company has to do more than merely act responsibly in certain situations. It must be perceptible from

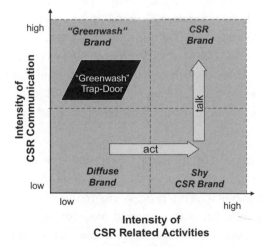

Figure 8.1 Classification of corporate brands in the CSR area. (Classification according to Ethical Corporation, 2007).

the outside, with self-awareness at the core of the company's decisions and upon which long-term targets and interests are the basis for the company's operations.

A CSR strategy should therefore be derived from the business purpose and the corporate strategy. A company's CSR mission statement or CSR guidelines publicly demonstrate that firm's basic principles, while a CSR road map illustrates the firm's long-term CSR intentions. It demonstrates how responsibility is being established in the core operations and which priorities are being set. The mission statement and the road map enable stakeholders to place individual decisions and activities in a greater context and illustrate the scope for a company's actions. Because of this they should be referred to again and again in a company's CSR communication.

Rule #3: Be prepared – critical questions and core operations

From a CSR point of view, the different levels of entrepreneurial action can be depicted as a pyramid. Extending the model of the London Benchmarking Group (www.lbg-online.net), we work with a flexible six-tiered model that reflects marketing topics as well as HR-related questions (see Figure 8.2). However, it is crucial for the communication of CSR that a company understands – and meets – its obligation to make concrete statements about the responsibility of its core operations. This is seen as the basis of its CSR.

Comprehensive corporate citizenship programmes tend to provoke critical stakeholders (or journalists) into asking questions about the treatment of employees, the manufacturing process environment or consumer protection. Social commitment is the optional programme of CSR but it offers great potential for differentiating a company from its competitors. However, such 'optional' CSR programmes will be ineffective without the required programme of CSR within a company's core operations. This is another

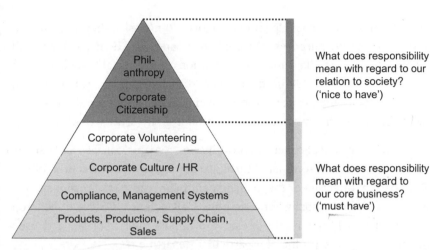

Figure 8.2 'Must have' and 'nice to have' CSR activities.

reason for communicating the overall picture and the corporate CSR culture at all times.

Rule #4: CSR must be a boardroom priority – merely being part of corporate communications threatens a loss of credibility

Where CSR policy is not handled by a department that reports directly to the board, CSR managers are faced with a dilemma, as the topic is interdisciplinary and affects most of the central business operations yet. Internal CSR projects require synchronisation and co-ordination so that the interests of individual departments are weighed up and evaluated comprehensively. Organisationally, the responsibility for CSR often resides in one department, and for historical reasons it is most often positioned in the corporate communications or HR department.

However, if too much emphasis is placed on the interests of corporate communications in CSR projects, one runs the risk of making the generation of 'stories' and 'pictures' the overriding task – they are, after all, very good for PR purposes. On the other hand, an HR department will emphasise aspects like employee retention or the establishment of an employer brand. But CSR needs to reflect the values of the entire company. In case of doubt, topics such as the environment and social standards should be preferred to other more 'communication friendly' CSR activities.

This is why cross-departmental co-ordination remains crucial – and usually succeeds if CSR is co-ordinated through steering groups or a central office. The board of directors or the management board must take responsibility, on behalf of the company, for a rigorous CSR policy. If CSR is to be a top priority it should not be the preserve of a particular manager and used merely to raise the profile of a particular department.

The behaviour of corporate management *vis-à-vis* CSR also serves as an example to the employees, and the commitment to the company by the management board should thus include an obligation for corporate responsibility. "The company's credibility with respect to CSR stands or falls on the basis of the attitudes of its corporate management. The commitment to providing resources for CSR budgets and capacities will reflect that attitude – and that commitment will, in turn, form part of the CSR communication."

Rule #5: Involve the employees – CSR communication moves from the inside out

Responsibility must become a reality within the company and must therefore also become a part of the corporate culture. In this context, the involvement of the employees is crucial. If a CSR measure manages to convince employees, they will, in turn, become witnesses and guarantors for the credibility of the company. If an action is viewed critically, or if the corporate management is accused of 'alibi actions', this can become very problematic for company communication. Currently only 21% of employees believe that their company takes on its responsibility fully, e.g. in the area of environmental protection.

This leads to two requirements with regard to employees. The first of these is that communication must take place from the 'inside out'. It is essential to inform the employees about a CSR project first – to 'bring them on board' – before the media and the public learn about it. If this is not done, CSR can quickly turn into a management issue that has nothing to do with everyday work. The second requirement is that CSR projects should be drawn up in such a way that they transform employees into 'doers'. The same goes for the corporate citizenship projects of a company. In the last few years a number of models for employee volunteering have developed, which demonstrate the value of involving employees.

With good employee communication and a low threshold for participation, employees' identification with the CSR targets and the company increases. In this way they become credible witnesses for the corporate engagement.

Rule #6: Extract messages – CSR issues must stand their ground in the economics of perception

Issues management is central to corporate communications. CSR issues such as environmental protection are in vogue at the moment, but the overall CSR picture of a company is complex and can only be communicated if there is already a basic sensibility among members of the target group in relation to this subject, or if one is nurtured. By means of strategic agenda-setting, a company can create a profile and a positive dynamic for the long term. Therefore, businesses have to choose the right CSR issues. An analysis of the significance of a topic for stakeholders and its business relevance should be undertaken, and in this way issues can be prioritised and a logical approach developed.

In the economics of perception, attention is the most precious good. More than 65% of the population feel 'continually bombarded with advertising messages' according to the Yankelovich Monitor. This environment makes

CSR communication especially difficult, because 'good' messages are often less attention-grabbing than not so good ones. This is why it is particularly important that those working in the complex field of CSR must extract clear messages and create plausible images and stories that are going to be newsworthy. At the same time, it is worth considering whether the general public is, in fact, the most relevant target group.

Rule #7: Everybody is different – address the CSR target groups according to their expectations and habits

As with any communication, when talking about CSR one must identify the correct target group. The more accurately a target group is defined, the easier it is to match the communication successfully. The general public is rarely the target group for complex CSR messages; this is more likely to be made up of local communities at the place of business, policy-makers, environmental groups, 'highly active or informed' groups of customers or future employees. The choice of communication tools needs to be appropriate for each target group, in line with the expectations and habits of its members. In coming up with these messages, CSR representatives should be able to draw on the company's usual resources.

In this respect, the CSR report is merely one way among many of disseminating information. It has its relevance as a supplement to the annual report and with respect to non-governmental organisations (NGOs), but for customers, employees and the public there are many other, more appropriate methods.

Two further aspects of CSR in corporate communications should be considered:

▶ A central CSR contact person in a company ensures stability, builds confidence and should also act as a 'first address' in communications.

▶ Apart from a very target group-specific communication with regard to certain CSR projects, the overall CSR approach must be transmitted across all communication instruments (see Rule #2).

Rule #8: Embrace dialogue – good CSR corporate communications focuses on exchange

The CSR communication of a company focuses on the various stakeholder groups (see Figure 8.3). This contact helps to identify opportunities and risks at an early stage. Opportunities for topic- or project-specific co-operation then open up. But co-operation can only succeed if the communication is on a partnership basis. At the same time, communication must follow a dialogue objective. In doing so, the companies don't have to initiate each dialogue themselves. For many different subject areas, there are sector-stakeholder dialogues, multi-stakeholder forums, discussion groups and other ways of communication exchange.

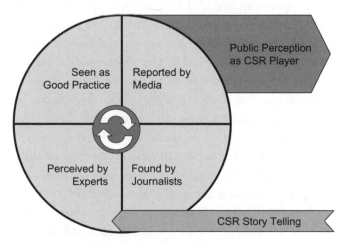

Figure 8.3   Instruments for stakeholder management.

Transparency, openness and a joint search for solutions are preconditions for successful dialogue with stakeholders. Only if stakeholders can also draw nearer to their own targets will they make a constructive contribution to the dialogue. Companies should therefore be familiar with the interests and expectations of their stakeholders. Topics must be identified that are relevant both to stakeholders and to the companies. In a strategic stakeholder management, the company defines the aims and the tools of a dialogue. These can be adjusted to suit the process of the dialogue.

A note of caution: dialogue always raises expectations and this should be channelled by the company. Not all of them can, or indeed should, be satisfied. This is why the area and the extent of stakeholder co-operation should be determined beforehand. The more precise the targets of the dialogue, the more transparent the process and the deeper the company can delve into it.

Rule #9: Become an example of good practice – benefit from the influence of opinion-makers

How does a company turn itself into an example of good practice in CSR? As long as the forming of opinion is created via the print media, TV and classic web communications, it is journalists and editors who decide on the CSR examples to be presented to the general public. As well-known CSR journalists do not yet exist in sufficient numbers, journalists primarily use two sources: their own research, which often means going back to older articles dealing with similar topics; or people they have identified as CSR experts. These tend to be academics, CSR consultants and CSR officers in companies and other organisations. As long as this group of people is small, a collection of good practices is generated, which reproduces itself again and again and which grows only slowly. Only when Web 2.0 formats gain in importance will this 'filter function' of experts and journalists be expanded to take in a wider account of the good or bad behaviour of companies.

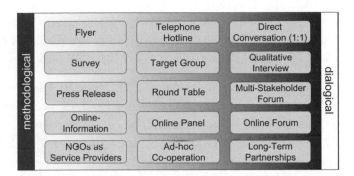

Figure 8.4 CSR experts as multipliers for a company's CSR perception.

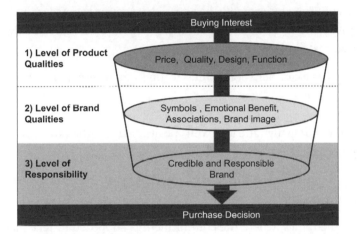

Figure 8.5 Responsibility as a buying incentive in relation to a product brand.

Rule #10: Responsible product brands – turn CSR into a selling point

Product brands can be enriched by a tag of social responsibility. As well as a product's features and values, a CSR-related factor can also influence consumers' purchasing decisions (see Figure 8.5). They may ask themselves: does the product count as a credible and responsible brand? This is an especially important criterion in the LOHAS (lifestyle of health and sustainability) segment. It is estimated that 12 million people belong to this consumer group in Germany alone (Spiegel 2009). The market importance of being responsible is also illustrated by the fact that sales of fairtrade products increased by more than 50% in 2008 (CSR News.net 2009).

The establishing of a responsible brand at the product level is a new opportunity for branded companies. On the one hand, they can introduce their own CSR commitments to broad sections of the population, and on the other they can build new groups of customers for their brand. In the last few years, the combination of donations with the sale of products has become popular. While this mechanism of cause-related marketing is quite successful in Anglo-American markets, the response in other places, such as central Europe for example, has been more tentative. Accordingly, more differentiated and comprehensive approaches are currently being developed and tested.

A quick check can help companies to find out whether they have brand CSR potential:

▶ Is the company already well positioned in the area of CSR in principle?

▶ Is the core business free of apparent risks that could turn into a target for the brand?

▶ Are the topics, where the commitment is supposed to take place, still vacant or are they already occupied by competitors?

▶ Is it possible to establish a plausible connection between the commitment and the core operations as well as the brand image?

If all these questions can be answered favourably, nothing stands in the way of establishing a responsible brand. Beside a convincing project concept, all marketing and communication channels can be made accessible for CSR issues – from below-the-line marketing to the 'eye-catcher' on the supermarket shelf. Figure 8.6 gives a handy checklist for avenues of communication in relation to CSR.

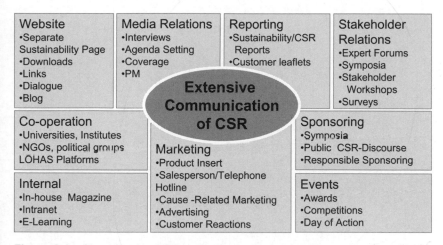

Website	Media Relations	Reporting	Stakeholder
•Separate Sustainability Page •Downloads •Links •Dialogue •Blog	•Interviews •Agenda Setting •Coverage •PM	•Sustainability/CSR Reports •Customer leaflets	Relations •Expert Forums •Symposia •Stakeholder Workshops •Surveys
Co-operation •Universities, Institutes •NGOs, political groups LOHAS Platforms	Marketing •Product Insert •Salesperson/Telephone Hotline •Cause -Related Marketing •Advertising •Customer Reactions		Sponsoring •Symposia •Public CSR-Discourse •Responsible Sponsoring
Internal •In-house Magazine •Intranet •E-Learning			Events •Awards •Competitions •Day of Action

Center oval: **Extensive Communication of CSR**

Figure 8.6   Checklist for CSR avenues of communication.

References

CSR News (2009) *Fairtrade wächst trotz Krisenzeiten*, 24.04.2009.http://csr-news.net/main/2009/04/24/fairtrade-wachst-trotz-krisenzeiten/.

Krauthammer (2009) Corporate Societal Responsibility 2009, www.Krauthammer.com.

Spiegel (2009) Lohas-Broschüre. http://media.spiegel.de/internet/media.nsf/1438C4FDE94F06B8C12575360033CFA6/$file/SPIEGEL_Broschuere_LOHAS.pdf.

University of Applied Sciences Wiesbaden and 2hm & Associates GmbH (2008) *CSR*.

Event project management best practice

Siegmar Ley

In this chapter we look at events (CSR, HR or volunteering) from a project management perspective, as increasingly such events are organised under the auspices of a CSR department. Here the emphasis is on the business plan and tools for developing good practice in the run-up to events. This is important not just in CSR terms but in order to communicate the business case and to align such events with other corporate goals.

Introduction

There are several different approaches to the topic of 'company events with a corporate or social commitment'. The main focus of this chapter is the company that has already embedded CSR into its corporate strategy or is planning to do so. The expression 'CSR event' takes in all types of company events – such as conferences, kick-offs, product presentations, incentives and trade show appearances – that are combined with a corporate or social event.

If the leading mission statement of CSR is defined as 'the sustainable success of a company with respect to environmental responsibility and economic efficiency', then the social commitment of a company – in relation to events – is an aspect of CSR that finds expression in concepts such as corporate citizenship (CC) or corporate volunteering (CV). When it comes to events like these, one must decide whether the targets are internal or external, i.e. whether it is a staff event or a customer event.

In addition to the many ways in which companies demonstrate a corporate and social commitment, the idea of combining events that are already taking place with a company's CSR commitment is slowly but surely growing in importance. The idea is that targets that correspond to the company's CSR targets will be met by participants within the context of the event. In order to discuss in detail this interesting variation on the CSR commitment, we must first ask why companies organise events at all.

Targets

Each event has as its target to instruct, educate or motivate participants to do something that is of use to the company! The interesting thing about the combination of CSR with the events of a company is that three different targets can be pursued at the same time, namely:

▶ the professional targets of the event

▶ HR or targets in marketing

▶ the company's CSR targets.

In order to achieve these targets, a functional chain must already be considered in the initial phase. This functional chain comprises four levels (see Figure 9.1). In the ROI (return on investment) method for the evalu-

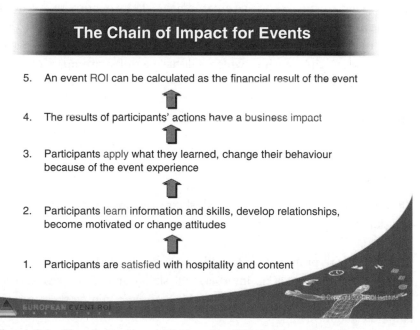

Figure 9.1 The chain of impact for events. ROI, return on investment.

ation of events, which is described later, measurable targets have to be set for each level:

▶ We have to create a *positive environment* at the event …

▶ … so that the participants are able to incorporate our message and to integrate it

▶ … in order to change their attitude afterwards

▶ … which will lead to the *desired benefit*.

If one continues along this functional chain, each attitude change requires a learning process that has to alter something in the minds of the participants. Therefore, if we fail to create a positive environment for the participants, they will not incorporate the message, their attitude won't be changed and we won't obtain the desired success. With regard to the first requirement, creating a positive environment, clarity of purpose is crucial. What exactly are the participants supposed to learn and what are they meant to draw from the event? Researchers have identified four types of learning in principle, each of which will have a different impact on what goes into an event:

▶ knowledge

▶ skills

▶ attitude

▶ other qualifications (e.g. social skills, relationships, interpersonal skills).

CSR targets are primarily to do with 'attitude' and 'other qualifications' (social skills, relationships, interpersonal skills) and, as is well known, these are best 'learned' in a team. In this respect, attaining these targets is mainly about:

► development of social skills

► strengthening identification with the company

► improving the working atmosphere

► team-building

► reduction of staff turnover

► improving the firm's image in the society/region.

Best practice

Although customer events are sometimes combined with a CSR commitment, such as the assembly of an adventure playground by a large German enterprise in co-operation with its key clients, staff events are particularly suitable for such projects, for example:

► sales conferences

► kick-offs

► company parties

► company anniversaries

► retailer conferences

► incentive competitions.

In traditional events, messages/learning targets are usually not realised until afterwards, and it is common for participants to find that, on returning to their busy daily routine, the resolutions fall by the wayside. In an event that includes a CSR commitment, the message is implemented in the course of that event and is experienced as a highly motivating team experience by the employees.

A good example of a staff event with a CSR commitment is a three-day kick-off meeting that took place in a German pharmaceutical company. On one afternoon, 350 staff members, assembled into small teams, carried out different projects in about 60 social organisations near the company's headquarters. The organisations included kindergartens, nursing homes, drug-counselling services, battered women's refuges, playgrounds and many more. The project work was recorded by a film crew and then screened before the participants and the management at a reception on the same evening. The enthusiasm of the staff was so great (as was the media interest) that all of them volunteered spontaneously to do a similar activity the next year.

Project procedure

The project procedure described below can be used as a template for each event with a CSR commitment and adjusted accordingly. It is divided into three major parts (see also Box 9.1):

▶ planning

▶ realisation

▶ follow-up.

Planning

▶ First of all the organising department has to co-ordinate the CSR targets of the event with the company's management or the CSR representative.

▶ The selection of suitable social organisations and projects comes next. It is advisable to co-operate with a partner who has good connections with the organisations and knows their needs (such as, for example, the UPJ in Germany, a national network of engaged

Box 9.1 Organisation of a CSR event

Planning

▶ The company's CSR targets for the event, based on the return-on-investment method (Jack Phillips, ROI Institute):

- level 1 (satisfaction): 80% of all participants should give the CSR activities a rating of at least 4 on a scale of 1–5 after the event

- level 2 (learning): three out of four participants identify with the company's CSR targets after the event

- level 3 (application): at least 50% of the participants volunteer for further CSR projects in their company after the event

- level 4 (impact): a minimum of three regional and two national daily newspapers look upon the company's CSR activities favourably with a PR/advertisement value of at least €100,000.00

▶ Choice of suitable CSR projects in co-operation with for example local community organisations, local government or educational centres.

Realisation

Compilation and realisation of the project planning, with details on:

▶ Project headquarters

▶ Tasks

▶ Personnel

▶ Responsibilities

▶ Deadlines

▶ Schedule

▶ Support

(Continued)

▶ Transport logistics

▶ Materials

▶ Documentation

▶ Media

▶ Cost budget

Follow-up

▶ Compilation of documentation for:

   − stakeholders

   − employees

   − social organisations

   − media

▶ Settlement of the event with all funding sources

▶ Evaluation (The financial comparison of target and actual business results) of the event regarding the CSR targets

   − level 1 (satisfaction)

   − level 2 learning)

   − level 3 (application)

   − level 4 (impact)

businesses and local non-profit intermediary organisations – see www.upj.de).

▶ Depending on the extent of the project it is also advisable to employ a full-service event agency with the necessary experience in realising CSR projects.

▶ Preliminary talks follow with the different social organisations about the realisation of the projects.

▶ Agreements with contractors (materials), service providers (transport, support) and craftsmen (expertise), if necessary, have to be reached and reservations made for the planned date.

▶ When all the different areas of planning have been covered, the agency (or the organising department) draws up a preliminary schedule.

▶ On the basis of this schedule and an associated cost budget, the decision about how to proceed is made.

Realisation

▶ If the project gets the go-ahead, a detailed project plan is drawn up, with the locations of the organisations, the contact people, the tasks, schedule, materials, staff requirements and possibly professional support for each organisaion.

▶ Detailed arrangements with the social partners about the tasks and schedule then follow.

▶ Contractors' services and the materials have to purchased.

▶ If necessary, a detailed plan is drawn up of the transport logistics to the social organisations.

▶ Setting up the project headquarters on location as a contact point for all participants for the co-ordination of the whole event, including transport, accommodation, catering, engineering and the social programme.

▶ Participants are cared for by hosts, professionals and craftsmen (if needed).

▶ Video and still photography of the work in the organisations.

Follow-up

This includes:

► compilation of documentation on all projects carried out

► detailed information on all participants and stakeholders

► comprehensive information on the relevant media

► a financial comparison between target and actual business results.

10

The role of IT in corporate sustainability strategies

Chris Preist

Responsible Business: How to Manage a CSR Strategy Successfully
Edited by Manfred Pohl and Nick Tolhurst
Copyright © 2010 Manfred Pohl and Nick Tolhurst

This chapter outlines the vital role that advances in IT – a key driver of economic growth – can play in achieving sustainability goals and reducing companies' carbon and ecological footprints. This is illustrated by examining how existing equipment can be used more efficiently and also how IT can be used proactively to develop more sustainable business models.

Introduction

Over the last 25 years, information technology (IT) has come to play an increasingly important part in commerce and society. It is recognised both by public policy-makers and business people as a key driver of economic growth and is integral to the way most companies function. For this reason, any sustainability strategy for a company must consider the role of IT.

When considering the impact of IT equipment on the environment, particularly CO_2 emissions, it needs to be approached from two perspectives. Firstly, what is the direct impact of IT equipment and services used by the company, and how can these be reduced? Energy use by IT equipment is a significant source of emissions. Gartner, for example, estimated that the manufacture and use of IT and communications equipment are responsible for approximately 2% of the world's CO_2 emissions (McNee & Weilerstein 2008). The growth of data centres, and their associated power consumption, is particularly important to consider. In the case of sectors focusing primarily on information, such as the financial sector, IT equipment can be the single largest source of power consumption and hence emissions.

However, it is not sufficient to focus only on the negative impact of IT. IT is an enabling technology, which has the potential to be used to change the way things are currently done, to reduce carbon emissions and to make companies more sustainable.

Reducing the environmental impact of your IT use

We can classify the ways in which a company can reduce the environmental impact of IT use into three categories. Firstly, the most immediate opportunities, and 'quick wins', for a more sustainable use of IT come in modifying how your company uses the equipment it already has. This can be done through a combination of awareness-raising and the deployment of appropriate management tools and policies across the company's IT estate. Secondly, the existing IT estate can be reorganised to be more efficient. There is often a redundancy of equipment, particularly printers and servers which are under-used. Thirdly, when upgrading equipment, the choice of new components, the way they are deployed, and the disposal of the old kit can take sustainability and energy efficiency factors into consideration.

Using existing kit in a more sustainable way

If someone enters an office out-of-hours, they might be surprised to see how much electricity is being wasted. The most obvious reason is the lights being left on, but the computers, printers and screens still operating also play a significant part. The first quick-win is to reduce this waste. Options here include:

▶ *Awareness-raising and encouraging people to switch off their kit when not in use* – in small, motivated offices this can be an effective approach, especially if there is a sense of working together to achieve it. There are two disadvantages, however. Firstly, in less motivated communities it is difficult to get many people to commit to this. The significant wait in the morning for a machine to power up will put many people off. Secondly, in some large organisations, maintenance and upgrade of software are carried out over the network during out-of-hours periods. If a machine is switched off when upgrading is taking place, it will interfere with the IT management processes of the company.

▶ *Setting the power management options on computers to ensure they enter low-power modes when not in use* – while not zero-power, these modes consume less power than a computer that is on but idle. Newer computers, particularly those that are Energy Star compliant, will already be set up to enter these modes relatively quickly. However, it is possible to improve on the standard settings. In corporate environments where machines are managed remotely, a power management policy can be rolled out automatically to all machines. In choosing what settings to use, it is important to balance power-saving with usability considerations. For example, it is best to power the monitor down for a few minutes before entering standby, warning the user and allowing them to intervene before the standby sequence commences.

In addition to energy consumption by PCs, office paper use is also a consideration when thinking about corporate sustainability. Paper recycling efforts have often been linked with the goal of 'saving trees' – in fact, if the paper is sustainably sourced, a more significant issue is the energy used to make it (whether or not it is recycled) and the associated CO_2 emissions resulting from this. The Environmental Defense Fund (see www.papercalculator.org) have estimated that the weight of CO_2 emitted during paper manufacture is two to three times the weight of paper produced. This means that reducing paper use should be a significantly higher priority than recycling, and IT policies can help here (though, of course, recycling remains worthwhile – according to the EDF, it reduces carbon emissions from manufacture by over 30%). One key means of reducing paper use is to make double-sided printing the default. There is no need for most printing that takes place in an office to be single-sided. While most printers are capable of duplex printing, it is common that this is not the default mode and must be explicitly requested. This, of course, is something people rarely think to do. For this reason, it is better to have the duplex mode set as the default printing option, and for people to have to request single-sided explicitly when needed.

As well as encouraging duplex printing, it is important to discourage unnecessary printing. It is quite common for print jobs to be printed and then forgotten about, ending up in the recycling bin next to the printer without ever being read. The most straightforward option here is education. However, technology can be used to 'enforce' a policy around this should it be desired. Some printers can be set up so that the job will not print until a user enters a code into the printer. When such an approach is adopted, it is surprising how many jobs are requested but never collected. Gartner has estimated that a 'pull printing solution' such as this can reduce paper use by around 10%. Hence, worthwhile paper savings can be made, but a company will have to weigh this against the irritation factor of having to enter a code and wait by the machine while a job is printed (McNee & Weilerstein 2008).

Upgrading kit

When it is time to upgrade kit, the following considerations should be borne in mind:

▶ What is the power consumption of the new machine? Is it Energy Star compliant?

▶ To reduce the overall carbon footprint, it may be appropriate to buy a more powerful machine but keep it longer. Upgrading is often required because advances in software mean that older machines no longer have the speed or RAM to run the software acceptably quickly. By opting for a more powerful machine, this software-induced obsolescence can be postponed for a year or two.

▶ Laptops are, in general, more efficient and have a lower carbon footprint than desktop machines, and modern LED screens are more efficient than CRT screens.

▶ Where mobility is not required, a 'thin client' solution throughout an office may be a good option to replace desktop PCs. In this case, most of the processing and storage are carried out on (more efficient) central servers, with the local machines used simply as user displays. This reduces power consumption and also requires upgrading less often. It does, however, increase the processing power of central servers, which we will discuss in the next section.

▶ In the case of printers, what is the printing requirement of the community being served and how can it best be met? It is often more efficient, environmentally and from a cost perspective, to replace a number of under-used desktop printers with a smaller number of workgroup printers.

▶ Is the machine chosen designed to be recyclable at the end of its life? Ideally, machines should be designed to be easily disassembled into its component parts, and these should be easily identifiable as to how they should be recycled. Processes which reduce the ease of recycl-ability, such as coatings and paints, should be avoided.

▶ Use of hazardous materials should be minimised.

▶ Supply chains for IT equipment are some of the largest and most complex in existence. This means that they have a significant impact, and therefore significant opportunity for positive action. How well is the provider of a potential solution making use of this power to raise social and environmental standards along its supply chain?

▶ What is the overall attitude to sustainability of the potential provider? Is it proactively engaged in improvements in products and in internal processes to reduce negative impacts and increase positive impacts?

When a new purchase is made, it is necessary to dispose of old equipment. If it is still usable, and security and legal considerations permit, it is best to encourage its re-use through the various schemes in which equipment is refurbished for use by charities or in developing countries. If this is not possible, then it should be disposed so as to maximise recycling of com-ponents. In the EU, the Waste Electrical and Electronic Equipment (WEEE) Directive means that this is increasingly provided for. Often, suppliers of new equipment will offer a take-back scheme for effective disposal and recycling of the old kit.

Networks, servers and data centres

So far, we have focused on IT equipment in the office – often the most visible part of the IT estate. However, most large companies will have a less visible, but significant, IT presence in the form of racks of servers in one or more data centres. In terms of energy use, these can be a significant contributing factor. The servers themselves are far more powerful than the average desktop or laptop computer, and are usually used much more intensively. Furthermore, in addition to the direct power use there is the knock-on effect of their activity. Servers produce a significant amount of heat and if this is allowed to build up, it could impair the servers' function or damage them. Hence they must be cooled, usually by air conditioning. The energy required to do this can be as much as that used to power the servers directly – effectively doubling their overall energy use.

There are two main kinds of inefficiencies which tend to occur in such systems. The first, associated with direct power use, is that there is often an over-provisioning of computing power for what is needed. Effectively, there are more servers than are necessary, and energy is wasted keeping them on but idle. The second, associated with the indirect power use required for cooling, is that the air conditioning system may not be set up to cool the servers in the most efficient way.

A corporation has a choice of whether to tackle these inefficiencies itself, or transfer responsibility to others. For smaller organisations, it is often more efficient and cost-effective to have their server needs hosted by a specialist company. The amount of data and computational power the company needs does not warrant an entire data centre, and hence the company can 'rent' use of computational power and storage as required to meet their needs. For larger organisations, it may be appropriate to maintain one or more data centres but consolidate and reorganise them to be more efficient. This can be done either in-house, in conjunction with appropriately trained consultants, or by outsourcing the management of the data centres to a specialist company.

In all the above cases, the reorganisation is likely to result in both energy and financial savings. Two current technologies, in particular, are driving these savings:

▶ *Virtualisation of servers.* This technology allows one single physical server to behave as if it were several, as far as the rest of the network is concerned. This means that several under-used servers can be consolidated into a single, more fully loaded one, reducing idle power consumption. The city of Copenhagen, for example, managed to reduce the number of servers it had from 700 to 80.

▶ *Thermal assessment and reorganisation.* Data centres can be assessed to identify 'hot spots' where cooling is inadequate, and 'cool spots' where excessive cooling is taking place. The relative position of chillers and servers can then be altered to be more optimal and hence reduce air conditioning costs. One solution, 'dynamic smart cooling', enables the local transfer of cool air to where it is most needed, in automatic response to the changing needs of the servers. Also, physical partitioning of a data centre allows cooling to be focused in the areas it is most needed.

Much of the motivation behind these solutions is financial, with sustainability benefits as a bonus. However, it is worth a CSR manager ensuring that carbon emissions are taken into account as a factor in such reorganisations. Upcoming legislation in the UK and elsewhere will place increasing pressure on companies to report their emissions and demonstrate that they are making savings over time. When using external hosting and outsourcing arrangements, companies should ensure their suppliers are able to report and reduce emissions in this way.

Other factors come into consideration when there is an opportunity to build completely new data centres:

▶ *Consolidation.* It is usually more efficient, both environmentally and economically, to build a smaller number of data centres.

▶ *Site.* Ideally, from an environmental perspective, a data centre would be sited somewhere cool to reduce the energy required to cool the servers. Direct access to renewable energy could also be considered.

▶ *Building design.* For new-build data centres, there is the opportunity to design the building itself to optimise the use of external air and/or water to reduce the need for air conditioning.

▶ *Container solutions.* For legacy buildings, a container-based approach where a building houses a number of data centre 'blocks' in shipping containers can be an option. This reduces cooling, in that the bulk of cooling effort is focused on the interior of the containers.

▶ *Back-up power.* Many data centres are considered mission-critical, and hence require back-up power. In countries with an erratic grid supply, this can be significant. Traditional back-up power solutions, such as diesel generators, are usually significant emitters of CO_2. Solutions should have their environmental impact assessed as part of the decision process, and ideally a low-carbon option such as a fuel cell should be adopted.

Using IT to reduce the impact of your business

In addition to considering the direct environmental impact of IT on a business or organisation's footprint, it is important to consider the role IT can have in providing solutions which support the monitoring and reduction of emissions. IT can be used to increase the efficiency of existing processes, to help re-engineer new processes, or to find new ways of meeting needs which are quite different from the current approach.

Logistics and manufacturing optimisation

Information technology already plays a key role in the optimisation of a firm's logistics and transportation operation. It is used to plan the location of warehousing, distribution centres, and so on. It is used to plan appropriate loads, vehicle choice and delivery routes. It can also be used to reconfigure dynamically in response to changing requirements, and communicate with drivers to inform them of this. In most cases, this optimisation is done to minimise costs with no consideration of environmental issues. And, in general, such cost minimisation will have a positive environmental impact, as in logistics the cost of fuel and storage is significant. However, this is not always the case – for example, the use of just-in-time delivery, where warehouse floor space is expensive in comparison with delivery costs, can mean that more smaller deliveries are made, resulting in greater fuel consumption per delivery. Some logistics planning tools now have embedded capabilities to report on probable greenhouse gas emissions resulting from a given set-up, which means that such factors can be incorporated alongside cost considerations when making decisions about the placing of distribution centres and the design of the logistics network.

Given that, in the future, carbon pricing will play an increasingly important role, it can make business sense to opt for a (currently) slightly more expensive set-up which is less affected by future increases in fuel and carbon costs. In a similar way to logistics optimisation, manufacturing processes can also be optimised, taking energy use and carbon emissions into account alongside price factors. Simply having a system which provides ongoing real-time monitoring of energy use in an industrial process can allow it to be managed more effectively and enable energy leakages to be spotted quickly. For example, the Turkish steel company Erdemir reported a reduction in power consumption of up to 5% after installing an energy monitoring system alongside its control systems.

Optimising publications

Many organisations produce huge amounts of printed material for broad distribution beyond the organisation, e.g. reports, publicity, brochures. The current economics of printing encourages over-production of such publications and results in waste from pulping what has not been used. Furthermore, when information in a small part of a publication becomes out of date, the whole thing needs to be replaced. The sustainability impact of the paper wastage can be significant. Redesigning an organisation's publications strategy can therefore yield significant benefits. There are several aspects to this:

► What information actually needs to be printed, and what can be delivered primarily in a 'pull' medium online? Some publications may no longer need to be printed, or can be printed in summary form referring to the online version for further details. It is important that the online version is browser-friendly and not simply a pdf document requiring printing by the user to be readable.

► Where documents do need to be printed (e.g. publicity for a sales show), a process can be set up allowing them to be digitally printed on demand in the numbers needed for specific events, at relatively local printers, and mailed to the person requesting them. This avoids large print runs being stored in warehouses and pulped when no longer needed. HP now uses this approach to manage much of its marketing material across Europe.

► In some cases, it is possible to personalise the material, missing out pages that are not relevant to a given customer. For example, Anglia Ruskin University allows prospective applicants to order a prospectus which only contains details of the courses relevant to them. It is printed and posted to them, saving paper and reducing the cost and weight of mailing.

Home working

Home working, or telecommuting, has the potential to significantly reduce the impact of the daily commute from a sustainability perspective, in terms of both emissions and driver frustration. It also allows businesses to reduce the need for office space – and the emissions associated with heating and lighting them. This is done by providing employees with broadband access, laptops and a software infrastructure that supports remote collaboration. It also requires creating a culture where team members are trusted to work in isolation and maintain good communication channels despite not being co-located.

In office working, the commute to work is often the factor that has the greatest environmental impact, so it is valuable to address this. However, there is some debate about the extent to which the gains of telecommuting are offset by other factors, known to as 'the rebound effect'. The home office needs to be heated, and this is often more inefficient than heating the workplace. Also, because employees don't need to travel to work, they may choose to drive elsewhere (e.g. to the shops) with the time that is freed up. There is also the longer-term impact on the overall system of a move to telecommuting. People may choose to live further from their workplace as they don't need to travel there every day, but when they do travel (say weekly) the emissions may be significantly greater than a daily commute.

Remote collaboration

In large and distributed organisations, where long-distance collaboration is important, remote collaboration and meeting technology can play an important role in ensuring effective team-working while reducing the need to travel. Different technical solutions, providing different 'qualities' of meeting and working, can be used depending on what is needed for a given interaction. Email and online chat can be used to interact formally and informally over the internet, and to build a sense of community remotely. Online meeting software, combining voice channels with the ability to share screens, can be used for more formal presentations. Video-conferencing also has an important role to play, in terms of building strong personal connections at distance. Recent advances in technology, offering telepresence solutions with very high quality and low delay, mean that for small meetings, the quality can be almost as good as being in the same room. In some ways, it has advantages over face-to-face meetings. There is the obvious reduction in travel emissions and avoidance of the need to spend time travelling, but it also allows flexibility. One research team used a three-site telepresence solution to meet with potential collaborators in two other locations. As the meeting progressed it became clear that at one location, New York, there were others who could make a contribution. They were able to be brought in to the meeting straight away, something that would not have been possible if the meeting had been face-to-face at a different location.

There is some evidence that remote collaboration can also have 'rebound effects', generating new travel needs as long-distance relationships build up. Hence, it is best used as part of an overall package to reduce travel use, which combines technology, 'soft' approaches, such as information and training, the rebranding of travel departments as meeting facilitation departments, and 'hard' approaches, such as the capping or reduction of travel budgets. Remote collaboration technology does not necessarily lead, in its own right, to a reduction in travel. However, by using it, it is possible for an organisation to implement a reduction in travel without compromising its effectiveness or the quality of relationships that develop remotely.

Other ways of reducing travel needs

Where a business needs to have employees travel to gather information, IT can potentially be used to reduce this need through the deployment of *in situ* monitoring technology linked to a network. For example, utility companies will be moving to a 'smart metering' infrastructure over the next few years. Smart meters in each home will monitor utility (gas, electricity) use and report back to the utility company over a network. This will provide customers with more transparency concerning their electricity consumption and also reduce or eliminate the need for utilities companies to send staff to read meters. Some boiler makers have installed a capability for their water boilers to be monitored remotely by the company, meaning their performance can be checked, and if an engineer needs to visit to carry out a repair, the correct part can be selected in advance.

Online services

IT can also be used to allow both customers and staff to engage in full 'self-service' in terms of the offerings of an organisation. This is currently most prevalent in e-banking and e-government, where online services can replace the need for postal or face-to-face interaction, and so reduce the need for transportation, travel and paperwork. For example, a study by WWF has estimated that if worldwide tax administration was carried out purely online, it could lead to reductions in CO_2 emissions of around 2.5

million tonnes of per year as a result of cutting paper use. e-Banking service can be very empowering for customers, allowing them more transparency and control over their affairs and the ability to gain access at more convenient times.

Such services can result in improvements in efficiency from both a cost and an energy/carbon perspective. When designed well, they can also give good customer satisfaction. However, there are some risks involved. They can be designed so as to make it difficult for a customer to connect with a member of staff. If the customer's request is relatively straightforward and the service is well designed and easy to use, this is not a problem. However, when a request is more complex, or the customer is less comfortable with technology, it can lead to frustration and irritation on their behalf. For this reason, it is important to design these services so that a member of staff is available to deal with more complex requests and to take responsibility for fulfilling them.

The same is true for web services inside a company; using online self-help and email services can allow the centralisation and improved efficiency of, for example, IT support and human resources. When well executed, a self-service approach to information can lead to more satisfied employees. However, if this approach is poorly executed or is used to make access to experts difficult in the case of more complex requests, it has the risk of making savings on headline support figures, but pushing hidden costs onto members of staff, who must compensate in their work for the poorer level of service. This damages both employee productivity and morale.

Using IT to develop more sustainable business models

The final, and potentially most significant, category to consider when thinking about IT's role in a sustainability strategy is its capability to allow business to take place in new ways, re-engineering and replacing existing business models. Can customer needs be met in new and original ways, with reduced environmental impact? The answer to this will be different for each business sector. However, here we give three examples of business models that have been enabled by IT.

Car clubs

Car clubs allow members of the public easy local access to short-term hire of a car. Their business model relies on IT to allow easy booking, access and payment for a car parked on a local street. Hence the service replaces car ownership. Research has shown that membership of a car club reduces emissions in a number of ways (see a summary of research results at http://www.ukerc.ac.uk/Downloads/PDF/09/0904TransCarClubsTable.pdf). Firstly, they reduce the number of cars owned. In some cases, membership of a car club means that a family doesn't need to have a car, and in others, it means they don't have to buy a second car. Secondly, membership tends to replace older, less efficient cars. Thirdly, members tend to reduce the number of trips they take by car overall, replacing them with alternate means of transport and combining several (inefficient) short trips into one longer one.

The example of 3M

The manufacturer of office products and other innovative goods, 3M, partnered with HP to drastically bring down the cost and environmental impact of its office printing. It replaced a large number of old, energy inefficient machines, including many desktop printers, with a smaller number of high-quality and efficient workgroup machines. It also introduced duplex printing as default. Over three years, the programme has resulted in an estimated reduction in paper use of 353 million pages, and a reduction in CO_2 emissions of 8,240 tonnes from this reduction together with increased energy.

Online shopping and home delivery

Online shopping has expanded substantially over the last few years. In principle, online shopping combined with home delivery should reduce the environmental footprint associated with travel to the shop. However, current savings are less than they could be due to several factors:

▶ The large number of local delivery companies working for different online retailers, alongside the comparatively sparse number of orders per company, means that local delivery is relatively inefficient.

▶ People are often out, meaning that re-delivery is necessary, or that customers must travel to a storage depot to collect their goods.

▶ In some cases, orders may be dispatched from outside a country for tax reasons. This can result in additional transport emissions, particularly when the goods are flown.

It is likely that over time, as home delivery becomes more widely used, these issues will be addressed and considerable savings will be possible. WWF has argued that with a substantial move to e-commerce, it would be possible to reduce the number of retail stores and travel infrastructure (e.g. car parks), resulting in a virtuous 'positive feedback' loop enabling further emissions reductions.

Digital goods

In addition to home delivery, online shopping also has the capacity to deliver digital goods direct to the customer – digital music, in particular, is becoming increasingly prevalent. This replaces both the manufacturing and transportation of a physical product, and so can result in significant savings even when taking into account the energy used to store and transmit the digital media. Analysis has shown that the retail purchase of a CD album in the US results in carbon emissions of around 3 kg through its life cycle, whereas online purchase of the same album would result in emissions of around 400 g (Weber *et al.* 2009).

These three examples all illustrate that IT has the potential to re-engineer business models in ways that allow them to be more efficient and more sustainable. Different businesses will have different opportunities open to them in this space, and it is worthwhile getting the innovators and strategists to think about what opportunities IT can offer for moving to a more sustainable business practice, in terms of both improving existing business models and moving to new business models. Points to consider in this respect include:

▶ What processes can be made more efficient through the use of IT? Which processes can be replaced by alternate ways of doing things? Further, can customers' needs be met in a different, more environmentally friendly way?

▶ What IT support will be necessary to do this? What additional impact will the IT equipment have? Is this significantly less than the benefits of the change?

▶ What are the broader impacts on the system of such a change? What potentially negative 'rebound effects' might come into play? What measures can be taken to reduce these? What positive additional impacts might result, and how can these be magnified?

Conclusion

A comprehensive CSR strategy should include consideration of IT. Firstly, it should consider the impact of IT on its energy use and climate emissions, and the impact of the manufacturing and disposal of this equipment from both a social and an environmental perspective. In this chapter, we have presented a number of considerations to help a CSR manager work with IT staff to minimise this impact, during both purchase and use of the equipment. Secondly, a strategy should consider how IT can be used to make its business operate in a more sustainable way, by increasing efficiency of processes and reducing the need for travel. Thirdly, it should consider whether IT can be used to innovate new business models which replace existing ways of meeting customer needs with more sustainable ones. In this chapter, we have provided a number of examples to draw inspiration from, as well as guidelines to use when considering what opportunities exist for a given company.

References

McNee, S. and Weilerstein, K. (2008) *Cost Cutting Initiatives for Office Printing*. Gartner RAS Core Research Note G00155489, 22 February 2008, Gartner, Inc.

Weber, C.L., Koomey, J.G. and Matthews, H.S. (2009) The energy and climate change impacts of different music delivery methods. Final report to Microsoft Corporation and Intel Corporation. Available online: http://download.intel.com/pressroom/pdf/CDsvsdownloadsrelease.pdf.

11

CSR in the hotel industry: the Accor perspective

Hélène Roques

In this chapter, a personal perspective of life as a CSR manager in the international hotel business is provided. The author details the various programmes enacted, offers an insider's guide to why specific CSR projects were undertaken and outlines the personal characteristics required by a CSR manager and the vital importance of CSR managers having operational experience in order to ensure success.

The Accor Group

Accor is a major global group and the European leader in hotels, as well as the global leader in services to corporate clients and public institutions. The group has 150,000 employees, operates in nearly 100 countries and has over 40 years of expertise in two core businesses:

▶ Hotels – including the Sofitel, Pullman, MGallery, Novotel, Mercure, Suitehotel, Ibis, All Seasons, Etap Hotel, Formule 1 and Motel 6 brands, representing 4,000 hotels and nearly 500,000 rooms in 90 countries, as well as strategically related activities, such as Lenôtre.

▶ Services – with 32 million people in 40 countries benefiting from Accor Services products in employee and public benefits, rewards and motivation, and expense management.

What did Accor hope to achieve by its CSR programme?

Over the last few years, Accor Group has mobilised its 150,000 employees to enact its new CSR commitments, guided, in the main, by the human resources (HR) and technical teams, but also by the purchasing department and, more recently, the marketing department – all in the service of our customers in 100 countries.

What was the reason for adopting this CSR policy? Firstly, because it is of obvious benefit in our business sector, as our employees and customers have a high degree of awareness of sustainable development issues. Hotel personnel are in contact with customers day and night, i.e. with people who have entrusted them with their comfort and safety. Many of the issues that are central to sustainable development have to do with well-being – e.g. the quality of the environment, health, water and food – and these are all factors that are integral to our business. Thus, showing concern for sustainable development means managing your hotel efficiently, motivating the teams well and thereby increasing the quality of the service offered to customers.

As part of the group's CSR programme, our employees have learned simple energy- and water-saving measures, and our hotel managers implement the group's environmental policy as laid out in a charter of 65 concrete actions, all of which have demonstrated their effectiveness over the last 15 years. Furthermore, 1,000 of our hotels offer fair-trade products approved by our purchasers; and in 38 countries, Accor is now helping to fight child sex tourism, thanks to training courses organised by the HR directors, something of which our employees are extremely proud. In Africa and Asia, not a month goes by without the organisation of AIDS committees to fight this disease, in particular through early detection programmes with our NGO partners.

These are just a few examples of the CSR work going on in the group. A team of six people is in charge of the operational deployment of an international sustainable development policy, covering the areas of corporate social and environmental responsibility. The specificity of this policy is a result of the group's size and the number of its partners. Leveraging the group's size allows us to maximise the application of best practices at a very large scale. This policy, which has been applied since 2002 in the hotel business, alongside Accor Services, Lenôtre and Compagnie des Wagons Lits, is based on a network of some 100 correspondents and performance measurement indicators. In collaboration with the group's IT engineers, the team has designed measurement tools for obtaining reliable results that can be used for international management.

How does a sustainable development department work?

Sustainable development is a true enabler of change in the company. Most of our time is devoted to managing overlapping projects, with quantifiable objectives, which concern all group professions in 100 countries. Thirty objectives, known to all group entities, are being pursued in two main areas: human well-being and the preservation of the planet's resources.

To make this approach more efficient, in 2006 we launched an action programme called Earth Guest, the motto of which was adopted across the group: 'As guests of the Earth, we welcome the world' (see Figure 11.1). The following are some of the actions of this programme:

▶ Commitment of all of the group's brands to a project for world reforestation and support to local economic development, in line with the United Nations Environment Programme, with the objective of planting three million trees by 2012.

▶ Organisation of training courses to fight against the sexual exploitation of children in tourism, in collaboration with the international organisation ECPAT (training of over 11,700 employees for risk prevention in 2008)

▶ Definition and deployment of a policy for fighting AIDS within the group: ACT-HIV (American Conference for the Treatment of HIV) training to allow the deployment of an AIDS prevention policy in each hotel; within the frame of the Global Business Coalition against AIDS, malaria and tuberculosis (GBC), launch and management of the Platform of Tourism Stakeholders against AIDS, bringing together around 10 international groups

▶ Commitment of 1,000 hotels to support fair trade

▶ Design and realisation for Accor Services (Ticket Restaurant®) of a world programme to deploy healthy and balanced menus to fight against obesity

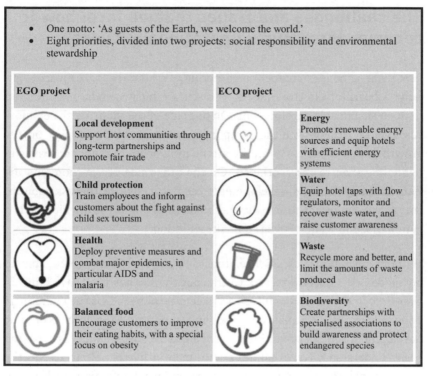

- One motto: 'As guests of the Earth, we welcome the world.'
- Eight priorities, divided into two projects: social responsibility and environmental stewardship

EGO project		ECO project	
	Local development Support host communities through long-term partnerships and promote fair trade		**Energy** Promote renewable energy sources and equip hotels with efficient energy systems
	Child protection Train employees and inform customers about the fight against child sex tourism		**Water** Equip hotel taps with flow regulators, monitor and recover waste water, and raise customer awareness
	Health Deploy preventive measures and combat major epidemics, in particular AIDS and malaria		**Waste** Recycle more and better, and limit the amounts of waste produced
	Balanced food Encourage customers to improve their eating habits, with a special focus on obesity		**Biodiversity** Create partnerships with specialised associations to build awareness and protect endangered species

Figure 11.1 Accor's Earth Guest programme.

▶ Commitment to the fight against climate change and the preservation of natural water resources: design and deployment of an environmental management tool allowing the consolidation of water and energy consumption data for 4,000 hotels in 100 countries, to reduce consumption by 10% over four years; launch in 2007 of a project to equip 100 hotels with thermal solar energy

▶ Deployment of methods for sorting and reducing waste in hotels

▶ Development of a group ethical charter, 'The Manager's Benchmarks', distributed to 50,000 operational managers around the world.

The challenges and issues that we face: how to convince the group's operational players?

"Let us imagine for a moment a gathering of a kind that takes place regularly: a board of directors meets to discuss a busy agenda, including an item on sustainable development. On one side of the room are the employees who are responsible the company's turnover, here to report on the growth of their business, with the attendant worries of reducing costs and lightening their teams' workload. On the other side of the room sits the director of sustainable development, keen to convince the assembly to commit to the bright future that he holds in his hands and which he has summarised in a slick PowerPoint presentation.

Without operational experience, that director is unlikely to be able to persuade other Accor directors to transfer the savings they have built up over time in the hotels business to projects – run by NGOs they have little knowledge of – for replanting trees and supporting the local economic development across six continents. The need for sustainability is clear and easily understood. For example, one human in five is able to live in the world thanks to the forests; they are essential for retaining fresh water, for our health, the quality of the air we breathe, and the medications we take. But when it is time for the company to decide what resources it can contribute to a sustainable project, only a precise understanding of the day-to-day operations will allow that director to put forward reasonable demands, engage in a constructive dialogue and obtain concrete results, such as those that have been obtained at Accor. This operational knowledge thus led us to adopt the 'step by step' strategy.

Sustainable development often means additional work and does not have the same direct results as other kinds of development. Seen from this angle, our profession could be reduced to simply organising the work of volunteers. It is therefore essential for CSR managers to have operational experience, of whatever kind, so that they are able to understand what it is that they are asking of their colleagues.

In the past, I was an operational employee, used to seeing experts from headquarters giving presentations, and that experience serves me well every day."

What are the factors of success?

Understanding operational constraints to be able to prioritise within a given budget or agenda is a prerequisite for success, but it is not the only one. It is necessary to be highly flexible and able to quickly understand the work of the other teams in the company. Sustainable development requires a certain level of expertise. But this expertise is shared with others: giving more weight to the opinion of the director of sustainable development than to that of a marketing director is no longer appropriate. Without our customers, there can be no sustainable development!

For example, when we committed Novotel hotels to Green Globe certification, we examined the commitments requested by the Australian certification body, line by line, with the Novotel brand's marketing team. Operating solely within the community of environmental certification experts would have been vain and counterproductive. The other qualities I consider useful are clarity of thought and purpose, energy and the ability to push an agenda forward despite constraints. Lastly, in the context of social responsibility, it goes without saying that honesty is absolutely essential.

What did the company learn?

The programmes deployed over the last few years have been extraordinarily well received by the employees. Last year, for example, Earth Guest day, a day of group employee mobilisation based around the eight priorities of the Earth Guest programme, was a huge success, with a very high participation rate among employees from over 77 countries. They demonstrated the whole group's commitment to sustainable development: with only limited resources, they deployed initiatives to save energy and water, plant thousands of trees, promote local development (e.g. financing a well in Burkina Faso through the sale of bottles of water on the Compagnie des Wagons Lits network), and carry out projects in the fight against sexual tourism affecting children in Thailand.

The main lesson of all this is that we have built something to last in our sustainability programme, and importantly, this corresponds to a deeply felt expectation among both group management and employees.

12
Microfinance: helping communities to develop

Hans-Ulrich Doerig

Responsible Business: How to Manage a CSR Strategy Successfully
Edited by Manfred Pohl and Nick Tolhurst

In this chapter, the background to one of the fastest growing CSR tools in the finance sector – microfinance – is provided through the perspective of Credit Suisse. The author outlines the aims, approaches and challenges of microfinance, as well as both the benefits for the recipients and the institution itself.

Introduction

The current 'best practice' approach in the areas of corporate citizenship and philanthropy involves linking development programmes with companies that have the necessary capabilities and expertise to help them succeed. Aid organisations define target sectors in which they can draw on the knowledge and support of the business community in order to have a measurable social impact and bring about change. In view of our role as a globally active bank, Credit Suisse regards the provision of support for the microfinance sector as an obvious focal point in our choice of philanthropic commitments. We have therefore launched a programme to support the training of microfinance professionals in Asia, Africa and eastern Europe. In addition, we are currently supporting two programmes in Africa that provide bank clients in rural areas with access to financial information and services that employ modern technology.

Microfinance at a glance

Microfinance dates back to the 1970s, when the concept of lending working capital – often amounting to as little as US$100, or even less – to the poor was first developed. Microfinance clients tend to have little or no collateral. Credit was initially granted to groups according to the principle of 'solidarity lending', so that the members could guarantee repayments. The interest paid by the borrowers provided the necessary capital to finance further loans to new micro-entrepreneurs. The straightforward nature of the concept is, unsurprisingly, one of the factors that contributed to its success. The range of microfinance services available gradually expanded from group loans to individual loans, with additional financial services such as insurance, savings schemes and fund transfers now being provided.

Microfinance is today regarded by many as a global movement to help individuals in poorer nations work their way out of poverty, and its huge potential is widely recognised. However, the microfinance sector still faces enormous challenges, despite the excellent progress achieved to date.

The World Bank estimates that approximately 40% of the world's population, or around 2.7 billion people, still live in extreme poverty and have to survive on less than $2 per day. It is also estimated that one-third of these people, i.e. up to one billion individuals, would establish their own small businesses and thus create their own employment if they had access to the right financial services and opportunities. With loan repayment rates averaging 97% and with no institutional defaults to date, microfinance has earned a reputation as a stable financial investment and an important building block for emerging financial systems.

According to a recent study by the policy and research consortium 'The Consultative Group to Assist the Poor' (CGAP), 47% of the funding in this sector originates from investors who are seeking a return on their money. Investments in microfinance often come from development finance organisations and institutional investors (pension funds and private equity funds), as well as from private investors via microfinance investment vehicles.

However, the majority of microfinance funding (53%) still takes the form of donations or grants. The grants are mainly provided by bilateral development organisations, multilaterals (e.g. the World Bank) and private donors. Donor funding is primarily targeted at sub-Saharan Africa and southern Asia. In eastern Europe, Central Asia, Latin America and the Caribbean, investments account for the clear majority of funding, with global banks such as Credit Suisse tending to act as both donors and investors in line with their commitment to promoting sustainable development in emerging economies.

Credit Suisse's contribution

As a financial services provider, Credit Suisse focuses primarily on serving clients at the top of the earnings pyramid. However, we are also committed to helping bridge the gap between the poorest section of the world's population at the base of the pyramid and those at the top. Our corporate citizenship initiatives reflect the principles of the UN Global Compact, which we have pledged to uphold, and they contribute to the realisation of the more broadly defined UN Millennium Development Goals of reducing poverty, improving health and providing equality for women.

With our microfinance programme, we are seeking to leverage our financial expertise and thought leadership to create a powerful philanthropic platform. We want to exploit our business capabilities to provide effective solutions for microfinance institutions (MFIs). At the same time, our microfinance programme enables us to satisfy the wish of many of our own clients to make investments that generate both a social and a financial return.

Employee participation is also a key element of our corporate citizenship activities. Although it is difficult to involve our employees in operations on the ground in the case of microfinance, we have nevertheless identified opportunities for our experts and managers to share their knowledge and experience with microfinance institutions in their capacity as advisors. In addition, Credit Suisse is interested in promoting innovation in the field of microfinance by facilitating research and fostering a dialogue about this topic.

Our philanthropic platform

Our approach to microfinance is based on our wish to exploit our financial know-how and business expertise in order to develop optimal solutions for MFIs (see Figure 12.1). This principle formed the starting point for our efforts in this field. Over a period of several months, a dedicated team of Credit Suisse professionals approached the question of how to support

Credit Suisse is committed to building bridges between the top and the bottom of the pyramid. Our approach integrates commercial interests, thought leadership and philanthropic contributions to find solutions for MFIs

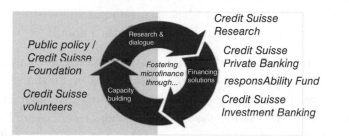

Figure 12.1 The Credit Suisse microfinance commitment: an integrated approach. MFI, microfinance institution.

the development of microfinance in the same way as they would a client mandate. One key aspect was clearly identified during this process: the need for capacity-building in the microfinance sector.

Speaking of the need for greater education in the microfinance sector, Bruce MacDonald, Vice President of Communications at ACCION International, a non-governmental organisation (NGO) with which Credit Suisse is in partnership, said: 'Training and capacity-building are among the biggest challenges facing microfinance institutions today, and are critical if microfinance is to reach the necessary scale and realise its full, global potential.' His statement is supported by our own findings. We have noted that loan officers, branch managers and the senior managers of MFIs usually have to execute a wide variety of tasks that require a broad range of interpersonal, managerial and financial skills. For example, the nature of the loan applications reviewed by loan officers can vary significantly. The officers meet groups of borrowers once a week to receive updates, keep records and collect repayments. Loan officers also have to make regular visits to individual borrowers in order to understand their short- and long-term needs and to provide targeted support and advice. Another important duty performed by loan officers is the verification of the identity of new clients and the assessment of their creditworthiness. During these types of meeting, a vetting or due diligence process is undertaken to check the suitability of the business plan, the borrower's references and other aspects. Once this information has been gathered and reviewed, the loan officer and branch manager will propose a loan amount.

The loan officers' field work is supported by a branch office, which maintains records, collects and reconciles repayments, and disburses loans. A loan or credit manager co-ordinates and controls the overall level of lending by the MFI and analyses the portfolio for performance and risk. The credit manager is generally responsible for reporting and maintaining records. A chief credit or risk officer may also supervise operations such as planning, co-ordination, risk mitigation and compliance. In addition, the officer may serve as a senior recruiter and trainer.

As MFIs rapidly expand their services and, in many cases, apply to the authorities to become regulated banks, there is a huge need to build their capacity by rolling out more sophisticated systems and appointing better-skilled personnel. To become a robust business, an MFI must often improve its internal systems in accordance with international standards. These improvements relate to aspects such as their organisational structure and ownership, governance, taxes, labour policies, reporting systems and management information systems (MIS). This often represents a major challenge for MFIs that don't have access to support and advice. Credit Suisse believes that supporting these capacity-building activities is even more important than supplying fresh capital to the MFIs.

Our approach

To realise our microfinance objectives, we decided to establish strategic partnerships with reputable, globally active NGOs. When selecting our partners, we looked for institutions with proven expertise and the necessary resources to drive capacity-building measures. At Credit Suisse, we consider a 'strategic partnership' to be a comprehensive form of co-operation, under which the relevant activities are jointly defined on the basis of each partner's needs and strengths.

Our experts examined a number of possible capacity-building activities that we could support, included the provision of tailor-made training courses for MFIs, education programmes offered by well-known universities, support for symposiums and conferences on specific topics, scholarships for MFI staff/academics, and study tours for MFI managers.

We considered it important to define a mission statement that would clearly convey the objectives that we want to realise in the field of microfinance to everyone within our company, as well as to our partner organisations and other stakeholders, including shareholders and clients. It was also intended that the mission statement would serve as a guideline for our longer-term commitments in this area. We defined the following mission statement:

> Through our partners, we aim to contribute to the high-quality training of thousands of microfinance staff and to provide improved access to financial services for hundreds of thousands of poor individuals and small enterprises in the developing world. By fostering research, innovation and a constructive dialogue, we aim to contribute to the spread of best practices and lessons learned around the world and to develop new solutions to drive further financial inclusion.

The selection process

Credit Suisse started by mapping the universe of strong microfinance organisations that were already working in this field and approached a selection of pre-screened and proven global partners. A clear focus was placed on two aspects: the potential for capacity-building and the geographical spread of the organisations. We requested concept papers from a number of the organisations that were shortlisted and subsequently conducted a formal submission and review process.

By March 2008, six global organisations had submitted proposals outlining different programmes for a three-year programme of co-operation. A committee reviewed these proposals according to the following criteria:

▶ the organisation's experience in providing microfinance/establishing training facilities

▶ programme design, including the organisation's ability to develop and successfully implement the proposed programme, the innovative nature of the scheme and the potential to leverage Credit Suisse's expertise

▶ the existence of a monitoring and evaluation concept that clearly tracks inputs, outputs and progress towards the programme's objectives and impact

▶ the scale of the programme and deliverables

▶ the organisation's management and technical capabilities

▶ branding and visibility, i.e. how the project/partnership will be communicated to the target communities as well as to a broader public, both locally and internationally.

We also wanted to obtain our partners' input and advice concerning Credit Suisse's volunteer work, including the question of how Credit Suisse employees could get involved (e.g. as trainers or mentors). We are currently setting up an educational programme in the Ukraine, under which retired financial experts and managers will act as teachers.

Based on our assessment of the industry and the findings of the review process, Credit Suisse subsequently entered into partnerships with four leading NGOs in this sector (see Figures 12.2 and 12.3; Box 12.1):

▶ ACCION International

▶ FINCA International

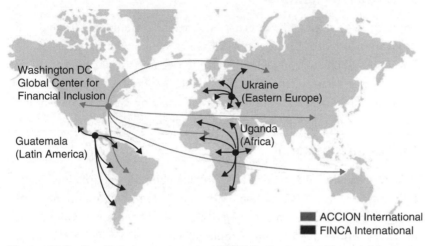

Figure 12.2 Credit Suisse supports ACCION's Center for Financial Inclusion and FINCA's regional training hubs.

Figure 12.3 Country programmes supported by Credit Suisse.

Box 12.1 Credit Suisse's NGO partners

ACCION International

Founded in 1961, ACCION International has been running microfinance programmes since 1973. Credit Suisse is a founding sponsor of the Center for Financial Inclusion, an action research and microfinance leadership centre launched by ACCION International. Credit Suisse also lends its support to the establishment of training centers in India and China. *www.accion.org, www.centerforfinancialinclusion.org*

FINCA International

FINCA International serves nearly 740,000 clients through a loan portfolio totaling over $345 million, with annual loan disbursements that exceeded $800 million in 2008. FINCA's clients have a repayment rate of 97.2%. With support from Credit Suisse, FINCA will implement a Global Leadership and Development initiative to evaluate training needs, identify best practices, set uniform standards and assist the monitoring and evaluation of training. *www.villagebanking.org*

Opportunity International

Opportunity International is one of the largest microfinance institutions in the world. It builds, owns and operates regulated commercial banking institutions serving the world's poorest people. Credit Suisse is one of the partners supporting the launch of an Electric Wallet Programme that utilises delivery channels such as mobile banks, ATMs and smartcards, coupled with biometric technologies, to provide first-time access for entrepreneurs who lack formal means of identification. *www.opportunity.org*

Swisscontact

Swisscontact is the leading Swiss organisation for private sector development. It supports small and medium enterprises (SMEs) in over 20 developing nations by providing advisory services and continuing education. Credit Suisse is sponsoring two programmes operated by Swisscontact. In the Ukraine, workshops are being provided by senior Swiss banking experts. In South Africa, a mentoring programme and awareness campaigns are being conducted to help improve the performance of small businesses. *www.swisscontact.ch*

▶ Opportunity International

▶ Swisscontact.

Setting targets and measuring goals

A programme manager was appointed to work with the four partner organisations over a period of three months at the start of the process to identify and agree the indicators that would be used to determine the success of the programme. Six months after the launch of the platform, the partners had defined the indicators and submitted target figures. The following results are expected for 2009:

▶ 400,000 of the world's poor will be directly and meaningfully impacted through improved services

▶ 1.6 million of their family members will benefit from improved quality of life

▶ 7,500+ local MFI staff will be trained

▶ 200+ training manuals will be designed

▶ 144,000+ transactions will be conducted in Africa via 'electronic wallets'

▶ Credit Suisse will become a founding sponsor of the ACCION Center for Financial Inclusion.

In view of the level of accountability and transparency we wish to achieve, there is a risk that we may not realise all the goals we have specified, but we are nevertheless determined to monitor our results. One of the most difficult questions to answer in the case of any capacity-building initiative is the question of its impact:

▶ If 7,000 MFI staff are trained, how are they actually improving services to clients and enhancing their quality of life?

▶ Are clients better informed about their risks and rights as a result of the training sponsored by Credit Suisse?

▶ How do outside influences such as the global financial crisis affect the success of the programmes?

Although these types of questions are commonly asked by international development practitioners, they remain difficult to answer. In fact, a sophisticated assessment process will be required to truly measure the impact that capacity-building measures have on clients. In order for a philanthropic platform to consistently have a measurable impact, the focus on deliverables and the collection of indicator data are vital. Credit Suisse intends to sponsor an independent assessment of the impact of our activities and the work of our partners in the third year of the platform.

Important lessons learned

We learned a number of key lessons while designing and implementing this platform:

▶ It is important to work with the resources you already have. If you have limited resources with which to manage and oversee a broad-based programme of grants, you should focus on external partners with a proven track record and strong capabilities.

▶ Ensure that you have a targeted strategy and a clear mission statement. This allows partner programmes to be responsive to your needs. It also enables you to have a measurable impact within a clearly defined sphere.

▶ You must be able to demonstrate your results through impact indicators. The labour-intensive process of defining indicators proves beneficial in the long run, when it comes to 'telling your story' and measuring the programme's success.

▶ Establish and clarify your needs as a corporate donor from the outset. Be absolutely clear from the start about the need for a specific degree of visibility to raise public awareness of the topic of microfinance as well as Credit Suisse's contribution.

The way forward

Microfinance is a sector that has experienced remarkable growth and is now moving towards a regulated, commercial banking model. For micro-finance institutions that rely on workers on the ground, this transformation process is creating enormous opportunities. However, their growth and development are also challenging the institutions' original mission of poverty alleviation.

Staff on the ground are crucial to the sector's success. Without sufficient numbers of fully trained microfinance employees who possess the necessary know-how to make well-reasoned decisions, growth in this area will inevitably be slow. Through our partners, Credit Suisse is contributing directly to the provision of high-quality training for thousands of micro-finance staff and is thus helping to improve access to financial services for hundreds of thousands of poor individuals and small enterprises.

The alleviation of poverty is a long-term issue. There is no magic formula or instant solution. This is why Credit Suisse is committed to supporting this sector not just today but in the future. We believe that, thanks to the support that our capacity-building initiative can give – in the form of train-ing for existing employees or the recruitment of new staff – MFIs will be able to greatly expand the scope and scale of their offering to benefit vast numbers of potential entrepreneurs. Many such entrepreneurs are today still desperately waiting for an opportunity to find their way out of poverty.

13

Sustainability management in the automotive sector

Gerhard Prätorius

Responsible Business: How to Manage a CSR Strategy Successfully
Edited by Manfred Pohl and Nick Tolhurst
Copyright © 2010 Manfred Pohl and Nick Tolhurst

In this chapter, CSR is examined in the automotive sector from the perspective of the work of the CSR manager, from stakeholder relations to supply chain management and the mission of the company. Special attention is given to the environmental challenges facing the industry, and issues such as carbon-neutral travel are outlined.

Introduction

No matter which of the world's pressing challenges you consider – global warming, shortage of energy and resources, demographic change, human rights, diversity and corruption – it will have an impact on the relationship between companies, the environment and the public. Companies are, in this respect, both the affected parties and the instigators. As such, it is incumbent upon them to seek solutions to the problems through their own efforts, as drivers of innovation and developers of technology. These solutions cannot, of course, be dissociated from a discussion about values. On the contrary, such discussions are actually strengthened by increasing globalisation, because there is no global order framework. This is reason enough, therefore, to expect a further growth in the importance of CSR.

Mobility that follows the precepts of sustainability must resolve the following contradiction: transport, i.e. the movement of goods or people, is a driver of economic development. Transport creates wealth and enables social participation. However, at the same time, it is a cause of environmental and climate damage. The key to sustainable transport lies in the provision and storage technology of the energy required for transportation. The more successful the efforts are for a largely climate-neutral and regenerative supply of energy, the more sustainable will be the transport system and mobility.

In a market economy, companies perform the function of a supplier of solutions to problems; in other words, in the system of labour division, they offer technical and economic solutions that are demanded by society. The perception of social responsibility by companies means, first and foremost, that they introduce their problem-solving expertise. For a vehicle manufacturer, this consists of the development and market distribution of technical and economic solutions for individual mobility that are in accordance with the precepts of sustainability. As one of the world's largest car-makers, Volkswagen is conscious of its social responsibility when developing new solutions for the future of mobility.

Global challenges

The current ecological challenges seem likely to transform the world as we know it. Above all the struggle against climate change will require considerable resources and lead to allocation conflicts and structural changes. A crucial issue will be whether the central findings of the *Stern Review* (Stern 2007) – that the cost of inaction will far exceed the cost of action – will ever be included in an internationally agreeable, post-Kyoto treaty that is based on binding objectives with effective and verifiable mechanisms. Although largely interwoven with climate change, the topics of biodiversity protection and the worldwide efficient use of limited water resources require their own eco-political priority. In this respect, companies are involved in a special way, both as major consumers and as suppliers of technology.

The major global challenges also include aspects of society and geopolitics. In society, the growing social inequality is becoming an ever more important topic. The advantages of a global economy for the economic and social development of every nation are in danger of being eroded if an appropriate level of participation by all income levels is not realised. Such cases can open the door to national political constellations that make it considerably more difficult for companies to operate in a global context. From a geopolitical perspective, the topics of terrorism and asymmetric wars will be at top of the agenda. If there is a rising number of regions around the world that threaten to cease as markets and, at least, as minimally protected legal areas ('weak zones of governance'), this will very substantially affect the action possibilities of, in particular, the global companies.

The global challenges as descriptions of future frameworks for companies are already significant; however, they will acquire a new quality of considerable dynamism through the globally effective interdependencies. In this respect, for example, the topic of energy not only concerns the growing demand and optimised efficient and climate-preserving usage, but also the increasing significance of energy security. Against this background, the call, for instance, for alternative fuels in the automotive industry adds a geopolitical dimension to the already existing climate-political aspects. Strategic investment decisions therefore also involve a further decision parameter that influences the prospective advantages of alternatives.

Corporate social responsibility as a perceived social responsibility of corporate activity is a response to these developments, signifying not only a company's reaction as an affected party but also its willingness to play an active role. It is perceived and evaluated in the public arena.

CSR drivers

If the main actors can be systemised as drivers of a CSR development, then four main groups can be identified: capital markets/investors, stakeholders, regulatory requirements and corporate values.

Capital markets/investors

According to a study by Mercer Consulting (2006), 70% of the surveyed investment managers expect that the integration of the so-called ESG factors (environmental, social and governance) will become mainstream within the next 10 years. Numerous further studies have since confirmed this trend as well as ascertaining a positive correlation between ESG performance and company value. This applies, above all, to the quality of risk management, customer and employee loyalty, and the possibilities of differentiation in competition.

Institutional investors such as pension funds are increasingly incorporating CSR criteria into their decision portfolios. Against this background, the CSR and sustainability indices are taking on a rapidly growing significance. The results of such ratings demonstrate that above-average CSR performance stands for both appropriate handling of risks and the perception of new corporate opportunities in the form of eco-efficient technology solutions, innovative personnel concepts and exemplary commitment to the regional structural development at the locations.

Stakeholders

Within the realms of the specialist public-domain discussion, institutional investors are regarded as very important in their capacity as CSR drivers. However, in the broader public domain, it is the other stakeholders, above all the so-called non-governmental organisations (NGO), and other actors of civil society that, through media work and other forms of public relations, critically scrutinise the ecological and societal profile of companies and call for their commitment.

Besides the NGOs, stakeholders include society in general, neighbours and local communities, shareholders, researchers, the public authorities and, of course, the customers. Additionally there are the internal stakeholders, such as employees and the trade unions.

Regulatory requirements

Whereas the previously described CSR drivers came mainly from the non-state area, regulatory requirements, both existing and anticipated, are responsible for the fact that CSR as a strategy and management process has become an essential element of corporate activity, particularly for the capital investment companies. In Germany, for example, management reporting in accordance with Section 289 HGB (German Commercial Code) requires the inclusion of the non-financial performance indicators in the report, such as information on environmental and employee issues.

In addition to statutory regulations, company environmental and social guidelines and standards are also important. Although these are not legally prescribed, they do nevertheless serve as a statement of recognised environmental and social responsibility with respect to (i) inter-company relationships, such as relationships with suppliers; (ii) relationships with investors or credit providers; and (iii) relationships with customers and the public. These include the International Labour Organization (ILO) standards for working conditions, the Organisation for Economic Co-operation and Development (OECD) guidelines for multinational companies and the principles of the UN Global Compact. In the environmental arena, the EMAS (Eco-Management and Audit Scheme) and ISO 14000 environmental standards apply. As an all-encompassing standard for CSR, the forthcoming ISO 26000 will make an important contribution towards the establishment of this topic. Its evolutionary process alone – which has already attracted very broad-based international and stakeholder participation – is indicative of the interest in and expectations associated with CSR.

Corporate values

If the previously mentioned CSR drivers can be described as 'outside pressures', one should also mention the 'internal' drivers, the level of self-understanding companies develop with respect to CSR, company values as guiding principles, codes of ethics and so on. In many cases, lines of continuity are evident, particularly with regard to companies that have a strong tradition and corporate culture. The corporate CSR concept is then the conscious link to this tradition combined with the integration of new topics and projects that result from the changed framework conditions. However, spectacular disasters can occur in this area when formulated principles and corporate reality diverge to some degree, or become completely disconnected, resulting in a considerable loss of reputation and economic damage.

Corporate social responsibility is a possible response by companies to the new demands and expectations from the various actors mentioned earlier. Beyond basic disputes over regulatory detail, the developments demonstrate that a minimum level of juridification and standardisation will promote the topic of CSR without allowing its substance as an ultimately competition- and innovation-driven concept to be damaged.

The Volkswagen CSR approach

The CSR concept as developed by Volkswagen can be demonstrated using a modified illustration of Caroll's pyramid (Figure 13.1). Building on the quality of the management of the core competencies in the operative business – including appropriate risk and compliance management – opportunities arise to develop CSR as a strategic concept. The task is, together with the corporate values, to understand and implement social responsibility in a targeted way so as to achieve competitive advantages. If successful, the required resources are also generated in a way that then enables the company, as a 'good citizen', to give something back to society. The best-managed companies lead the way. The converse also applies: poor or average management seldom offers the opportunities to develop and implement a convincing CSR strategy.

Corporate culture

The Volkswagen Group boasts a long-standing tradition of social responsibility and environmental protection, elements that form part of the corporate culture. The special sense of responsibility for its employees and

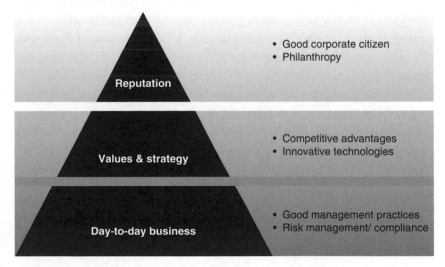

Figure 13.1 Corporate social responsibility.

the concept of a strong participation orientation stem from labour regulations of 1947, when manufacturing recommenced at Volkswagen after the Second World War. This manifested itself in the first social reports, produced during the 1970s, as well as innovative concepts for securing employment and a commitment to regional structural development at the company's sites in the 1990s.

Social Charter

With the signing of the European Social Charter by the management board, the global group works council and the International Metal Workers Union in 2002, the system of particular social responsibility was extended to include the global activities of the company. Volkswagen's understanding of social responsibility also includes the equal ranking of economic goals and employment goals.

Environmental protection and sustainability

The environmental commitment by Volkswagen is also based on this long-standing corporate culture. In this respect, in the 1990s the group became the first large German company to appoint its own environmental board member – a step that highlighted Volkswagen's early recognition of the strategic importance of this topic. Through the development of the corporate environmental principles for the manufacturing operation and the products, a sustainability mission statement was able to be compiled at a relatively early stage in which economic success, environmental protection and social competence were formulated as core elements of a modern and responsible corporate policy. A corresponding system of sustainability reporting was also established.

As one of the original participants in the United Nations Global Compact, Volkswagen aligned their model of sustainability to the principles of this inititive: human rights, labour standards, environmental protection and working against corruption. Another important orientation framework for Volkswagen's global activities is the OECD *Guidelines for Multinational Enterprises*.

Group values

The core values of the Volkswagen Group include – in addition to customer nearness, high performance, added value and renewability – respect and responsibility, i.e. respect for the achievements of others both within our company and outside it, responsibility for ambitious goals and realistic and honest reporting. Sustainability is also one of the group's values. It prescribes the agreed, long-term aims of the company into consideration in the daily work and the responsibility for the long-term success in the balancing of economic, ecological and social goals and the consideration of securing the future in all aspects as a core task.

CSR management: co-ordination and steering

In spite of excellent individual performances, the company's sustainability profile began to lose its definition at the beginning of this century. Critical signs of a phase of stagnation were positional losses in some important sustainability indices. Consequently, in 2006 a group office 'Coordination of CSR and Sustainability' was set up with the central task of strategically aligning and optimising CSR and sustainability management within the Volkswagen Group. This group co-ordination strengthens the exchange processes between the specialist departments. Steering groups and project teams focusing on topics such as CSR, sustainability report, CO_2 and supplier management ensure that the topic is integrated into the working procedures and decision processes. The office reports to the high-level CSR steering committee, to which all central group departments and the group works council belong.

ESG factors

In addition to improving the internal exchange processes, the co-ordination unit is also responsible for the corporate profile with regard to the sustainability rankings and indices. They are an important medium for illustrating the performance of the company in the areas of ecology, social policy and economics/governance (ESG factors). During the past two years a trend reversal in Volkswagen's positioning has been achieved in this domain. Volkswagen was able to regain a leading position in the industry in the most important international sustainability ratings and indices.

CSR performance

This concerns, in particular, the Dow Jones Sustainability Index (DJSI), which was set up in 1999. Companies that demonstrate special activities and achievements within the area of sustainability and social responsibility are eligible for possible inclusion in this index. Acting on behalf of Dow Jones, the Swiss asset management company SAM conducts an annual assessment in which the companies must qualify for inclusion. Twenty criteria, encompassing topics such as environmental management and climate strategy, working conditions, health and safety, supplier management, risk management and commitment, are assessed. After having successfully secured readmission to the DJSI World in 2007, Volkswagen was the only vehicle manufacturer in 2008 to qualify for the narrower-based DJSI STOXX index. In addition to the acknowledged accomplishments for highly efficient technology solutions and environmental protection, the current assessment specifically highlighted progress in personnel work and social commitment.

Volkswagen's claim to a leading role in CSR and sustainability can be demonstrated through various spheres of activity which are described briefly in the following section. The most important media channels concerning CSR are, of course, the sustainability report, the annual report, the internet and specific stakeholder media.

Sustainable mobility

For an automotive company, sustainability means to consider the product life cycle as the whole. Accordingly the sustainable strategy has two fundamental pillars: the environmental standards of production, i.e. the infrastructure and the production processes; and the environmental standards of production, i.e. fuel and resource efficiency, recycling, safety and so on.

The central objectives of Volkswagen, therefore, are to continuously improve the eco-friendliness of the products and reduce the consumption of natural resources. The goal is to make advanced technology available around the world while giving due regard to eco-conservation and the social acceptability of the company's activities.

The aim of the Volkswagen powertrain and fuel strategy is to develop technological solutions that will, in the long term, provide the basis for largely carbon-neutral private transport. The first steps on the way to achieving this will be to make further improvements to the efficient powertrain technologies that are already in existence. These technologies are helping customers to make the most efficient possible use of petrol and diesel fuel and so reduce their CO_2 emissions. In parallel, the need for second-generation biofuels, natural gas, hydrogen and electricity is obvious.

There is no 'silver bullet' on the road to sustainable individual mobility and further reductions in the levels of consumption and pollutants. A strategic overall concept therefore requires several options. These include the hybrid concepts as well as, in particular, electro-traction based on the lithium-ion battery. In addition to technical propulsion elements, other items playing a role in the quest to reduce consumption further include new lightweight materials and alternative fuels.

New vehicle concepts represent an important part of the sustainability strategy. These include, for example, a new generation of city cars, i.e. compact, space-efficient vehicles that are designed for different propulsion concepts and which take into account the particular mobility requirements of large conurbations.

In addition to product-based innovations for sustainable mobility, the transport system, i.e. the interplay of vehicles and infrastructure, also takes on an important function. An overburdened infrastructure and traffic jams lead to considerable environmental pollution and economic damage; hence communication technology-based intelligent traffic management (including 'road works and traffic congestion management') can provide significant efficiency gains. The improved collaboration of all transport carriers (inter-modality) can also make an important contribution towards the sustainability of transportation.

A specific element of Volkswagen's CSR: democratisation of technology and innovations

Volkswagen, as a multi-brand and volume manufacturer offering all vehicle types, from small cars through to luxury limousines, has the unique opportunity to transfer innovations rapidly and efficiently from the up-market segments to the volume models. An extremely successful example of this is the DSG double-clutch gearbox that helps to reduce fuel consumption. This is an element of Volkswagen's sustainability strategy that no other vehicle manufacturer possesses. It can be described as the democratisation of technology and innovations in order to make a contribution towards sustainable mobility through highly efficient technology solutions.

The integration of CSR into the daily business

Sustainability is very much an integration task, meaning that as a live corporate reality it is part of the day-to-day business. In this respect, the investments in technology take into account the employment and location effects as well as the qualification requirements of tomorrow. Sustainable in that sense also means investing today in the qualifications for tomorrow. This creates and secures jobs and supports the economic development within the location environment.

Sustainability in supplier relationships

Responsibility and sustainability do not end at the factory gate. Particularly for an industry such as the automotive industry, in which around two-thirds of value creation is produced by suppliers, the structuring of this topic in the context of supplier relationships takes on an important role. The core elements of the Volkswagen concept are as follows:

▶ the requirements placed on the suppliers with respect to ecological and social standards as well as anti-corruption

▶ informing suppliers, and acknowledging their requirements, via the group-wide B2B platform

▶ the early detection mechanism for risk

▶ the range of support by the company's team of experts

▶ the range of qualification projects.

Volkswagen also incorporates these experiences with its CSR supplier project into its relationships with other companies. In this respect, Volkswagen, together with other international companies, plays a leading role in the CSR Europe project 'Responsible Supply Chain Management', which has created a joint information and training portal for suppliers. The project's first achievement was the creation of a portal with easy access to, and information about, international guidelines and training materials (www.csr-supplychain.org).

CSR as social commitment worldwide

Social commitment – in the sense of giving and helping – is the traditional understanding of CSR. Instead of becoming obsolete as a result of the strategic concept outlined here, the two concepts in fact merge. In doing so, a stronger association between the topic of commitment, on the one hand, and corporate self-interest, on the other, is sought for an effective CSR profile, i.e. the projects are selected such that they address a social problem as well as fitting in with the company's strategic CSR concept – which, if successful, leads to a win-win situation.

For a company such as Volkswagen, which boasts a strong corporate tradition of social commitment as well as having embarked on a path of internationalisation from an early stage, these considerations are therefore not fundamentally new. Twenty years ago, foundations were set up in South Africa and Brazil which are devoted to the process of qualification and education in the regional environment. Through this commitment, Volkswagen contributes to the social and economic development of the region and its population as well as simultaneously improving its own location prospects by being able to draw on qualified workers. The concept also underlies the commitment to HIV prevention and therapy. These joint projects were carried out by Volkswagen in conjunction with international institutions such as the Deutsche Gesellschaft für Technische Zusammenarbeit (GTZ) and the ILO, and the company received several awards for their exemplary performance.

Another example of this social commitment is an accident research project in China. In co-operation with Chinese research institutes, hospitals and local authorities, Volkswagen is addressing the tremendous increase in accidents and fatalities on China's roads. This social project also helps to strengthen the image and reputation of the company.

An early example of a strategic CSR concept can be seen in Volkswagen's long-standing commitment to regional structural development at its German locations. Location development was combined with job security and a strengthening of a region's scientific and technical infrastructure through regional development agencies and innovative public private partnership (PPP) companies. For example, in a joint venture between Volkswagen and the city of Wolfsburg – Wolfsburg AG – more than 10,000 jobs were created over a 10-year period in the Wolfsburg region through the settlement of 100 supplier companies and the establishment of around 400 new companies.

Other areas of Volkswagen's CSR commitment include conservation and biodiversity, and the voluntary commitment of employees and former employees.

Volkswagen integrates its long-standing social commitment as a 'good corporate citizen' into a strategic CSR understanding that systematically links with the firm's corporate self-interest, connecting the spheres of activity with the company's core economic processes (innovative technology, personnel work, corporate values).

Conclusion

The preceding discussion clearly shows that for a CSR approach to succeed, it needs to move beyond the short-term thinking of a public relations exercise. Indeed, the concepts that have the best prospects of success are those with substantiated content that fit into a long-term, strategic corporate understanding of social responsibility. CSR will establish itself and continue to develop, irrespective of whether the term itself remains. There are three primary reasons for this prediction:

▶ In a globalised economy, companies are required to operate in a political environment, particularly as there is no global order framework, and the challenges for companies are becoming increasingly political; the environment, human rights and civil-societal participation are just some of the key words that are forcing companies into the political arena. The more convincing a company's responses and actions are in this respect, the higher will be its acceptance as an actor.

▶ Corporate activity requires an ethical foundation. Economic management is problem-solving action for overriding purposes and not an end in itself. Strategic CSR is the implementation concept for ethically founded corporate activity and thereby the contribution by companies towards a sustainable social market economy.

▶ Finally, as the experiences of recent years have shown, CSR as an appropriate management of ESG risks contributes towards corporate value. Furthermore, it offers the opportunity for companies to differentiate themselves from their competitors. It thus meets the expectations of customers, employees, the general public and the financial markets, which increasingly view specific performances and accomplishments in the areas of sustainability and social responsibility as compulsory elements of corporate activity.

Reference

Mercer Consulting (2006) *Fearless Forecast*. www.mercer.com/riforecast.

Stern, N. (2007) *Stern Review: The Economics of Climate Change*, Cambridge University Press.

14
Beyond marketing: CSR as a business strategy for SMEs – the Betapharm story

Nick Tolhurst

In this chapter, innovation, marketing and CSR as company strategy for small and medium-sized enterprises (SMEs) are discussed through the experience of Betapharm, a trail-blazing company in the field of CSR. Also the issue as to what extent a small or medium-sized company can use CSR as a strategy with similar or even generic products is examined. The chapter is based on a series of interviews with Betapharm's founders and present managers.

Introduction

The historic Bavarian town of Augsburg is not a place one would normally associate with modern, cutting-edge business practice. Rather, the picturesque town is known more as the one-time medieval weaving centre of Germany. Since 1993, however, a small generic drug firm has increasingly challenged the ways one traditionally views firms' business strategies. Betapharm, which was founded barely 15 years ago, has striven not just to follow accepted responsible norms but also to pursue a complete CSR-based strategy, even when this goes against immediate profit calculations. The reasoning behind this, at first seemingly counter-intuitive, strategy is that as a producer of generic and non-patented drugs the company has virtually no product or monopoly power to leverage market share or profits. With this in mind, the founding father of Betapharm, Peter Walter, and head of the Beta Institute, Horst Erhardt, realised that the only way to create a sustainable business, and to stay ahead of the competition, was to concentrate on building up the firm's reputational and cultural value even before immediate profit calculations.

The 'model Betapharm' has now become an oft-studied example of CSR, although crucially, and rather tellingly, there is no real CSR department to speak of, as the broad strategy of the company encapsulates CSR thinking within all aspects of business. In order to obtain an insight into how this works, we conducted a series of interviews with Horst Erhardt as well as Betapharm's CSR manager, Christine Pehl.

Interviews

Nick Tolhurst:

Mr Erhardt, CSR is often dismissed as mere 'window dressing' – how does this charge apply to Betapharm?

Horst Erhardt:

"The usual view of CSR is of branding. But the question is, whether we aren't an example of a form of ethical marketing, beyond the actual brand, in terms of dialogue marketing and partnership marketing. Basically CSR is one of the causes – if not the main cause – for the success of this company. It is not only a good name, but also many aspects of the brand appeal and will play a decisive role in the future, if you have absolutely identical products offered by different companies, and this is especially the case in the generics branch.

'...the art of CSR is to be socially responsible while this strategy also helps a company to differentiate itself within the market'

"This is why awareness is increasing within our marketing department. Some have understood this from the beginning. But basically the question is, whether CSR was in essence the company in the first place – CSR as intelligent and ethical marketing. Here CSR is not only an inner structure, but it can also be a mindset that requires a certain attitude; it's actually about investing in CSR. And then there is the question, don't we have to be honest and have to say that the art of CSR is to be socially responsible while this strategy also helps a company to differentiate itself, to become more successful, to produce different degrees of popularity and to create different connections. A professor I recently spoke to said, 'CSR is something that you do, even if you're not doing well.'

"I laughed and said one can only do CSR if it is embedded in a strategy. It can't just exist somewhere and you do it, no matter what state your company is in. But that's what most people think. It is part of an overall strategy. You cannot dissociate it and say, this is 'my CSR bit'. This is something most people don't understand. And I say, 'I'm CSR, it's me in the way I interact with the employees, the way I deal with resources, the way I deal with this or that.' If that's the way I think, and if I visualize this, then these projects are parts of my company marketing, not part of the product marketing, but part of the increasing brand appeal. It is both internal as well as external; for example, it is the way the marketing and corporate culture identifies with its employees.

"The marketing or the statement of corporate communications is to say, 'Here you can tell whether you can trust me, here you are able to see that I'm responsible, here you can see my sustainability' and all these points which are necessary for companies in times of globalisation. In order to test whether they fit the picture or not, new marketing strategies and new forms of marketing will develop."

Nick Tolhurst:

What are these new strategies and how are they developed?

Horst Erhardt:

"These are dialogue marketing strategies which build on connections, credibility and trust. Of course, the service of a company plays a role as well: delivery capacity and product quality. But I believe that marketing needs to win the market over, so that the decision for a product is in my favour. And here I can make something of CSR, and every single subject of our conversation today basically has one aim: that is to say, by which means can I occupy the market and the relations in such a positive way, to make us and our brand, our existence, appear in a positive way, even if our quality or our service [has flaws]. If I have flaws, the customer still says, 'But this is an appealing company.'

'...dialogue marketing strategies build on connections, credibility and trust'

"The brand appeal must be attached to something, though. If it is true what I'm saying, then I can explain by means of each project why I'm doing it, why I'm doing it the way I do, how it is embedded into a model and why it works. I once defined this model not as win-win, but as win-win-win. I believe that a lot of people think that CSR means one single deed or even a collection of 'good deeds'. Our view is different. Once we have presented ourselves as a CSR company, we simply cannot stop this later. So, I can talk about 'win-win-win'.

"Within the relationships that we establish there is the company that has to get something out of it. There is, as well as the company, the customer on one side and the society on the other. This network exists, because business exists. The kind of network, in which a company commits itself to the society, has been there for a long period of time. Social responsibility has existed for a long time. The secret is to understand how to create the link between society and the customer, so that the company benefits from this. Indeed, most pharmaceutical companies don't want to be concerned with the patients. Our 'usual' customers are doctors, pharmacists and health insurance companies. This is why we do something by saying that the interests of this target group can be found at the Beta Institute. We act as advocates for these interests. At the Beta Institute we attend to the needs of the patients and thus the society. And now I create a link between the two.

"An example: if one looks at the counselling of patients in association with their illness. If you suffered from cancer, then you would learn something about your medical, therapeutic, surgical matters, but who tells you how to solve other problems such as your job or your journey to the therapy? Who takes care of your elderly father whom you visit every evening, etc? The questions that emerge are infinite. We are talking about the patient's concerns in the context of his therapy, the target group and issues.

"What we're doing here actually comes back to the company in a positive way. Anyone can do this and I can do this with any class of business as well. If I ask what the direct/indirect target group is, what is the customer target group, how much marketing do they need from me? What can I do in order to help him find a better solution? In which way am I able to create a higher level of attractiveness for his customers. Everything we do at the institute deals with this. And the aim of everything we do is patient management. Patient management is undertaken by mammaNetz. MammaNetz is a case management model with seven employees working there. The doctor in private practice gets in touch with mammaNetz and says, 'I have a patient who is in need of support.' Within 48 hours the patient has contact with the case manager, the doctor has a solution and the hospital has one as well.

'The secret is to understand how to create the link between society and the customer, so that the company benefits from this'

"We manage the path, the entire procedure as well as the patient during the entire treatment. The health insurance company pays for it, because an improvement of quality evolves from it. It is easier for the patient to move through the system, it is a classical case management path. What we are doing is case management and we deliver it to the doctor."

Nick Tolhurst:

And what happens under the umbrella of the Beta Institute. Where is the Betapharm link?

Horst Erhardt:

"Betapharm provides the funding, so that we can develop these ideas. If we are able to finance or refinance these projects, then Betapharm withdraws. Betapharm invests so the institute can do its work. But this principle can be applied to every project. We train care assistants for German general practitioners, for example. If the government says that general practitioners need care assistants, then we're present and we see to it that we are part of the development of concepts. In co-operation with the association of general practitioners we now start to train thousands of care assistants on a big scale. I'm doing something here which at first seems like it has nothing to with the company and its products, but I strengthen this relationship. The stronger this relationship is, the more light will be shed on the company as a whole.

"We published a book, for example, the only dictionary for social issues in Germany. The most recent edition had a circulation of over 500,000 copies. For eight years this has been the only book in Germany that you would find in pharmacies as well as medical practices – the dictionary for social issues and patient management. There you have the knowledge of social security regulations, information on what works and what doesn't work. Once it is in the system, the doctor gets in touch with us, if he has got a question, because we have call centres and internet chat rooms."

Nick Tolhurst:

Ms Pehl, if I could just ask you as a CSR manager of a small company, how can a company of Betapharm's size take CSR seriously as a corporate strategy?

Christine Pehl:

"I think the main thing before one even considers CSR this or that – the starting and end point is attitude. Let's say we produce something, and I decide that I will not discharge my company's pollutant waste into the sea. This means that it always has to be that way. And I think that this is the problem with the CSR experience of large corporate groups, because people take a closer look at them and say, 'Here you are behaving very well, but not in South Africa.' There has to be not just a canon of values, that is good, but there has to be a 'CSR attitude'.

'...before one even considers CSR this or that – the starting and end point is attitude'

"This is something which I am certain addresses small and medium-sized companies, because these companies usually say that there is little they can do with the 'superstructure of CSR' or 'I cannot afford a CSR advisor in the first place' and then 'I have to go through every process.' But to say, 'I will start at one point, which will also lead to an economic benefit', then one has quite a lot already!"

Nick Tolhurst:

I've seen quite a concentration of media and academic interest in CSR in large companies, especially as a corporate group can afford a big-budget, well-resourced CSR department with CSR managers, CSR assistants and so on – but what about smaller companies?

Christine Pehl:

"It is a lot easier for a small or middle-sized company to pursue CSR than it is for a large company! It doesn't happen that often that a CEO of a company group appears and says, 'Now I want a completely new CSR strategy for the whole group.' Even if they have good projects already, it's not easy. This is actually a business chance for small and middle-sized companies and I think that in public there is too much reporting about CSR being something which is done by large companies, such as building a nice school in Africa.

> *'It is a lot easier for a small or middle-sized company to pursue CSR than it is for a large company'*

"Of course this is great, but these are singular projects. What I wanted to say is that it is less difficult for small or middle-sized and they benefit more from it. The acceptance in the United States or in Europe still is rather small. The small or middle-sized companies are insecure. They believe – wrongly – that they are too small for CSR."

Nick Tolhurst:

Mr Erhardt, You said that CSR enhances the degree of Betapharm's popularity. Are there also other advantages, is this is measurable at all?

Horst Erhardt:

"In 2006 the situation changed in Germany that the health insurance companies offered discount contracts to the pharmaceutical companies. For years we had the most discount contracts, because the road to the health insurance companies was effortless for us. We have always been a preferred partner in the contracts, because the relationship was there already. It was easy for me or for Mr Walter to get in touch with a person at one of the health insurance companies, a contact which resulted from this relationship, and to say, 'Do you want to close a contract with us?'

"In the minds of our target groups the Beta Institute is clearly a research and development institute, but it comes from the Beta brand. And if you do something with the Beta Institute, people are aware of the fact that the institute is able to do something, because Betapharm is there. This alliance is logical, it is clear. Nevertheless we are a gateway within this system because of the independence of the non-profit institutes, and because we are a charitable institution we are able to open every door. The Beta Institute is not a part of the business, but it is a great network. It is credible, it is stable and, what's one of the biggest strong-points, it cannot be copied. No other pharmaceutical company has been able to copy our competitive advantage and to put us out of business."

Nick Tolhurst:

Many companies want to 'own their good works' within their CSR projects. At Betapharm a large part of CSR was relocated at the Beta Institute. Of course this has a lot of advantages – how does this work?

Horst Erhardt:

"It is not that easy. Our company also wanted to pretend that our marketing was that of Betapharm. I always had to rap on their knuckles and I had to say, 'No'. I like to refer to the example of a cook. You're the host and you invite your friends for dinner. A cook prepared the meal. Yes, you've bought it. Now you can say you've got two possibilities, you could say, 'Look what I have prepared for you,' or you could say, 'Look I've had this made for you. This is my cook.' There is merely a small difference of meaning, but it is crucial within the CSR scene. Betapharm had to learn this; the employees had to learn not to say that 'I'm doing something for you here.' Not 'I'm doing something', but 'I'm taking care of it, it is my duty', that the Beta Institute is active, that they get something from it.

"My dedication is to make it possible. And if we do marketing today, then the joker is not to say, 'I will give a book to you', that's wrong. Pharmaceutical books are worthless; instead I would say, 'I'm glad that you will receive this book from us.' It is completely independent. I saw to it that the Beta Institute was able to publish one again this year. This is a different message and this subtlety is much more credible; because somewhere each pharmaceutical company has a few people who do something for the market."

Christine Pehl:

"Now we're getting to the subjects of partnership and sharing of knowledge. For our idea of CSR to work means that we have to find and trust partners. I have to say, there are people – and here we have the link between the economic and the social world again – there are people who are able to do this. I enter into a partnership at the same eye level; this is the original idea of a civic involvement, and this works here.

> *'....For our idea of CSR to work means that we have to find and trust partners'*

"And this is where most companies still want to do everything on their own. And this goes to such lengths at the Beta Institute... the institute has so many partnerships that we have to integrate them again. One cannot have a proper relationship without this – this is important even in little things. For example, if you publish a press report, you can't just put the Betapharm logo there, this would be dishonest; we have to include all the partners. It is very exhausting, challenging, but that's the quality that makes it worthwhile."

Horst Erhardt:

"We also cultivate independent partnerships, actual alliances. We have developed the model of a care assistant with the German general practitioners. Through this we developed the so-called 'Veras'. Vera is an abbreviation for 'Versorgungsassistentin in der Hausarztpraxis' (care assistant in a general practice). If we educate them, then I have the possibility to arrange their further training. But I could also connect them to a long-lasting support, the call centre, the book, everything we have got here. It is very, very complex. Betacare is a knowledge system and I interconnect it. You receive a newsletter, you receive further training twice a year, and you receive all the information on innovations you should know about. This is how the quality management with Vera and the Beta Institute develops.

"The Veras mostly are the top assistants in the medical practice. They have an influence on how a doctor learns about cases. But the doctors cannot be manipulated by us, if he prescribes a medication. There is no letter saying now that we supervise Vera, you have to prescribe drugs made by Betapharm. This is too crude. He himself knows that the company gives something to him. And he can do something for that. The sales force can talk to him about that. But this isn't a precondition. In the history of Betapharm, this is the reason for the growth of the company since the beginning of this development. Our rise from the 28th biggest pharmaceutical/generic drug company to the fourth biggest in Germany is due more or less completely to our CSR strategy, not because we have different products. We had the same products, the same sales force, equal chances for development.

"One example: Betapharm is a pain specialist in its drug portfolio. I would like to do something in the area of palliative medicine; 80% palliative is a pain issue. This means that we have a target group in common: the doctors that take care of palliative patients are specialists for pain as well. At first he says, 'This is my portfolio, this is my issue' and I say, 'Palliative medicine is my topic as well.' This is why we develop the largest database on palliative issues – this isn't an exaggeration – for these doctors. We are WHO-accredited and so on. The largest project in Europe runs in our house at the moment.

'....Our rise from the 28th biggest generic drug company to the fourth is due more or less completely to our CSR strategy, not because we have different products'

"You wouldn't think that this small house is capable of doing something like that. But you don't need much more if you develop a knowledge portal. We've discussed these issues, we've discussed the target groups and we connect the subjects 'target group' and 'development'. This is the only time when we [Betapharm and the Beta Institute] co-ordinate our efforts. This is also a result of being independent. I say, 'I would to build up a database with doctors, with publishers, with knowledge no one has collected so far.' Then I draw up a proposal and, if agreed, establish a programme. Then Betapharm says 'You will receive €1.6 million.' This is the budget for the database for several years. This is something other companies don't get as well!"

Nick Tolhurst:

What about the finance for these projects. How does it work? Does it mean that the Beta Institute receives certain shares of the company's profits?

Horst Erhardt:

"No, Betapharm funds the platform. We have a sponsoring contract. This contract says that the institute receives a certain amount regularly. I think it's a minimum of €1.5 million annually. We receive a minimum amount and from this we have to pay our basic expenses to begin with. Basic expenses are the expenses within the company, all the operating expenses, everything. Now I can come and say I've got Betacare. This is a knowledge service for the market and Betapharm pays a fee for this, which has been calculated by me. This means Betapharm is the only one who can now say, the knowledge service, funded by Betapharm, comes from Betapharm, from the Beta Institute, because Betapharm pays for it. There are projects for which Betapharm doesn't pay anything, mammaNetz for example. MammaNetz is self-financing. Perhaps about €500000 or more and the service pays for itself."

Nick Tolhurst:

Project expenses could come from the health insurance companies then?

Horst Erhardt:

"They came from others, ministries of research and development, federal ministries, Bavarian ministries, other foundations. And we earn our own money! Papilio, for example, earns money by selling materials on further education and by offering further training, but not that much. We finance the internet ourselves, two-thirds comes from Betapharm. And if we want to do this, we have to apply for this, just like with every other organisation. If I apply for a grant at the federal ministry, then I apply for a programme, which is announced by the Federal Government. Here it's the same procedure. Yes, if Betapharm says, 'I would like to have something which deals with osteoporosis' then I can make a proposal. I draw up an application or, as you said, 'We need something which deals with the subject of pain,' I said, 'Let us do something that deals with palliative medicine, pain is included in this.'

"I submit an application, I present the application, I outline the concept, a synopsis, and I apply for subsidies. I am part of the executive team, of course, part of the senior management level and I say, 'Let us do this in this or that way.' But, under strictly formal aspects, Betapharm grants the subsidies for the duration of the project application. It's the same for anybody; it's the same everywhere, no matter whether it's outside of or within the company. We describe and develop the idea, there is an application and an official notification and a report in the end."

Nick Tolhurst:

This means that it is easier for you to get into touch with health insurance companies and with departments of state than for other companies. Thus you get better contacts, better networks than other companies?

Horst Erhardt:

"Yes, exactly. Usually the pharmaceutical companies use classical lobbying. Betapharm does not do this, cannot do this. The funny thing about it is, due to our position we receive invitations and calls for advice from the federal president, health insurance companies and certain ministries, which perceive Betapharm as an equal partner because of our strategy and positioning. Thus, we therefore have access and popularity in different ways which can be as good as, if not better than, those of more classical lobbying. And we are able to introduce new topics into conversations, because we are credible."

Nick Tolhurst:

Are there other ways one can benefit from CSR strategies, benefits which are easily missed?

Christine Pehl:

"Yes indeed there are! Most people go the classical way, from lobbying to marketing and even to bribery. Betapharm does not just avoid all bribery, the company does not even have company logo pens nor does it offer disguised 'educational trips' to Hawaii. All that Betapharm offers is here; you can it see on this list and we have a telephone hotline here.

> *'Betapharm does not just avoid all bribery, the company does not even have company logo pens nor does it offer disguised "educational trips" to Hawaii'*

"The doctor can call the hotline, if he has difficult questions like, 'I have a patient who draws unemployment benefits and what do we do with sick pay?' and so on. And even a search machine! This is all that our sales force can deliver. And there is the triad if we say, 'Yes we have quality drugs.' But this is something they all have, and the customer service belongs to this as well. But this actually is standard, and we have an ethical marketing here, which comes out here plus several other things – let's say, a kind of overall bonus for CSR, if one hears of 'Papilio', or a stroke project, where the customer unconsciously says, 'Oh, this is great, I like this.' "

Nick Tolhurst:

How have recent health care and state reforms affected Betapharm and its strategy?

Horst Erhardt:

"There really is socialism in the pharmaceutical industry, in the generics industry, since the reforms! The prices are fixed, the maximum price is fixed, the price levels are fixed, the contracts and public tenders are coming up by and by, classical tenders, European tenders, approaches… but we will score there as well, because the new tender criteria demand award criteria in the evaluation. They're not completely monetary. The DAK (Deutsche Angestellten Krankenkasse), a health insurance fund, starts with this already, because the assessment criteria tell you how dependable, how credible, a company is, and which add-ons the company can offer to the product; this is increasingly evaluated in the tenders. This means 70% price – but who gets the tender in the end is also depending on his expertise, his quality, his delivery capacity and the other award criteria he can make appraisable. And this is a modern European public procurement regulation, it has not been adopted completely; now tenders will no longer be merely monetary, but the whole company will be examined."

Nick Tolhurst:

There have been discussions in the EU about whether CSR should be regulated by Europe-wide criteria and carried out in all industries, with the aim here not just because it's good from society's point of view, but also as an anti-dumping measure against companies from outside Europe which might well not respect social or environmental criteria.

Horst Erhardt:

"Yes, I believe, if we did regulate it, then every company would have to do something. However, this is not the same identity as if someone would do it on his own accord, because he says, 'This is an advantage for me.' Because if they all have it, where is the advantage then? If it is part of the competition and if one says, CSR is a matter of competition, of how to stand out, brand strategy, and so on, and you don't regulate it, but let's say you create open criteria and you say these are qualifications which can be considered in the tender procedure, which are to be considered by the party issuing the bid, then it turns into a competitive advantage."

"It must be possible to use CSR as an advantage of distinction. And this brings us back to marketing, our initial point. CSR must be an advantage for the company, and not just because it is supposed to be socially responsible. It must be a real advantage that CSR entrepreneurs score better than others and that one can make use of it in tenders, for example. Today we have a disadvantage in tenders because of our company expenses. Our margin losses are much higher compared to companies that don't invest in CSR. If some company enters the market, for example, that doesn't invest anything into this area, then we have the situation that they offer prices which are dumping prices for us. We cannot keep up with these prices. We could, if we only produced medicine. But with CSR, with a sales force, with our responsibility for people, with our investment in cars that use less petrol, with all these things which carry weight here, we could not compete only with respect to price. We would always lose, because the expenses, the cost of goods and the inter-company costs are higher because of the way we are. This is why they need companies that contribute something to our society, which serves the public spirit, the creation of meaning in a sustainable and long-term way; so that business does not descend into wheeling and dealing alone, but that it is part of a social entity, of a social life, where people meet, where values have to develop, where credibility has to exist.

'...more and more the complete company profile is being considered not just by NGOs or consumers but by governments and corporate buyers'

"If you want to do this in business, you have to be able to award the companies which do this and to let the companies that don't feel as if they have been punished. Our company would survive, but where tenders are concerned I think CSR could and should play a role. But I think this is coming anyway: more and more the complete company profile is being considered not just by NGOs or consumers but by governments and corporate buyers. This is a chance for CSR, if CSR works, if there is a reference to the product, not just service. Then it's about what the CSR company brings into a complete supply system. If this is appraisable, then we all win."

Nick Tolhurst:

This is exactly the point I wanted to address, because the Indian company, Dr Reddy's, has taken over Betapharm and surely you wondered, whether this would change the business model or culture?

Horst Erhardt:

"The history of Betapharm, why we started, was initiated by Peter Walter, the former CEO, and I. When we met, I was just looking for funds for a project and Peter Walter said, 'Yes, this is something that could motivate my people, could prop them up and create meaning.' As Peter Walter has always said, his bottom line has always been his view that 'Companies are there to serve people, not the other way round.'

"He was looking to create meaning for his company. This relationship soon turned into a personal friendship, but in the first place it was a success that the employees were proud of, they picked themselves up, they went into the market saying, 'We're nothing like all the others.' Then he said, 'We will make more from this.' And then we were sold on the peak of this development. It was always said that because Betapharm was looked upon as the 'jewel of the pharmaceutical industry', as a role model, the selling price suddenly was a lot higher than the analysts had predicted – €270 million was not the original price; the analysts said €220 million is the maximum value. It was always said that the institute is worth €70 million – subjective, not actually. For Betapharm it is a brand value of €70 million. And 3i never really understood this, the British chairman told me later. He did think about saving the money occasionally. He didn't dare to do it, though; there was a kind of mystique involved! He didn't know what it was, but it worked! Betapharm benefited from the institute and didn't lose anything.

'Companies are there to serve people, not the other way round'

"Therefore it was worth the money, it was better than placing an advertisement. When the Indians came, we went through this due diligence phase and then we had the conversations with Ren Bexin and Mr Singh, the CEO, who was most impressive. We introduced our work and who we are and yet they always knew everything! They had a whole team, 10 or 15 people, who didn't do anything aside from observing us for two years. This is what I was later told. So they analysed us and then they came to a decision. From an analyst's point of view Betapharm was completely overrated! I was told, it is very difficult for an Indian company to buy something somewhere on earth without knowing beforehand whether the cultures will succeed, whether the mix will succeed, whether the communication will work, whether it will work to get into a high-quality country like Germany from the position of a developing country, whether this relationship will work. Many takeovers and mergers fail because of this.

"Then they concentrated on that: what Betapharm is, its culture, the institute, the philosophy, which resemble what they are doing in India; they have their own foundations, they have a strong social commitment. In a way they have more CSR, I would say, and they have more 'triple bottom line' concepts than we did. But, well, you couldn't picture Betapharm as a business model without the institute at the moment. Betapharm would be nothing. Betapharm has its position in the market because of the way it is. Otherwise it would only be one among 20 others, without a profile or a face."

Nick Tolhurst:

What comes first: CSR or the business culture?

Horst Erhardt:

"It is inseparably linked for us. The culture of this company was shaped by the CEO, Mr Peter Walter, who said, 'I want to prove two things: one can be successful without torturing people, because the sales forces of other pharmaceutical companies are being tortured, and I am able to do it without bribery.' This was the fundamental culture, this is the overall image of a company of this man, who said, 'I will do this in a different way.'"

Christine Pehl:

"And of course you need a certain amount of courage for that. One university research team examined pattern breakers as business innovation drivers. And they interviewed top executives and they found out that it was strongly linked to self-image. Then there is the strong element of their relationship with people. We don't have a classical hierarchy here. You can enter Mr Walter's or Mr Erhardt's office and you complain about something! We are in a team together. It could have gone wrong. And one has to repeat this again. This developed more from a certain instinct, but it was nice that business academics came and said, 'What you are doing actually is CSR.' And it was already here!"

Nick Tolhurst:

What has the feedback been, post-takeover, between Betapharm and Dr Reddy's?

Horst Erhardt:

"We are now developing concepts in co-operation with India. Papilio is to be applied to India as a concept for disease prevention in co-operation with the foundation there. The first German–Indian research application is already on its way for mammaNetz. It's about analysing in which way case management can be placed within a developing health system in the next years. This can grow more rapidly in India than in Germany, because we have politically directive structures here. It is a free market in India. If you table €10, you can get a case management. It's as simple as that. All of these co-operations with India are in the pipeline, are under way. It is exciting because now Betapharm has an owner that wants to build on the experiences here and extend them to India. It won't be exactly the same but I'm optimistic it will work. We shall see!"

15
Sports sponsoring and CSR: lessons from HypoVereinsbank

Clemens Mulokozi and Klaus-Peter Storme

Responsible Business: How to Manage a CSR Strategy Successfully
Edited by Manfred Pohl and Nick Tolhurst
Copyright © 2010 Manfred Pohl and Nick Tolhurst

This chapter will examine the advantages of sponsorship in business terms as well as how it can fit into a CSR strategy. Also outlined are the dilemmas and challenges facing sponsoring – in this case, sport – which can involve political and social sensitivities. The authors also address questions regarding the active role that sports sponsorship can play in terms of social responsibility, including where to engage and what to avoid.

Introduction

As one of Germany's leading financial institutes, HypoVereinsbank can boast a long-standing commitment to sustainable development. With its 23,000 staff, 800 branch offices and four million customers, HypoVereinsbank sees itself very much as part of society and therefore takes its social responsibility very seriously. The bank's Integrity Charter contains six principles – fairness, transparency, respect, freedom to act, trust and reciprocity (www.hvb.de/integrity) – which constitute the basic set of values for its economic conduct.

These values determine our treatment of our colleagues within the company, as well as those groups that are essential to our success: customers, suppliers and investors as well as the representatives and citizens of the towns and communities in which we operate. And these values are also reflected in the activities we use to cultivate our business and to contribute to the sustainable development of our environment and society.

As part of this commitment, HypoVereinsbank has, over the years, sponsored many sports and cultural activities. Now, by directly combining our sports sponsorship with our social responsibility, we are trying out a new and promising solution. We believe it has great potential for the following reasons:

▶ Sports sponsors are frequently asked about their social responsibility.

▶ Sports show great potential as a platform for social responsibility – providing role models, offering opportunities to identify with others, attracting much interest and appealing to wide target groups.

► Sports sponsorships have often fallen into disrepute because of doping and corruption scandals, and so it is necessary to regain trust.

► The combination of successful sponsorships with social issues creates new synergies both for the company and for the sponsorship partner.

Sports and social responsibility

Sponsors of large-scale events such as the 2008 Beijing Olympic Games or 2010's Football World Cup in South Africa are often asked how they reconcile their commitment with their social responsibility. At the same time, they are expected not to intervene in the interests of the sponsored parties. The study *What Role Does Responsibility Play in Sports Sponsorships?* (Scholz & Friends 2008) highlighted the predicament sports sponsors find themselves in nowadays. In that study, only 22% of German respondents were in favour of a link between sports and politics, yet 71% of them thought that Olympic sponsors should publicly voice their opinions on the political situation in China and make statements about human rights. The study also concluded that the undisputed strengths of sports sponsorship, such as high publicity and a broad target group appeal, can also pose risks for the sponsor's reputation, especially if there are negative incidents.

But even away from large-scale events and doping and corruption scandals, sports sponsors are being forced to re-establish themselves and secure acceptance in a changed world in which companies must increasingly show responsibility. It is a fact that, 'In public perception, supporting professional sports is not associated with accepting social responsibility' (Sports & Market 2008). According to many stakeholder groups, such as customers, suppliers, non-governmental organisations (NGOs) and politicians, the often large amounts paid for professional sports can no longer be justified by its particular marketing effects or by an improved image, especially for companies that explicitly recognise their social responsibility.

HypoVereinsbank's commitment

Upon conclusion of a sponsorship agreement with Bayern Munich in 2003 (see Box 15.1), HypoVereinsbank also had to ask itself a lot of questions and justify its commitment *vis-à-vis* its shareholders. But it was possible to show that the company greatly benefits from this arrangement: thanks to our co-operation with Germany's best-known football club, we have acquired more than 70,000 new customers, and our Bayern Munich savings card, which allows fans to increase their interest rate with every tenth goal scored by the club, has been a great success to date – so it is time not only to devise further co-operation products but also to use this successful sponsorship as a platform for the company's social concerns.

Box 15.1 Sponsoring Bayern Munich

HypoVereinsbank has set up a premium partnership with the German record-holding champions Bayern Munich until 2010. It is thus not only Bayern Munich's primary bank but also its exclusive partner for financial matters and its consortium bank in the case of an initial public offering. The development, marketing and distribution of innovative financial products for the community interested in football is a further business target that is central to our co-operation. The image transfer and close co-operation with Bayern Munich in the product development area enable HypoVereinsbank to acquire new customers, more business and to generate more revenue, because, by co-operating with Bayern Munich, it benefits from the best-known club with the largest following, the best opinion ratings and the largest media presence in Germany. Ninety-five per cent of all Germans are familiar with Bayern Munich, which has around ten million fans and 120,000 members. Bayern Munich can boast a history of success not only in terms of football but also as a business model: economically, it is the most successful football club in the world.

The topic of social communication and integration ranks highly among these concerns – because not achieving this can have a negative affect on the economic development of a region and therefore also the business and future prospects of the financial institute. In the larger German cities, in particular, the integration of migrants has become a hot topic. Studies show that there is often little integration at all, and so society and companies miss out on much-needed new blood – a social challenge that HypoVereinsbank must face in the interests of a forward-looking development.

Munich, where our head office is located, has the second highest percentage of foreigners of all German cities, standing at 23%. More than 300,000 migrants from a wide range of countries live here; 52% of children under six years have a migration background, and 60% of them have no basic knowledge of the German language. In this way, their fate of becoming marginalised is often sealed. In order to break this circle of inevitability early on and to provide equal educational opportunities for children and adolescents, the city of Munich has started a number of initiatives. HypoVereinsbank has now seized on one of them and linked it to its successful sports sponsorships and to the Unidea 'migration programme', the foundation supporting UniCredit Group's charitable goals (see Box 15.2).

Supporting 'Colourful Teams Kick Well' (see Box 15.3)

By sponsoring the Colourful Teams Kick Well initiative for an initial 12 months, HypoVereinsbank not only provides financial aid to the tune of €95,000 to organise the street football league, but it also gives creative support due to its partnership with Bayern Munich. For instance, by providing 'Colourful Teams Kick Well' with rights from our co-operation with Bayern Munich, they get:

▶ the chance to set up information desks in the fan shop at the Munich Allianz Arena

Box 15.2 Joint commitment: Unidea and HypoVereinsbank

Unidea, the company foundation of the UniCredit Group, to which HypoVereinsbank belongs, supports social projects and is dedicated to annually changing social issues. It provides the subsidiaries of UniCredit Group not only with the financial means to enable implementation but also with the necessary expertise. In the past year, Unidea has launched a 'migration programme' in order to address one of the hottest topics of the moment, and also to support the company's sustainable development. The 'Colourful Teams Kick Well' (see Box 15.3) project was thus also able to benefit from the foundation. HypoVereinsbank has joined this programme and it also encourages and supports those employees who are happy to volunteer.

Box 15.3 'Colourful Teams Kick Well' project ('Buntkicktgut')

The Colourful Teams Kick Well project has set itself the goal of achieving a social and cultural reciprocation between young people from different cultures and of different nationalities, thus giving them a meaningful and healthy pastime. The idea of an inter-cultural street football league in Munich was born in 1997, arising out of child and youth care work in Munich's hostels for refugees of civil war and asylum-seekers. Football is a medium that allows understanding, especially where people don't have a voice. Today, the street football league 'Colourful Teams Kick Well' has become an inherent part of the city's sports events and has often received awards – such as first prize in the Integration Competition 2002, awarded by the Federal President. Goalkeeper-legend Oliver Kahn from Bayern Munich is its patron.

▶ the use of the HypoVereinsbank box at the Allianz arena for press conferences

▶ the chance to use banner advertising for Bayern Munich home matches

▶ an opportunity to meet and train with the Bayern Munich players

▶ an opportunity to use the Bayern Munich training area for their final league matches.

Anyone who has ever seen a child's eyes light up upon meeting their football hero will understand what what these opportunities mean. And anyone who has ever experienced the amount of press surrounding the likes of Luca Toni or Philipp Lahm will be able to imagine the attention that the 'Colourful Teams Kick Well' project will receive on such a platform.

In addition, the HypoVereinsbank sports sponsorship opens up a new dimension. Because 'Colourful Teams Kick Well' clearly shows what sports are capable of achieving in the interests of society: street football, which is known in all countries of the world, is a better and more direct way for this project to reach children and adolescents than any other activity. It not only provides them with a sensible and healthy pastime but it also opens up opportunities to practise social and cultural togetherness in a fun way – and removed from all language barriers.

At Colourful Teams Kick Well, children and adolescents are appreciated for who they are, regardless of their circumstances and their cultural background – supplemented only by 'approachable' ideals and role models represented by the foreign players at Bayern Munich. At the same time, workouts and tournaments allow them to learn about rules and values – without finger-wagging – that are essential for a successful life and for a forward-looking community: fairness, tolerance, participation and non-violence. Nowhere in our society are rules communicated more clearly, and accepted more readily, than on the football pitch.

The combination of Colourful Teams Kick Well, HypoVereinsbank and Bayern Munich was first put into practice in the league tournament at the

Bayern Munich training ground in summer 2009; 32 teams of different age groups, both from Munich and from Colourful Teams Kick Well twin towns (from Germany and other European countries), spent two days playing for the trophy. Just meeting the Bayern Munich football players and attending the award ceremony was an incentive for the youngsters, but the location was also extremely motivating.

Perspective: sports and responsibility

To put it simply, in spite of all the crises and scandals, sports – and, in this case, football – are still, for the majority, the most favourite pastimes in the world. At the same time, companies are increasingly required to show more responsible behaviour and a commitment to a forward-looking society. As a result, social responsibility has become a key component of company policy, as shown in the study *Sponsor Visions 2009* (Pilot 2009), and therefore also of sponsorships. Almost half of the responding companies already implement CSR programmes as part of their sponsorship agreements; a quarter expect to redeploy finances for CSR programmes due to tight budgets.

Even though the smallest percentage of respondents in the Sports & Market (2008) study believed that CSR and sports sponsorships go together, we believe the opposite is true. This is because, in spite of all negative aspects, this study found a general acceptance of the connection between CSR and sports sponsorships. We therefore see a great opportunity in combining these two central social issues. According to the study, however, in order to reconcile the two, it is necessary to successfully transfer the media presence from professional to amateur sports.

By linking our Bayern Munich sponsorship to our social commitment and to our support of Colourful Teams Kick Well, as set out above, we want to show that this is true, and that it works, because we are convinced that such a combination will become increasingly important not only due to tight budgets but also to strengthen confidence in companies.

In conclusion, in our opinion, there are four core reasons for a company to consider sports sponsorship as a part of a company's CSR strategy:

▶ Much more so than cultural sponsorships, sports sponsorships have the potential of reaching a wide target group and simultaneously offer a platform for social commitment which must above all, given current problem analyses, focus on minors and adolescents.

▶ Sports, as long as they are 'clean', offer invaluable potential to communicate values such as respect, tolerance and fairness. These values are essential for successful social integration and also for the economic success of a society, and in the current crisis they are justifiably demanded by all concerned.

▶ Employee volunteering (corporate volunteering) can also be easily combined with sports. In many sports clubs, adults already volunteer to train children and adolescents and offer them emotional support, and this can often be complemented by further arrangements, such as helping with homework.

▶ Corporate responsibility for the environment and society requires increased visibility but also comprehensibility, which sports can provide. Naturally, CSR must be applied in the core business as well. Whenever this is the case, customers, employees and other stakeholder groups should be involved and inspired to take part – in the interests of their own business model as well as in the interests of the sustainable development of society.

References

Pilot study "Sponsor visions 2009". www.pilot.de/node/661.

Scholz & Friends (2008) *What Role Does Responsibility Play in Sports Sponsorships?* on behalf of the sponsorship association S20 (www.s20.eu).

Sports & Market (2008) *The Connection between Corporate Social Responsibility and Sports Sponsorships*, on behalf of the sponsorship association S20 (www.s20.eu).

Five rules for sustainable supply chain management

Anselm Iwundu

Responsible Business: How to Manage a CSR Strategy Successfully
Edited by Manfred Pohl and Nick Tolhurst
Copyright © 2010 Manfred Pohl and Nick Tolhurst

In this chapter, the author explores the increasing importance of supply chain management as a part of a company's overall commitment to responsible business and provides a five-step practical guide to ensuring that companies' supply chains are sustainable. Real-life business examples are provided from the agri-food industry sector, which has become a leader in supply chain good practice.

Introduction

Sustainable supply chain management (SSCM) is arguably one of the most important topics in today's discourse on business CSR strategies and one to which corporate managers are increasingly paying attention. Two points argue the need for managers' growing interest in SSCM: the increasing evidence that a company's financial performance can be linked with their environmental and social sustainability performance; and the fact that stakeholders, now more than ever, hold companies accountable for their suppliers' behaviours, especially as there are growing indications that supplier actions can pose numerous risks for companies' bottom line.

In itself, a supply chain is notably very complex, and strategies to manage it nowadays are hugely influenced by several factors, among them the growth in environmental, social and economic sustainability concerns. Several of these concerns, such as ill-treatment of workers and labour exploitation on farms and in factories, toxic production waste and emissions, soil and water contamination, use of hazardous chemical substances, deforestation, chain bribery and corruption, discrimination and other forms of human rights violations, relate to suppliers and can easily be associated with the companies doing business with them. Corporate managers therefore find ways to ensure that proposed responsible business practices or programmes intending to address any or all of these concerns extend beyond internal operations and are sufficiently integrated into their supply chains and distribution spheres by engaging SSCM. This chapter provides five steps that should guide CSR managers in establishing and managing a sustainable supply chain, using the agri-food industry as case examples.

Step #1: Establish and manage an internal sustainability or CSR programme

To ensure the successful establishment of SSCM, companies first need to ensure that their internal operations are carried out using responsible practices. Companies must identify, understand and manage their own internal sustainability-oriented risks before extending similar programmes to suppliers. Thus a good place to start is to build a functional internal sustainability or CSR programme, as follows:

1. Assign a team with sufficient leadership and decision-making capacity within the organisation to handle this programme.

2. Determine what CSR aspects and risks to address, based on the degree of importance to the company and its stakeholders.

3. Develop policy and implementation strategy for the programme and communicate it to staff as well as to other relevant stakeholders.

4. Establish a monitoring and evaluation system as well as a management feedback loop.

Note that a functional internal sustainability or CSR programme is the start of and a necessary part of the build-up towards SSCM.

Step #2: Extend CSR programmes into your supply chain

Supply chains increasingly account for the social and environmental impacts of companies. Therefore, incorporating social responsibility programmes and risk management into a company's supply chain plays a crucial role in reducing social and environmental impacts and risks as well as protecting its reputation and brand value. The following is a guide to how one can extend a firm's CSR programme into its supply chain:

1. Develop a vision for responsible supply chain management and unveil it to staff and suppliers.

2. Identify relevant supply chain activities engaged in from time to time (e.g. procurement/ sourcing) and map products and services usually obtained from suppliers.

3. Evaluate existing internal CSR policy and extend it to include relevant supply chain activities.

4. Communicate this CSR policy to suppliers, highlighting the critical areas of focus.

5. Incorporate the policy into suppliers' contractual agreements.

6. Provide platforms of support for suppliers to comply with the CSR policy directives.

7. Establish a monitoring and evaluation system as well as a management feedback loop.

Step #3: Know your suppliers and map your entire sphere of engagement

Sourcing/procurement, product design and development, processing, manufacturing and transportation are important areas in a company's operations which often utilise several suppliers. To establish and manage their supply chains effectively, managers need to know their suppliers. Aside from delivery costs, location and time, some companies know very little about their suppliers, and the aim should be to find out as much additional information about them as possible, such as how these suppliers conduct business with their own suppliers, what measures are in place for product quality, and what the working conditions are like for their staff. In addition, companies must map their sphere of engagement. Most companies often build their supply chain management around the first tier of suppliers with whom they have established direct relations. However, it is important to determine, and include, subsequent suppliers with whom the direct supplier does business. This is often a challenge, especially with global and complex supply chains, where direct suppliers in turn source their components and raw materials from a complex range of tertiary suppliers, perhaps located in different countries (Visser *et al.* 2007). The ability to influence these tertiary suppliers naturally diminishes greatly with size and location. The steps involved in this process are as follows:

1. Know more about your direct suppliers.

2. Identify your tertiary suppliers up to the last tier (where possible).

3. Map potential priority sustainability issues that may come from your supply chain against where they are likely to occur and which suppliers might be involved.

4. Determine likely corrective measures.

Step #4: Establish a responsible sourcing programme

Commitment to sustainable sourcing

The demand for sourcing of sustainable food products or ingredients is steadily increasing. Companies are therefore finding it relevant to make commitments towards sourcing sustainable food ingredients, especially from suppliers engaged in one of the numerous certification schemes (see Box 16.1). Such a commitment is not only made to the companies' shareholders but also targets the consumers of their end-products and other relevant stakeholders.

Several companies have recently made commitments to source sustainable food and beverage products. Mars Inc. recently made a commitment to have its entire cocoa supplies certified by the Rainforest Alliance by 2020. And Starbucks, in an effort to boost its commitment to attain a goal of 100% responsibly grown, ethically traded coffee by 2015, recently

Box 16.1 Supply chain partnerships for sustainability (source: www.fairfood.org)

Co-operation aimed at enhancing sustainability within companies' supply chains is increasing. Companies nowadays are establishing partnerships with their suppliers to ensure minimum socioeconomic and environmental measures for products they trade in. Furthermore, NGOs often engage in subtle partnerships with companies towards establishing sustainable production and supply chains *vis-à-vis* the sustainability level of their end products. Fairfood International is an example of this.

With a lobby focus, Fairfood International approaches several food and beverage companies (over 1,000), particularly ones that sell their brand products in mainstream markets within the Netherlands, Germany, Belgium, the UK and France. Its aim is to engage these companies in a reasonable and reliable partnership towards achieving successful product sustainability. Fairfood's strategy is first to engage in purposeful visits and constructive dialogues with brand owners, requesting information on how sustainable the main ingredient of their brand products is and encouraging them to make such claims by providing documented proof (in what is referred to as an 'assurance procedure').

The final goal is to willingly promote products with sufficient sustainability claims in their well-publicised 'buy list' or to have brand owners place Fairfood's logo on the specific product for marketing purposes as well as to stimulate other brand owners without such claims to engage in a list of researched initiatives. A successful example of these partnerships for Fairfood is with a Dutch egg brand owner, *Natuurfarm de Boed*. Fairfood encouraged this brand owner to ensure that only sustainable soy is used in the feed for their animals – they adopted this measure and consequently had their products listed on Fairfood's 'buy list'.

announced an increase in sourcing Fairtrade-certified coffee in 2009 to reach £40 million.

Certification labels and schemes

Sustainable sourcing, as defined by the London 2012 Olympic Games Committee, which is committed to hosting a 'sustainable Games', is 'ensuring that goods and services are sourced and processed under a set of internationally acceptable environmental, social and ethical guidelines and standards' (London Organising Committee of the Olympic Games 2008). Certification labels and schemes are increasingly becoming fundamental instruments for monitoring and communicating the sustainability of products. Due to seemingly perceived consumer assistance, 'fair trade' and 'organic' certification labels and schemes are steadily moving from niche levels to the mainstream; products bearing certification labels of the most prominent schemes – Fairtrade (Flo), Utz Certified, Rainforest Alliance – have begun to capture not only significant market share, but also significantly greater value than comparable agri-food commodities (Potts *et al.* 2007; Liu 2008).

Supplier policy, guidelines, standards or codes

Companies should develop a sustainable sourcing policy, guidelines or set of codes for their suppliers to adhere to. These should ultimately guide a company in deciding on appropriate suppliers with respect to compliance with certain social, environmental and economic sustainability criteria. Several companies have developed sourcing policies that strictly guide their buying trajectories. Cadbury Schweppes, for example, has developed ethical sourcing standards for its suppliers (Cadbury Schweppes (2009). The company maintains that these standards will be part of their general supplier selection, helping them to choose suppliers based upon an assessment of economic, quality, environmental and ethical factors. Amongst others, it expects that suppliers will commit to core labour rights, health and safety in the workplace, fair remuneration, diversity and respect for difference.

In 2003 Starbucks developed a supplier code of conduct that is intended to guide the types of suppliers they buy from (Starbucks Coffee Company 2003). Their suppliers are required to sign an agreement pledging compliance with the code of conduct which outlines specific standards, such as commitment to the welfare, economic improvement and sustainability of the people and places; adherence to local laws and international standards regarding human rights, workplace safety, and worker compensation and treatment; meeting or exceeding national laws and international standards for environmental protection; and minimising the negative environmental impacts of their operations.

Furthermore, some companies have also developed specific corporate programmes connected with sourcing and sustainability claims for their suppliers. A few examples are: Nespresso AAA (Box 16.2), Starbucks C.A.F.E. (Coffee and Farmer Equity) Practices and Tesco Nature's Choice.

Box 16.2   Nespresso's responsible sourcing programme (source: www.ecolaboration.com)

Nestlé Nespresso recently launched Ecolaboration, its platform for developing sustainable innovation throughout its operations, especially in coffee, capsules and machines. Through this platform, Nespresso has committed itself to enhancing its sustainability performance by  2013 by sourcing 80% of its coffee from its AAA Sustainable Quality programme and Rainforest Alliance Certified farms. Nespresso also commits to putting systems in place to triple its capacity to recycle used capsules to 75%, and to reducing its overall carbon footprint required to produce every cup of Nespresso by 20%.

In 2003, Nespresso announced the launch of the Nespresso AAA Sustainable Quality™ Coffee Programme together with Rainforest Alliance. The main focus of this programme is to enable farmers to achieve a high quality of coffee that serves to help Nespresso achieve its mission of delivering quality coffees, whilst at the same time helping to improve the standard of living for farmers and their families and conserving the natural environment. The programme combines sustainability principles (economic, social and environmental) with food quality principles.

Nespresso and Rainforest Alliance developed the Tool for the Assessment of Sustainable Quality (TASQ), a user-friendly tool that enables coffee farmers in the Nespresso AAA Programme to improve on-farm practices related to producing the highest quality coffee in a manner that is socially, environmentally and economically sustainable. This tool has four basic processes:

1. Farm assessors and agronomists are trained by Nespresso and Rainforest Alliance on how to use the tool for formal assessment.

2. Farmers and growers are provided with an easy self-assessment checklist for self-examination on performance prior to formal assessment against the TASQ criteria as well as help and advice on how to carry out the self-assessment.

3. Formal assessment against all indicators in the TASQ tool, including quality aspects such as the strain of coffee plant, soil type, harvesting practices; environmental aspects such as the use of fertilisers, biodiversity and water conservation; social practices such as adequate housing and access to education and health care; and economic issues such as yields, productivity and pricing.

4. Farms that do not sufficiently address some of the criteria will not qualify for the programme. However, other farms that do qualify will become partners of the AAA sustainable programme and will be assisted to develop a plan for sustainable production of coffee to be supplied to Nespresso.

To summarise the approach towards developing a supplier policy, guidelines, standards or codes:

1. Make a commitment towards sourcing sustainable food products/ ingredients or buying certified ingredients.

2. Develop a responsible sourcing policy or code for your suppliers.

3. Ensure that a trusted employee is directly responsible for this programme.

Step #5: Establish chain transparency and traceability

Establishing and nurturing transparency in commodity supply chains is crucial to achieving favourable results in sustainable supply chain operations. Transparency within a supply chain is usually enabled with traceability tools and systems that track and provide vital information about the state of goods and services in an entire chain. In the food and beverage industry, traceability tools track an entire food chain from farm through to processing distribution and retail parts of a production chain. Some examples include the Global Reporting Initiative (GRI) transparency reporting initiative for supply chains (see Box 16.3), the UTZ certified traceability tool for commodity products, Product Authentication International (PAI) Group's Pyramid tool, TraceAssured, Sedex, CSR Europe's Portal for Responsible Supply Chain Management, Nature and More Track & Tell tool.

Steps towards establishing chain transparency and traceability are as follows:

1. Engage in sustainability reporting of both internal operations and supply chain activities.

Box 16.3   Supply chain transparency through sustainability reporting – Global Reporting Initiative (source: www.globalreporting.org)

Global Reporting Initiative (GRI), in collaboration with Deutsche Gesellschaft für Technische Zusammenarbeit (GTZ), initiated a project aimed at exploring how reporting can promote sustainabil-  ity and transparency within supply chains of multinational enterprises (MNEs). The pilot project featured four companies that mentored 11 of their suppliers in India, Turkey, Thailand, China, Chile and South Africa in sustainable reporting. These suppliers were supported by training and resources to start up a reporting process using the Reporting Framework and the guidance of the reporting handbook, *The GRI Sustainability Reporting Cycle: A Handbook for Small and Not-so-small Organizations*. To further promote transparency through sustainability reporting, GRI launched a Global Action Network for Transparency in the Supply Chain (GANTSCh). This network enables companies to provide support to their small and medium-sized enterprise (SME) suppliers in measuring and reporting on their social, economic and environmental performance, thereby enabling a transparent sustainability reporting framework throughout their chain.

To participate in the Global Action Network, MNEs are expected to become one of the GRI Organisational Stakeholders and pay annual membership fees of €10,000. This fee ensures free scholarship for between five and 10 of the suppliers that MNEs nominate to be trained by GRI-certified training partners based on the G3 sustainability reporting framework. Current members of the network include Energias de Portugal (EDP) and Puma.

2. Request suppliers as part of the CSR policy to report their social and environmental impacts.

3. Engage effective traceability tools and programmes.

References

Cadbury Schweppes (2009) *Ethical Sourcing Standards*. http://www.cadbury.com/SiteCollectionDocuments/EthicalSourcingStandards_wordversion.doc.

Liu, P., ed. (2008) *Value-adding Standards in the North American Food Market – Trade Opportunities in Certified Products for Developing Countries*, FAO: Rome.

London Organising Committee of the Olympic Games (2008) http://www.london2012.com/news/media-releases/2008-04/london-2012-commits-to-sustainable-sourcing.php.

Potts, J., Wunderlich, C. and Fernandez, G. (2007) *Sustainable Trading Practices of the Coffee Sector*, International Institute of Sustainable Development, Winnipeg, Canada.

Starbucks Coffee Company (2003) *Starbucks Supplier Code of Conduct*. http://www.starbucks.com/aboutus/csrreport/Supplier_Code_of_Conduct.Pdf.

Visser, W., Matten, D., Pohl, M. and Tolhurst, N. (2007) *The A to Z of Corporate Social Responsibility: The Complete Reference of Concepts, Codes and Organisations*, John Wiley & Sons, Chichester, UK.

Public private partnerships
in corporate responsibility

Judith Kohler

Responsible Business: How to Manage a CSR Strategy Successfully
Edited by Manfred Pohl and Nick Tolhurst
Copyright © 2010 Manfred Pohl and Nick Tolhurst

In this chapter, the various applications and benefits of public private partnerships (PPP) will be outlined. Furthermore we will present solutions to existing management challenges, which may affect the successful implementation of PPP. Finally you will learn about the latest PPP developments – the PPP programme develoPPP. de and Capacity Development for Partnerships with the Private Sector (CDP).

Why establish public private partnerships[1]?

How to attain a goal in a faster, more efficient, cost-effective and sustainable way – development partnerships with the private sector

'Partnerships are the most effective way to address sustainable development challenges' – this is the key result of an international survey of more than 2,200 sustainability professionals in early 2009 (Globescan/ SustainAbility 2009). Those surveyed were asked about the private sector's contribution to sustainable development, what is often described by terms such as corporate social responsibility (CSR), corporate citizenship (CC) or corporate responsibility (CR). This involves a responsible corporate transaction, creating windows of opportunity for a sustainable development.

Such a commitment within the private sector is also of great relevance to governmental development co-operation. In order to improve the economic, ecological and social situation of partner countries in co-operation with the private sector, Germany's Federal Ministry for Economic Co-operation and Development (Bundesministerium für wirtschaftliche Zusammenarbeit und Entwicklung, BMZ) initiates public private partnerships (PPPs) via its develoPPP.de scheme.

Companies create employment and income, they are able to introduce innovative ecological and environmentally friendly technologies and they are instrumental in designing global supply chains. Equally, they can play an important role in the fight against corruption and in the assertion of human rights. The basic idea of develoPPP.de is that the partnership

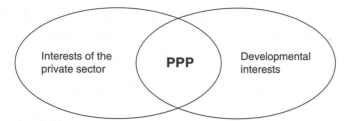

Figure 17.1 In public private partnerships (PPPs) joint projects between the private sector and government agencies are of mutual interest and benefit.

Box 17.1   Criteria to be met by public private partnerships (PPPs)

▶ They have to be compatible with the development goals of the Federal government.

▶ Complementarity – the public and the private contributions have to complement one another in such a way that both partners will attain their goals more quickly and with more cost efficiency and greater impact.

▶ Subsidiarity – a public PPP contribution can only be performed if the private partner would not carry out the PPP measure without the public partner or if the measure is not required legally.

▶ The company's contribution is at least 50% of the total costs: the company must make a considerable financial contribution and/or a contribution in manpower to the PPP measure.

between the private sector and the government agency leading development co-operation are of mutual interest and benefit (Figure 17.1). In jointly planned, financed and realised actions, goals can be attained in a faster, more efficient and more sustainable way (see Box 17.1). However, it is important that there is an economic interest in the partnership on the part of the company, because the more significant the reference to economic success, the more likely it is that the measure will lead to lasting improvements for the people in the partner countries. This win-win situation encompasses a multitude of CSR topics, such as human rights, working conditions, education, health and the environment.

develoPPP.de offers a platform to companies to realise their CSR commitment within specific sustainable measures, such as the following case studies from the portfolio of the Deutsche Gesellschaft für Technische Zusammenarbeit (GTZ) GmbH.

Case study 1: Energy-efficient refrigerators in Brazil's favelas

In the socially disadvantaged city districts of Brazil, the so-called favelas, outdated, climate-damaging refrigerators are not the exception. The inhabitants cannot afford to buy environmentally friendly appliances and use the 15- to 20-year-old refrigerators as long as possible. Poorly fixed, they often leak, so that climate-damaging gases such as chlorofluorocarbons (CFCs) can escape. Additionally, they waste a lot of energy, resulting in enormous costs.

In the past, companies did not have an incentive to develop profitable models for the distribution of energy-efficient refrigerators in low-income districts. Moreover, the market is characterised by massive socioeconomic challenges. This is where the development partnership between GTZ and BSH Bosch and Siemens Hausgeräte GmbH comes in. The partnership uses the 'Clean Development Mechanism', an instrument of the Kyoto Protocol, which offers companies in industrialised countries the opportunity to obtain greenhouse gas emissions credits by creating energy-saving projects in developing and emerging markets. The partners jointly develop projects in order to provide the inhabitants of favelas around São Paulo with new, environmentally friendly devices and thus generate certificates from these replacements.

So far BSH has exchanged 50,000 units. Local NGOs are being specifically trained for this purpose and for the professional disposal of the old refrigerators.

Mutual benefit (Figure 17.2)

The economic interest of BSH is to obtain emission certificates. In the long run the company aims to become the market leader for the distribution of energy-efficient refrigerators in Brazil. The progressive political interest in the partnership is based on the increase in incomes, which results in cost savings of the energy-efficient devices for private households, and the exchange of the old refrigerators for the local waste management companies. The measure also contributes to the reduction and the avoidance of climate-damaging environmental impacts.

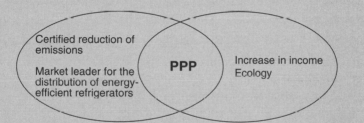

Figure 17.2 Mutual benefits for the public private partnership between Deutsche Gesellschaft für Technische Zusammenarbeit (GTZ) GmbH and BSH Bosch and Siemens Hausgeräte GmbH in Brazil (case study 1).

Case study 2: Micro-insurances for low-income population groups

In most developing and emerging countries, people on low incomes rarely have the possibility to protect themselves against elementary disasters and risks threatening their survival. On the one hand, public safety nets are mostly underdeveloped and, on the other, the majority

(Continued)

of the population is employed in the informal sector. In Indonesia barely 3% of the approximately 230 million inhabitants have life insurance. Disasters often lead to an almost complete loss of income and the uninsured families are usually not equipped with financial reserves they can draw on.

In the past, the micro-insurance market was not profitable for insurance companies. The premium was too low and the existing distribution channel was not suitable for the vast geographical spread and the large number of those to be insured. Allianz and GTZ met these specific challenges through PPP measures in 2005.

'Payung Keluarga' (Family Umbrella) is the name of the (credit) life insurance that was developed by the partners in co-operation with the United Nations Development Programme (UNDP), local microfinance institutions and NGOs. This insurance contract with an annual premium of US$0.66 is also affordable for those on a very low income. In addition, the access to micro-credits has been improved, as the Allianz takes on the outstanding premiums in case of the death of the credit user. Thus the providers of micro-credits no longer have to bear the risk of a shortfall in payment, whilst the subsequent payment obligations for the surviving dependants are waived.

The three-year partnership between Allianz and the GTZ draws a successful balance of more than 35,000 contracted insurances. Allianz's plan to extend their range of products by a health and educational endowment insurance speaks to the viability of the concept.

Mutual benefit (Figure 17.3)

The commitment in Indonesia enabled the Allianz Company to collect valuable knowledge of a formerly unexploited market and to enter an intensive dialogue with public policy makers and different private institutions.

(Continued)

In terms of development policy the insurance offer is an effective protection against extreme risks for especially disadvantaged population groups. Apart from that the conditions for the extension of micro credits are improved, which is also connected with a positive impact on the development.

Figure 17.3 Mutual benefits for the public private partnership (PPP) between Deutsche Gesellschaft für Technische Zusammenarbeit (GTZ) GmbH and Allianz in Indonesia (case study 2).

How to ensure that projects are successful

Partnerships can benefit from the thematic overlaps of CSR and development co-operation (see Figure 17.4 for the interfaces between the two). But what should be considered in the realisation of these partnerships? The co-operation within these projects differs from other forms of co-operation. They are not comparable to the usual commercial principal–agent relationship, nor is it a matter of a sponsorship or a non-binding declaration of intent. Based on GTZ's experience of more than 1,000 development partnerships, the following decisive factors have to be considered in order to ensure that a PPP project is successful.

Co-operative road to success

A PPP can only be successful if all the participants are open to the prospect of a co-operative collaboration. In the initial stages, there are often many

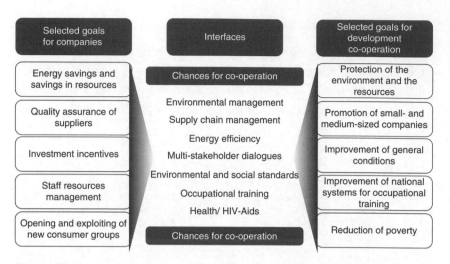

Figure 17.4   Interfaces between development co-operation and CSR.

stereotypes to be challenged. The public sector is commonly regarded as slow and bureaucratic, while the private sector is seen solely as profit-oriented rather than development-oriented. The acceptance of differences and of the legitimacy of each party's motive for action, which often involves a different use of language by the partners, is important. The respect for principles such as equity, transparency and give-and-take plays a crucial role. A working development partnership must have clearly defined targets and has to be of mutual benefit. It requires an especially open and broad-minded attitude from all participants. It is fundamental that this is emphasised at the beginning of the co-operation and that management structures are created to enable the co-operative supervision and financing of the project.

Management for successful partnerships

Targets and strategies

Partnerships make sense, when one cannot achieve one's targets alone and if there is a win-win situation for all the partners. That is why it is important that each partner articulates their interests and expectations clearly and that the partnership's contribution to sustainable development is precisely expressed.

The development and determination of the shared targets are part of a negotiation process that has to consider the interests of every partner. The more openly interests, expectations and apprehensions are communicated between partners, the more thorough the grounding of the partnership will be. It is important to keep records of the targets and the respective indicators, as they form the basis of the effect-oriented monitoring for measuring the success of the partnership.

A helpful tool for the development of strategies is a results chain (Table 17.1). On the basis of these, it becomes apparent where the participants have to render services in order to hit the targets.

Project management

One conclusion that is drawn from all development partnerships is that a professional project management is decisive for the success of the measures. Apart from the classical, operative management of projects, the project management in non-hierarchical contexts must also be mastered in partnerships. Different cultures of the partners, such as organisational cultures, play a role here. The joint planning of activities, a joint process of co-ordination and a clear assignment of roles and responsibilities within the co-operation are important, if misunderstandings are to be avoided and the project's course is to be successful. Commitment and transparency are created by a jointly developed operation plan. In the last few years, different approaches and tools for project management have been developed taking these special requirements into account, e.g. the steering and monitoring tool for partnerships (*Steuerungs- und Monitoringinstrument für Partnerschaften*, SMP) of GTZ.

Co-operation management

Co-operation management covers the internal consultation processes and rules, and also the organisation of external relations of a development

Table 17.1 An example of a results chain for developing strategies and targets

Term	Definition	Central questions
Impact	Positive and negative, primary and secondary, often long-term changes, caused by development measures, directly or indirectly, intended or unintended	Which political, economical and socially important changes have occurred in the sector, in the country, to which the direct result contributes?
Outcome	The presumably or actually achieved short- or medium-term changes as a result of the use of outputs of an intervention	Who benefits from the change that results from the use of the project outputs? What changes exactly?
Use of output	Participants use the created products, goods, services and institutions/guidelines	What do the users change, if they integrate the use of the project output into their (professional) routines permanently?
Output	Products, goods, services and institutions/guidelines, which have been created by the DC	What exactly does the project offer to the surroundings? What is the effect of the activities?
Activities	Entirety of actions that have been carried out within a DC	What does the project team do? Who participates? Who is the target of the activities, who is the beneficiary?
Input	Financial, personal, material contributions and funds, which have been provided by different participants and instruments within the DM	

partnership. The agreed 'guidelines' of the partnership must be known to all, and responsibilities, functions and decision-making powers must be defined precisely. Communication plays a key role here. The partners have to deal in a sensitive way with the fact that each has their own 'language'.

To a certain degree, each partner therefore has to adapt their use of language to reach a common understanding. A good communication culture also means that conflicts are dealt with openly. Methods of conflict resolution should already be included in the design of the PPP, e.g. how to react if a partner does not meet the deadlines.

External protagonists, e.g. the professional and general public, can also have a strong influence on the success of a partnership and will have to be included accordingly. Transparent communication is essential in order to convince external protagonists of the target of this measure – this includes the ability to respond to criticism quickly and with one voice. Key external stakeholders are, of course, the beneficiaries and it is crucial that they are involved right from the start.

Continuous reviews and adjustments

Another important factor in successful partnerships is to have a continuous review of the progress of measures. Right from the planning stage, regular co-ordination meetings must be agreed upon that are no more than six months apart. In the course of these meetings, the partners jointly review the progress, which gives them the opportunity to make any necessary adjustments promptly. During the joint evaluation, differences in the assessment should not be dismissed, but they should be discussed and overcome.

Control questions that have been developed as part of the SMP can serve as a basis for these meetings. They refer to the targets of the measure, the project as well as the co-operation management and they allow a comprehensive monitoring of the partnership. Figure 17.5 gives examples of control questions that work with a traffic-light system.

Partnership opportunities: develoPPP.de

The PPP programme develoPPP.de of the BMZ rests on three pillars: two categories of ideas competitions and the so-called strategic alliances (three

Comprehensive evaluation	◓	○	●
Has the model of the partnership proved its worth and would it be preferred to troubleshooting with the help of a protagonist in the future?			
I. Targets and strategies	◓	○	●
Have the targets of the partnership been documented and will they be communicated to internal and external stakeholders?			
II. Project management	◓	○	●
Have the partners executed the defined activities in the operational plan and have the appointed resources been procured?			
III. Co-operation management	◓	○	●
Were conflicts between the partners discussed in time? Were they addressed and dealt with openly?			

Figure 17.5 Control questions for the validation of the partnership using a traffic-light system.

implementing organisations execute the programme, Deutsche Investitions- und Entwicklungsgesellschaft, GTZ and Sequa GmbH). These pillars are described below.

develoPPP.topic

In this category, companies have the possibility to submit proposals for joint measures on selected topics several times a year. The commitment of private industry is actively supported in developmentally important sectors, where there is a special need for action, but where there are special opportunities as well.

develoPPP.innovation

The second category consists of innovation competitions. Companies are invited to give their own input independent of the competitions linked to different topics. Entries that show an exceptional commitment or great entrepreneurial creativity have the best prospects. If a proposal meets the criteria of the ideas competition, joint elaboration of the itinerary follows. Before a measure is executed, it is subject to an internal examination.

develoPPP.alliance

The third constituent offers opportunities for particularly ground-breaking approaches. They are generally applied cross-nationally, include several partners and can develop a broad, constructive impact, because they go far beyond the environment of a single company.

The proposals with the best concepts and the most efficient approaches in the ideas competitions can be co-financed with up to €200,000. For projects in this category, BMZ allocates more funds, as PPP alliances make high demands on project planning and management and because their developmental impact is stronger.

Every one of the three pillars is suitable for co-operation within the context of CSR. Up-to-date information and current deadlines for all competitions can be found at www.develoPPP.de.

Capacity Development for Partnerships with the Private Sector (CDP)

For some time, public partner organisations from BMZ and GTZ have shown interest in starting their own programmes for co-operation with private sector. Ministries or governmental authorities in developing countries and countries in transition have increasingly recognised the potential offered by partnerships with the private sector. The crucial question is: which structures, skills, resources and instruments are required for a successful partnership, in order to contribute effectively to sustainable development? The German development co-operation answers this question with a new approach: 'Capacity Development for Partnerships with the Private Sector' (CDP) stands for consulting and training services of GTZ. Through CDP, GTZ wants to enable governmental organisations, the private sector and civil society to co-operate in the context of sustainable development.

Footnote

1 This chapter is not about private sector participation or private participation in infrastructure. The term public private partnership (PPP) in the context of German development co-operations stands for 'development partnerships'.

Reference

Globescan/Sustainability (2009) *Sustainable Development Challenges and the Role of Companies: Findings from the Sustainability Survey*, Globescan. http://surveys.globescan.com/tssebrief/tss_eBrief.pdf.

CSR in developing countries

Isaac H. Desta

This chapter provides an overview of CSR in developing countries. The author discusses relevant environmental, social and ethical issues in developing countries affecting CSR, and goes on to elaborate on the benefits of CSR for firms from developing countries. Later there is a discussion on the relationship between CSR practices and supply chains. Here, supply chain is considered as a major environmental factor shaping the practice of CSR in firms in developing countries.

Environmental, social and ethical issues in developing countries

The goals of firms in developing countries are mostly profit-making. They pay little attention to their social responsibilities. Firms focus on elements in their environment which are necessary to their success and pay less notice to the social, environmental and ethical implications of their actions (Okafor *et al.* 2008). But in circumstances where their customers or other external factors (such as local or national institutions) require them to meet certain social, ethical or environmental standards, they implement measures to comply in order to maintain their market share (UNIDO 2002).

It should be noted, however, that specific historical, political, economic and cultural factors determine the level of CSR of firms in the various developing countries. For example, Indonesian companies, especially those operating in the global market, have become aware that they are required to balance the social, economic and environmental components of their business while building shareholder value. Thus, the main driving force in Indonesia for firms to adapt CSR is involvement in the international market. By contrast, in the Philippines the major drivers of CSR behaviour in corporations and private institutions have been market forces. Here, corporations and private institutions organise and involve themselves in CSR activities not only as tactical responses to potential crises but also in acknowledgment of the fact that businesses could not possibly thrive in an environment where the majority of the population are poor.

A different picture emerges in Singapore and Vietnam, where the state is the major driving force for the introduction of CSR. In this case, there is much emphasis on compliance with legislative requirements as a means of achieving and regulating socially responsible behaviour. In Thailand, on the other hand, the practice of CSR is at an early stage of development and is substantially influenced by religious beliefs and traditional norms of ethical practice.

Nevertheless, some generalisations regarding the practice of CSR in firms in developing countries can be made, and these are discussed in the following section.

Features of CSR in developing countries

Corporate social responsibility in developing countries has the following basic features (Visser 2008; Blowfield & Frynas 2005; UNIDO 2002):

▶ CSR is formally practised by internationalised national and multinational firms (and these firms mostly set the local CSR agenda).

▶ CSR codes, standards and guidelines tend to be issue-specific (e.g. HIV/AIDS, poverty) or sector-led (e.g. mining, agriculture).

▶ CSR is commonly related to philanthropy or charity.

▶ Firms perceive making an economic contribution (e.g. investments and job creation) and provision of social services (e.g. housing) as the most effective way of making a social contribution.

▶ The practice of CSR is strongly influenced by traditional community values and religion (e.g. humanism (*ubuntu*) in Africa, co-existence (*kyosei*) in Japan, and harmonious society (*xiaokang*) in China).

The most unique feature of CSR in developing countries is the role played by community values and religions as drivers in shaping the CSR environment. For instance, *ubuntu* teaches concepts such as respect, trust, compassion, empathy and, above all, the notion that individual success is dependent on the success of the group. This does not mean, however, that individual progress is subordinate to the success of the group. It is simply the recognition that individual success is possible only by promoting the good of others (Panse 2006). This example shows that the concept of CSR is not new to the developing world. It existed as part and parcel of the value system before the advent of CSR in the Western hemisphere.

Additional drivers of CSR including international markets and multi-national enterprises are elaborated in the following section.

Drivers of CSR in developing countries

International markets are among the strongest drivers of CSR, given that the regulatory and governance systems in developing countries are weak. An example given by Lyon & Maxwell (2007) on the Colombian cut-flower industry serves to clarify this point. This industry, which caters to customers in the USA and Europe, has been affected by consumers' opposition to the use of pesticides. This shift in market demand has allowed the enforcement of pesticide regulations, which were promulgated but not enforced due to weak government.

Other important drivers of CSR are multinationals and their supply chain (Blowfield & Frynas 2005). In recent years, multinationals have begun including social and environmental criteria, which are referred to as supply chain standards or codes of conduct, to engage in business relations with local firms in developing countries (UNIDO 2002). Since a number of these indigenous firms are engaged in business relations with multinational firms in the form of subcontracting, licensing and joint ventures, multinationals are now one of the major driving forces behind the proliferation of CSR activities in developing countries. Multinationals may develop CSR standards due to internal or external pressures.

The rise in CSR activities as initiated by multinationals is not necessarily a positive development. For instance, UNIDO (2002) points out that multinationals may force CSR standards on firms in developing countries in order, among other things, to pass on costs for monitoring and auditing social and environmental practices. Therefore, multinationals may have ulterior motives when developing CSR standards. Even in circumstances where multinationals do not have a hidden agenda, it is doubtful whether CSR standards developed in the context of a Western socioeconomic environment by Western firms (including international institutions) can allow indigenous (developing countries') firms to design and implement effective CSR policies unless local businesses in developing countries are involved in the setting of CSR standards.

Additional drivers of CSR are effectively summarised in Visser (2005) as follows:

► political, social and economic environment

► governance systems

► increased internationalisation of local firms

► stakeholder activism.

In cases where the political system pursues prudent economic and political liberalisation, there is an automatic shift of responsibility – including responsibility for social, ethical and environmental issues – away from the state towards the private sector. In addition, the socioeconomic environment shapes the type of CSR activities undertaken by firms. For example, in Africa, where HIV/AIDS is prevalent, firms tend to focus on providing social services that reduce the spread of that disease, including the provision of educational services. Furthermore, CSR in developing countries is often considered as a response to governance challenges. CSR activities articulated in the form of various social services (e.g. utility provision) are aimed at bridging the governance gap. One of the negative effects of the governance gap is that business practices in developing countries are not closely monitored by the state. Therefore, ethical issues are generally not considered when doing business and thus ethics is not a major CSR driver for businesses.

Increased internationalisation of firms in developing countries is another CSR driver. As these firms have become more internationalised, they are increasingly being forced to consider international CSR standards in order to gain access to Western markets. Furthermore, stakeholders (e.g. NGOs, media and business associations) are playing an active role in forcing firms to adapt environmentally friendly practices.

Benefits of CSR

Even though it is important to discuss the need for CSR, every firm will always ask:

▶ Why do I need to have CSR programmes?

▶ Of what benefit are CSR programmes to my organisation?

▶ How will CSR ultimately affect the balance sheet and shareholder value?

This section attempts to address these issues.

One of the strongest arguments for CSR is that firms in developing countries can gain competitive advantage by improving the quality of their service delivery and innovation capabilities. This in turn helps firms achieve positive customer, supplier and employee responses *vis-à-vis* the competition (Mendoza & Torralba 2004; Matura 2004). For example, Opondo (2005) points out that Kenyan flower companies have adopted CSR successfully, which has resulted in a dramatic improvement in employees' working conditions. Koestoer (2007) also observes that CSR has helped companies in Indonesia to enhance business sales, improve quality of services and gain public trust.

Additional benefits of adopting CSR include (UNIDO 2002; Graafland & Smid, 2004; Hohnen 2007):

▶ improved affiliation with current and emerging customer concerns and greater access to markets, especially markets in developed countries – CSR can help companies establish sustainable relationships not only with consumers but also with multinationals or firms entrenched in Western markets where international market standards include CSR standards

▶ decreased operational costs resulting from environmental efficiency measures (e.g. energy efficiency and reduced labour turnover) and enhanced productivity and better management

▶ increased local reputation and public image – good reputation, among other things, enhances job satisfaction, employee commitment and the overall quality of firms' workforces. Additional benefits include increased customer base, and price and quantity premium.

Some specific examples of the benefits of CSR are given in Box 18.1. As these examples illustrate, although it is seems that CSR may be expensive to companies and may affect the balance sheet negatively, it is not actually true. In fact, if it is managed prudently, CSR is a smart way of improving the overall position of any corporation.

CSR and supply chains

The prudent management of CSR for firms in developing countries requires the development of ethical supply chains. So why is there a need for this? Owing to increased globalisation, businesses are now outsourcing and relocating their manufacturing bases to cheap high- or low-skilled labour markets. This outsourcing and relocating has resulted in the creation of global supply chains which facilitate commerce between firms around the globe. Even though these supply chains have allowed companies to reduce their costs and increase their profit margins, they have brought about new challenges to both multinationals and subcontractors (in developing

Box 18.1   CSR and return on investment (Gray 2009)

Amanco

Amanco, a plastics producer in Brazil, has saved $580,000 through a variety of eco-efforts at its numerous company plants. Its heavy promotion of environmentally sustainable efforts has allowed Amanco to win contracts from a range of organisations throughout Latin America.

DQY Ecological

DQY Ecological, an egg producer in China, is strongly committed to environmental and safety performance. This commitment, besides attracting foreign investment from the likes of the Global Environment Fund and the International Finance Corporation, has increased DQY's sales from $600,000 in 2002 to $6.7 million in 2006. The increase in sales was even observed during the infamous SARS (severe acute respiratory syndrome) outbreak of farm-borne pneumonia.

Anglo-American

Anglo-American opened HIV-AIDS clinics near its mining sites, paying $125 per month for retroviral drugs for every HIV-infected Anglo-American employee. This measure, coupled with the provision of sex education to its workers, has helped to reduce the infection rate, reduced employee absenteeism and saved Anglo-American $200 per month for each infected worker.

countries) in the form of public pressure, which is forcing companies along the supply chain to introduce ethical, social and environmental practices (Valentino 2007).

In response to this challenge, a number of companies have introduced corporate codes of conduct that require suppliers to adhere to certain CSR standards, including high employment standards and other forms of fair human resource management practice (Valentino 2007). However, as Valentino correctly notes, despite these measures, unfair labour practices (such as the use of child labour) persist in developing countries. Given the increased pressure from NGOs, activist groups, the media and other interest groups, such unfair labour practices are damaging the profitability of firms in both developed and developing nations. Therefore, given the urgency of the matter, what should firms in developing countries do to work harmoniously with firms in developed nations?

For an efficient and transparent ethical supply chain system to be in place, it is essential for firms in developing countries to set up a framework for ethics and risk management. CSR facilitates this framework by helping companies (Valentino 2007):

► establish value statements and codes of conduct

► facilitate the adoption of internationally accepted processes and develop measurable performance indicators

► co-ordinate the different units of the firm so as to develop an ethical business environment

► develop programmes for building awareness and need for CSR.

However, it is important to note that the form that CSR takes in the supply chain is based on the structure of the industry. Following UNIDO (2002), we identify three types of supply chain based on the relationship between firms from developing and developed nations (along the supply chain): supply chains neither dominated by buyers or producers; buyer-driven supply chains; and producer-driven supply chains.

Supply chains not influenced by buyers or producers

In industries where the relationship between brand owners and producers is weak, e.g. agriculture, industry-level initiatives need to be put in place, which includes product standards, monitoring and certification systems (e.g. industry protocol on child labour and organic standards). In such cases, firms in developing countries need to build networks and form associations that co-ordinate and monitor CSR practices within the industry. These firms can form a multi-stakeholder partnership whereby industry sectors adopt a common code of conduct and work with various interest groups to achieve an acceptable monitoring system. For example, the Kenyan Flower Council has developed its own codes of conduct and certification systems in order to help its members meet international standards.

Buyer-driven supply chains

In buyer-driven supply chains, such as labour-intensive consumer goods (e.g. textiles), brand owners have a closer relationship with manufacturing firms in developing countries. In this case, firms from developing countries need to establish individual monitoring systems and CSR strategies, given the pressure they face from brand owners to maintain good relationships with buyers (in such industries, buyers/brand owners, have a strong influence on the behaviour of local firms).

Before establishing a CSR strategy, firms need to conduct a CSR assessment (Hohnen 2007). This involves gathering relevant information about the firm's processes and outputs to determine the status of the firm with regards to its CSR activity. Key stakeholders need to be involved in this process. The process of CSR assessment includes assembling a CSR team, developing a context-specific definition of CSR, identifying legal requirements, reviewing relevant proprietary documents, and identifying and engaging with key stakeholders.

Once a CSR assessment is made, possible steps to develop a CSR strategy are as follows (Hohnen 2007; Sturdivant 1985; Jamali 2007):

1. Build support with the CEO, senior management and employees.

2. Research what others (including competitors) are doing and assess the value of recognised CSR instruments.

3. Prepare a matrix of proposed CSR actions – in the process, it is essential for firms to understand that CSR has to be integrated into its operations, which involves addressing the following questions:

   – What CSR initiatives has the firm undertaken already?

   – How have the current CSR initiatives affected (positively or negatively) the organisation?

   – What are the firm's CSR goals?

   – What are the fundamental social, environmental and ethical issues relevant to the firm's sphere of operations?

   – How can proposed CSR changes be organised into short-, medium- and long-term deliverables?

   – How can these deliverables be measured, what resources are required to accomplish them and what changes need to be made within the organisation to achieve them?

   – What are the benefits and costs of the proposed CSR changes?

4. Develop options for proceeding and the business case for them – here, the potential gain in competitive advantage, profits, opportunities for cost reductions and new development has to be investigated.

5. Decide on direction, approach, boundaries and focus areas:

   – Direction: the overall course the firm could pursue is decided at this stage, given prominent issues specific to the industry. For example, an apparel firm would probably decide to emphasise the health and safety of employees

   – Approach: refers to how a firm intends to move in the direction identified. At this stage revision of mission, vision and values and ethical statements might be in order

   – Focus areas: the firm decides to prioritise CSR activities based on its objectives.

Producer-driven supply chains

In producer-driven supply chains, consumer durables with higher technology input are produced (e.g. automobiles and computers). Here, there is a strong relationship between brand owners and their suppliers, as partnership is essential in the designing and production process of these high-tech products. A close relationship between brand owners and suppliers in the form of shared management systems, training and strategic alliances is the norm in these supply chains. Thus, firms from developing countries in producer-driven supply chains must adapt CSR standards, mainly in the form of efficient management systems and effective utilisation of resources (e.g. technology, finance, material and human), to stay in the partnership. Firms in producer-driven supply chains must align and simulate their activities to mirror those of their partners based in the developed nations.

Therefore, although we observe that CSR initiatives taken by firms vary based on the nature and structure of the supply chain, companies from developing countries need to integrate CSR into their supply chain management for sustainable development.

Conclusion

Corporate social responsibility in developing countries is in its early stages. However, the current pace of globalisation is forcing firms from developing countries to adopt CSR strategies. Thus, firms need to consider this changing environment and take proactive CSR measures to stay competitive in the global market. In addition to the issue of competitiveness, CSR initiatives also ensure the sustainable utilisation of national and international resources. Given the current levels of depletion of resources, CSR is an invaluable concept that can ensure the survival of firms from developing countries.

References

Blowfield, M. and Frynas, J.G. (2005) Setting new agendas: critical perspectives on corporate social responsibility in the developing world, *International Affairs*, **81**(3): 499–513.

Graafland, J. and Smid, H. (2004) Reputation, corporate social responsibility and market regulation, *Tijdschrift voor Economie en Management*, **XLIX**(2): 271–308.

Gray, K. (2009) *ROI: Companies See Financial Benefit in CSR Programs*. Online: http://www.shrm.org/hrdisciplines/ethics/articles/Pages/ROICompaniesSeeFinancial BenefitinCSRPrograms.aspx.

Hohnen, P. (2007) *Corporate Social Responsibility; An Implementation Guide for Business* (ed. Potts, J.), International Institute for Sustainable Development (IISD), Winnipeg.

Jamali, D. (2007) The case for strategic corporate social responsibility in developing countries, *Business and Society Review*, **112**: 1–27.

Koestoer, Y.T. (2007) *Corporate Social Responsibility in Indonesia*. Online: http://www.aseanfoundation.org/seminar/gcsg/papers/Yanti%20Koestoer%20%20Paper%202007.pdf.

Lyon, T. and Maxwell, J. (2007) *Corporate Social Responsibility and the Environment: A Theoretical Perspective*, Kelley School of Business, Indiana.

Matura, B.O. (2004) *Profit Maximization and Business Social Responsibility Objectives in Business Management. Shareholder Value and the Common Good*, Don Bosco Printing Press, Nairobi.

Mendoza, A.M.E. and Torralba, C.T. (2004) *The Challenge of Business: Going beyond Wealth Maximization and Profit Maximization. Shareholder Value and the Common Good*, Don Bosco Printing Press, Nairobi.

Okafor, E., Hassan, A. and Doyin-Hassan, A. (2008) Environmental issues and corporate social responsibility: the Nigeria experience, *Journal of Human Ecology*, **23**(2): 101–107.

Opondo, M. (2005) *Emerging Corporate Social Responsibility in Kenya's Cut Flower Industry*. Online: http://www.unisa.ac.za/contents/colleges/col_econ_man_science/ccc/docs/Opondo.pdf.

Panse, S. (2006) *Ubuntu – African Philosophy*. Online: http://www.buzzle.com/editorials/7-22-2006-103206.asp.

Sturdivant, F.D. (1985) *Business and Society: A Managerial Approach*, 3rd edn, Richard D. Irwin Inc., Homewood, IL, USA.

UNIDO (2002) *Corporate Social Responsibility: Implications to Small and Medium Scale Enterprises in Developing Countries*, UNIDO, Vienna.

Valentino, B. (2007) *MBA Toolkit For CSR: Supply Chain Management And Corporate Social Responsibility*. Online: http://www.chinacsr.com/en/2007/12/12/1938-mba-toolkit-for-csr-supply-chain-management-and-corporate-social-responsibility/.

Visser, W. (2005) *Corporate Social Responsibility in Developing Countries*. Online: http://www.waynevisser.com/chapter_wvisser_csr_dev_countries.pdf.

Visser, W. (2008) *CSR in Developing Countries: Distinctive Characteristics*. Online: http://csrinternational.blogspot.com/2008/10/csr-in-developing-countries.html.

19

Carbon offsetting as a CSR strategy

Nick Tolhurst and Aron Embaye

Responsible Business: How to Manage a CSR Strategy Successfully
Edited by Manfred Pohl and Nick Tolhurst
Copyright © 2010 Manfred Pohl and Nick Tolhurst

In this chapter, an introduction to the growing trend of carbon offsetting is provided, outlining a business that increasingly influences many different industries. We consider both the business case and the CSR implications of carbon offsetting as well as providing real-life examples and recommendations for best practice.

Introduction

One of the most pressing environmental issues facing global society today is climate change. Changes in ecosystems, resulting in extreme hazards such as floods, droughts and storms, with consequent damages to human health, buildings, livelihoods and infrastructure are among the dire effects of climate change. As business organisations are part and parcel of the larger social environment, they are equally influenced by the consequences of climate change. According to the UN Intergovernmental Panel on Climate Change, business risks from climate change include, among other things, increasing legal and regulatory pressures, mounting public and shareholder activism, changes in consumer and supplier markets, and increased costs of doing business now and in the future.

Whilst international policies for climate change are debated, technological breakthroughs are still evolving and the green lifestyle is still in its infancy, companies are mapping out strategies to help them deal with the risks, opportunities and responsibilities associated with climate change. Along with their own in-house emissions reduction measures, more and more companies are buying carbon offsets to help meet their environmental objectives. As a financial tool, carbon offsetting allows companies to achieve their emission reduction targets either through the purchase of carbon credits or through financial support of projects that reduce the emission of greenhouse gases in the short or long term.

In addition to the main role carbon offsetting plays in reducing emissions, a carefully designed carbon-offsetting strategy also allows companies to achieve their CSR objectives in meaningful ways. In this chapter we discuss how investment in carbon-offsetting projects gives companies the opportunity to secure their own competitive advantages while contributing towards economic, social and environmental sustainability.

Brief overview of strategies for reducing emissions

The climate change strategies, goals and policies followed by companies depend on the nature of their business and the scope of the risk identified. Generally speaking, companies use strategies that combine internally focused emission reduction measures and externally available emission reduction approaches.

Internal measures

As a matter of principle, a company's carbon or emissions management strategy should at first focus on internal initiatives that reduce or limit greenhouse gas emissions at source. Such internal initiatives that help companies to cut their carbon footprint include:

▶ identifying new processes that improve operational and energy efficiencies

▶ increasing use of alternative energy sources

▶ developing new products and services that reduce greenhouse gas emissions or help to mitigate impacts of climate change.

However, in cases where the internal reductions fulfil only a certain portion of a company's reduction target, where companies lack technological capability or the cost of the in-house measures are too great, they can still meet their environmental objectives through externally available greenhouse gas emission reduction measures. One such externally available measure, established by the Kyoto Protocol, is carbon offsetting.

External measures – carbon offsetting

The basic idea behind carbon offsetting is that regardless of location, a reduction in emissions will have a net positive effect in combating climate change. This is possible because climate change is not a localised problem; greenhouse gases spread evenly throughout the atmosphere, so reducing them anywhere contributes to overall climate protection.

Carbon offsets are measured in tonnes of carbon dioxide equivalents (CO_2e) and may represent six primary categories of greenhouse gases. One carbon offset represents the reduction of one tonne of carbon dioxide or its equivalent in other greenhouse gases.

According to many sources, the demand and supply for carbon offsetting are growing rapidly in both the compliance and voluntary markets. For example, in 2006, about $5.5 billion of carbon offsets were purchased in the compliance market, representing about 1.6 billion tonnes of CO_2 reductions. In the compliance market, companies, governments and other entities buy carbon offsets in order to comply with caps on the total amount of carbon dioxide they are allowed to emit.

In the same year, about $91 million of carbon offsets were purchased in the voluntary market, representing about 24 million tonnes of CO_2e reductions. The voluntary market consists of companies, governments, NGOs and individuals buying or selling carbon credits for reasons other than regulatory compliance. Although the voluntary market is still small, it is growing at a very fast rate, with various estimates putting this at 200% growth per annum.

Carbon offsetting, CSR and sustainability

Against the backdrop of rising global concern for the environment and climate change, the global demand for carbon credits will continue to increase. This growing trend makes a discussion on how companies can use a carbon-offsetting strategy in conjunction with their CSR strategy a timely topic.

Most definitions of CSR in the business and society literature tend to emphasise the role of business in sustainable development. For example, the World Business Council for Sustainable Development (WBCSD) defines CSR as 'business's commitment to contribute to sustainable economic development, working with their employees, their families, the local community, and society at large to improve their quality of life.' Similarly SustainAbility (2004) describes CSR as 'an approach to business that embodies transparency and ethical behaviour, respect for stakeholder groups and a commitment to add economic, social and environmental value.' Similar definitions by the EU, the UN and many others also establish the role of CSR in sustainable development.

The Clean Development Mechanism (CDM) is one of the main features of the Kyoto Protocol. The mechanism emphasises that beyond the expected climate benefits, carbon offsetting should serve as a vehicle to support projects with sustainability and development goals. Similarly, important voluntary carbon offset standards such as Gold Standard (GS), the Voluntary Offset Standard (VOS), the Climate, Community and Biodiversity Standards (CCBS) and the Plan Vivo System also focus on carbon-offsetting projects that generate social and economic co-benefits along with the carbon mitigation process.

This potential for generating projects that contribute towards sustainable development connects carbon offsetting with the broader objectives of CSR. Therefore, if companies are to utilise carbon offsetting as a strategic CSR mechanism, they need to direct their investments towards projects that deliver rich sustainable development benefits.

The business case that supports a company's engagement in CSR also exists in well-crafted and executed carbon-offsetting projects. For example, Business for Social Responsibility mentions the following business benefits associated with the voluntary practice of offsetting carbon emissions:

▶ improved reputation and environmental credibility, particularly for customer-facing companies

▶ increased experience in voluntary carbon markets in anticipation of a carbon-constrained economy, particularly for large companies and those in emissions-intensive sectors

▶ enhanced credibility, dialogue and networks with industry groups and regulators in order to gain a hand in shaping policy

▶ more internal attention on the environmental balance sheet

▶ employees who are inspired and prepared to conserve and innovate

▶ opportunities to become a net emissions reducer and sell offsets to retail or compliance markets at a profit.

The following discussion will present some strategic carbon-offsetting projects that companies might consider to bolster their CSR activities.

Carbon-offsetting projects that complement a CSR strategy

The websites of the Clean Development Mechanism and other organisations that provide voluntary carbon-offsetting services, such as The CarbonNeutral Company, PowerTree Carbon Company, Carbon Footprint Ltd and Carbon Catalog, mention various renewable energy, methane abatement, energy efficiency, reforestation and fuel-switching projects as sources of offsetting that help companies to leverage a higher level of CSR.

Renewable energy offset projects

Generally speaking, renewable energy offsets include investments in wind power, solar power, hydroelectric power and biofuel. Renewable energy projects are crucial for the long-term protection of the global climate because they are the key to moving away from fossil fuel-based economies towards economies that grow on more sustainable forms of energy.

In particular, renewable energy projects based in developing countries have multiple impacts on both climate change and sustainable development. Energy use and development patterns in developing and emerging economies will have a large impact on the climate in the middle and long term. For example, according to a recent study by the Netherlands Environmental Assessment Agency (PBL), the share of global CO_2 emissions from developing countries is slightly higher (50.3%) than that from industrialised countries (46.6%) and international transport (3.2%) together.

Therefore, if developing countries are to leapfrog the fossil-fuel phase for economic development, they need assistance to make renewable energy a key part of their development strategies. In this regard, any kind of investment including renewable energy offsets will have a big role to play.

Energy efficiency offset projects

The main objective of energy efficiency projects is to reduce the overall demand for energy. The World Future Council notes areas such as efficient energy production and transmission, large-scale combined heat and power systems, smart urban transport systems, efficiency standards for vehicles, buildings and appliances, and energy-efficient light bulbs and cooking stoves as measures for energy efficiency. Therefore, companies that seek carbon offsets in this category could fund such projects.

Most of the energy efficiency offsetting projects can be implemented at large industrial facilities. However, smaller projects such as the Efficient Cook-stoves Projects in Darfur and the Democratic Republic of Congo, supported by Carbon Clear Ltd, and JP Morgan Chase's investment in energy-efficient cooking stoves in Uganda have far-reaching sustainability benefits for the local communities in addition to reducing greenhouse gas emissions.

In many developing countries, the main source of fuel is wood, which is used for cooking on an open fire. This fills the kitchen with smoke and creates severe health problems, particularly for mothers and children.

According to the United Nations Population Fund (2001), exposure to indoor pollutants kills more than 2.2 million people each year, over 98% of them in developing countries. Therefore, the effectiveness of such projects in terms of their contribution towards the achievement of the millennium development goals makes them appealing CSR investments for companies.

Land-use and forestry offset projects

Projects that deal with improved forest and agricultural land management, re-forestation and re-vegetation play a very significant role in combating climate change. According to an International Panel on Climate Change (2007) report, deforestation is responsible for the largest share of additional CO_2 released to the atmosphere due to land use changes, approximately 20% of total anthropogenic greenhouse gas emissions annually. Much of the deforestation responsible for CO_2 releases occurs in tropical regions, specifically in developing countries such as Brazil, Indonesia and DR Congo (Sheikh *et al.* 2008).

Forestation projects such as tree planting in India, Eritrea, Kenya, Brazil and the Philippines are among those that generate greenhouse gas credits for companies. Furthermore, such projects can also provide tangible benefits to local communities in terms of transforming their land, crop yields, food security, income and standard of living. Moreover, forestation projects protect the habitat for at-risk species in all parts of the world and specifically in some of the world's most diverse and impoverished places. Both the environmental benefits and the associated sustainability co-benefits support the CSR objectives of companies.

Conclusions and recommendations

While carbon offsetting is establishing itself as one of the major environmental strategies by companies around the world, there are experts and environmental bodies who have concerns about the strategy. Much of the concern emphasises that if companies depend heavily on carbon offsetting to achieve their environmental obligations, they may neglect the internal emission reduction procedures, which have the potential to bring real changes to business environmental behaviour. Therefore, companies should use carbon offsetting as the next option after exhausting their own internal emission reduction procedures.

Moreover, the extent to which companies can benefit from their carbon-offsetting investments depends on the criteria they follow in their decision-making. According to Broekhoff (2007), adhering to the criteria in Box 19.1 will help companies to invest in carbon offsets that have both credibility and effectiveness.

Finally, in order for companies to strengthen their image as leaders in CSR and capitalise on the benefits such as position can bring, they need to give a strategic look on their carbon offsetting investments. The economic and social benefits generated by carbon offsetting projects are indeed valuable sources for corporate reputation and legitimacy which open the opportunity for licence to operate in various corners of the world.

Box 19.1   Criteria to help companies invest in credible and effective carbon offsets

▶ **Real** – offsets should be quantifiable. Greenhouse gas reductions should represent actual emission reductions from tangible sources

▶ **Surplus** – greenhouse gas reductions should be a response to the buyer's promise to purchase them, not reductions that would have happened anyway under 'business as usual' conditions (i.e. they should be 'additional').

▶ **Verifiable** – greenhouse gas reductions should result from projects whose performance can be readily monitored and verified

▶ **Permanent** – greenhouse gas reductions from offsets should be permanent, with safeguards that ensure and replace any reversals

▶ **Enforceable** – offsets should be backed by contracts or legal instruments that define their creation, provide for transparency and ensure exclusive ownership

References

Broekhoff, D. (2007) *Linking Markets for GHG Reductions: Can It Be Done?* International Network for Environmental Compliance and Enforcement. Online: http://www.inece. org/emissions/dublin/Broekhoff.pdf.

Intergovernmental Panel on Climate Change (2007) *Climate Change 2007: Synthesis Report*. Online: www.ipcc.ch/pdf/assessment-report/ar4/syr/ar4_syr.pdf.

Sheikh, P.A., Gorte, R.W. and Sidener, J. (2008) *Climate Change and International Deforestation: Legislative Analysis*, Congressional Research Service (CRS) Reports and Issue Briefs, Congressional Research Service.

SustainAbility (2004) *Gearing Up: From Corporate Responsibility to Good Governance and Scaleable Solutions*, Sustainability, London.

United Nations Population Fund (2001) The State of World Population 2001. Online: http://www.unfpa.org/swp/2001/english/.

Websites

Carbon Catalog – www.carboncatalog.org

Carbon Footprint Ltd – www.carbonfootprint.com

PowerTree Carbon Company – www.powertreecarboncompany.com

The CarbonNeutral Company – www.carbonneutral.com

The Clean Development Mechanism – cdm.unfccc.int/index.html

The World Future Council – www.worldfuturecouncil.org/startseite.html

20

Implementing profitable CSR: the CSR 2.0 business compass

Oliver Laasch and Ulises Flores

Responsible Business: How to Manage a CSR Strategy Successfully
Edited by Manfred Pohl and Nick Tolhurst
Copyright © 2010 Manfred Pohl and Nick Tolhurst

This chapter deals with the relationship between CSR and management, and its potential role in successful business. The authors examine why businesses very often do not have a clear definition of what they are searching for when trying to implement CSR, as well as looking at advanced management tools and real-life examples from international companies.

CSR 2.0 and 3D management

There is a welter of terms to describe attempts to implement corporate social responsibility (CSR) for the creation of tangible benefits and profit. Prominent examples include the very fashionable term 'strategic CSR', the traditional 'search for the business case for CSR', the profoundly scientific 'instrumental CSR' and 'corporate social opportunity'. Each of these terms comes with a rather theoretical set of frameworks, models and ideas. These contributions are undoubtedly valuable on a academic level, but business practitioners in charge of CSR are in urgent need of a practice-oriented and easy-to-understand but extensive management framework for the profitable implementation of CSR. This chapter proposes the CSR 2.0 business compass as the appropriate tool, perfectly appropriate for this task. We will discuss how the CSR 2.0 business compass connects cutting-edge scientific insight with the best practice of some of world's leading corporations, and then introduce a straightforward checklist that every business can use to implement CSR profitably. This chapter contains two central terms, both of them serving to facilitate a very practice- and profit-oriented understanding of CSR:

▶ **3D management.** The general understanding of CSR in this chapter is that of an umbrella term for business disciplines managing not only the business dimension but also the social and environmental dimensions connected to business activity. Referring to these three dimensions, we call this umbrella concept three-dimensional (3D) management. Using this broad definition we can unify various disciplines such as business sustainability, environmental management, business philanthropy, corporate citizenship, business ethics and many others under the broad umbrella of 3D management. That means when we are talking about CSR we are talking about all the topics under the umbrella. This way we can escape the endless discussion about the definition of CSR, which is of little value for its practical application. At the same time 3D management is not a discipline that is only relevant to big corporations, but to any kind of business, whatever the size. For the sake of simplicity we will use CSR interchangeably with 3D management throughout this chapter.

▶ **CSR 2.0.** This is an advanced version of CSR conduct with respect to 3D management with the creation of business value at its heart. At this point a conflict with the term responsibility in CSR arises. As soon as businesses do earn money from practising CSR, it begins to look like a business opportunity rather than a sense of responsibility. As we will see in the following case studies, this is the reason why, for example, Procter & Gamble rarely uses the term CSR and Deutsche Bank even separates responsibility and opportunity in its organisational structure.

In summary, readers will learn about a radically practical and inclusive understanding of CSR – 'corporateSR' that does not talk primarily about corporations but about any form and size of business; 'CsocialR' that not only has a social dimension but environmental and business dimensions as well; and 'CSresponsibility' that is about more than just responsibility, but seeks a business opportunity as well.

The CSR 2.0 business compass

Probably the most innate characteristic of businesses is to strive for profit. Hence, any compass giving guidance to businesses has to point to this very natural business outcome. This is precisely what the CSR 2.0 business compass does. It consists of two opposite poles, CSR 1.0 and 2.0. CSR 2.0 unifies all the different features in the conduct of CSR with all forms of 3D management, which potentially leads to business value creation and profit in one common framework. This CSR 2.0 framework is the positive pole, which the compass helps you to reach. At the same time this framework also includes the opposite type of CSR conduct, which instead hinders business value creation from 3D business activity. This negative pole is called CSR 1.0. The following description is the practice-related summary of an extensive scientific analysis of cutting-edge CSR theory, which will be published in the near future.

The CSR 2.0 business compass uses these two opposite poles in CSR implementation to orientate businesses in terms of what concrete type of CSR conduct they should seek to create business value (CSR 2.0). At the same time it shows which conduct to avoid, since it is unlikely to create value for the business (CSR 1.0). We defined an open list of 23 different statements (see Figure 20.2, p. 305) to be consulted in order to find out whether a business is operating the 1.0 or 2.0 version of CSR. Agreement or otherwise with the statements will help you to determine whether your firm is spending money on CSR or earning money from it. At the same time they give guidance on what to change if you want to move your business towards CSR 2.0. The statements can be grouped into six distinct dimensions. Three dimensions analyse CSR conduct from a business's internal perspective. The other three analyse it from an external perspective. Each of these six dimensions of CSR implementation may be fulfilled in either a 1.0 or 2.0 manner. The following description of these dimensions is based on Figure 20.2.

The three internal dimensions are the type of 'business effect' (I1), the 'mindset and drivers' (I2) and the 'internal implementation' (I3) of CSR. A business can claim to do CSR 2.0 in the 'business effect' dimension when CSR in the company adds high value to the core business, supports and complements the core business functions and demonstrates the characteristics of an investment, yielding tangible financial returns. The typical 'mindset and drivers' of CSR 2.0 are characterised by a viewpoint on CSR as a business opportunity, driven by an innate company interest and pursuing the basic goal of actively generating profit from 3D management.

The 'internal implementation' dimension becomes 2.0 as soon as CSR is closely aligned with the business strategy, not only superficially implementing good values but achieving tangible activity and impact throughout all business functions. These activities should not be financed by philanthropy funds but from the budget of each business unit. Contributions should be done in a physical way, e.g. by employee volunteering or the development of sustainable products.

The three external dimensions include 'location, environment and interaction' (E1), the type of 'stakeholder relationship' (E2) realised as well as the 'causes covered' (E3) by the business. Doing CSR 2.0 in the 'location, environment and interaction' dimension means to tailor the CSR activities to local circumstances and opportunities, to be a driver of change towards more sustainability in the communities in which the company operates and to actively seek local support and innovative input for its activities. A CSR 2.0 stakeholder relationship is characterised by an active engagement, with stakeholders having strategic importance and being granted transparent access to internal company information, which allows for a productive relationship, often even exceeding stakeholders' expectations. The way businesses act in the 'causes covered' dimension is CSR 2.0 when there is a clear focus on one or few causes, which are strategic and close to the core business. The choice of cause should take all three dimensions into consideration, i.e. the social, environmental and business impacts of the cause.

Unlike a normal compass, the CSR 2.0 business compass does not guide the way to a location external to the compass, but instead to its centre: business value and profit. Closest to this business value is CSR 2.0, which is represented by the ring directly surrounding this centre point on the compass. CSR 1.0 is located on the ring on the outer edge of the compass (Figure 20.1). In order to realise value from pursuing CSR, business have to move to the inside of the compass, towards CSR 2.0 and business value in each and every one of the six dimensions. Hence, the task is to manage as many dimensions as possible in a CSR 2.0 instead of CSR 1.0 manner.

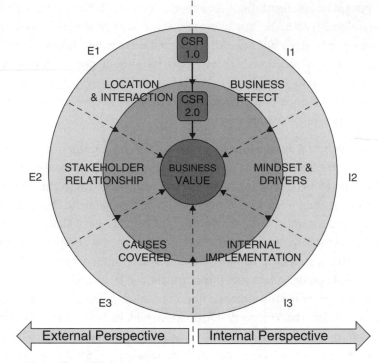

Figure 20.1 The CSR 2.0 business compass.

Due to the versioning characteristics and its parallels with Web 2.0, the CSR framework presented here has been called CSR 2.0. In spite of justified scepticism about the (mostly unrelated) over-use of the term 2.0, the similarities between Web 2.0 and CSR 2.0 are too striking to be neglected. To begin with, the role of internet users has shifted drastically from a passive-receptive content-taking role in Web 1.0 towards an active-creative content-making role in Web 2.0.

This development parallels the shift of businesses, as users of CSR, from a receptive-passive role, doing the things demanded by outside pressure, towards a creative-proactive usage of CSR based of an innate interest. Of course, such a role shift can only occur when the users are equipped with the technical prerequisites facilitating such a shift. In Web 2.0 this prerequisite was the emergence of significantly different web pages and technologies allowing for such user behaviour. In a similar manner CSR 2.0 is based on the development of effective corporate management instruments enabling businesses to take an active role in managing CSR. Shaping the worldwide net according to their own preferences, wants and needs increases the perceived utility for net users. The same effect is seen when companies manage CSR in order to create business value, increasing their own utility from CSR.

The advanced characteristics of Web 2.0 applications have been the reasons for its survival and unquestioned success after the 'new economy' bubble had burst. This catastrophe has been the trigger for the amazing triumph of Web 2.0 over its predecessor, a kind of Darwinian survival of the fittest. This pattern looks set to repeat itself when analysing the current financial and economic crisis and its effect on CSR. It seems reasonable to assume that the deeply implemented, revenue-creating and flexibly managed CSR 2.0 will be sustained and will thrive. Certainly the shallowly integrated, cost-creating, inflexibly managed CSR 1.0 will undergo serious drawbacks. A great deal of evidence for this is already visible. This development calls for a drastic assumption: CSR 1.0 will die during the crisis and make way for the era of CSR 2.0. Borrowing from the traditional proclamation announcing the accession of a new monarch – 'The king is dead, long live the king' – we will experience a historical shift in the way CSR is being conducted – 'CSR 1.0 is dead, long live CSR 2.0'.

CSR 2.0 in practice

This section will serve to provide practical insight into how some of the world's leading corporations in the conduct of CSR manage CSR 2.0 and create business value from it. We have deliberately selected worldwide leaders in the widest range of sectors from vastly different regions. This way we hope to convince on one point: it is possible to implement CSR 2.0 profitably under almost any circumstances, independently of industry parameters, culture or location. In the following you will get to know six corporate role models, each of them being leader in one of the six dimensions of profitable CSR implementation. As you will see, along with the successful business implementation of CSR, the enterprises discussed here are able to make a real difference for their respective social and environmental causes.

Business effect – the Toyota Prius driving sustainable business value

Toyota is not only one of the world's biggest car producers, it is also in the vanguard for CO_2-friendly vehicles. Most notably Toyota developed the first mass-produced hybrid vehicle, the Prius. After 15 years and three model generations of the Prius, an analysis of its business effect, as one of the most successful sustainable innovations, is an intriguing topic.

Colin Hensley, general manager, Corporate Affairs & Planning at Toyota Motor Europe, says the Prius started as a principle and turned into a profit. He refers to the change in perception from the first model Prius 1 to the Prius 3. The Prius 1 was a trailblazer for CO_2-friendly cars, being of undoubtedly high value for sustainable development. The newest model, the Prius 3, also offers a set of features that are attractive to a wide range of different customers and therefore has the basis for real commercial success. This has even led to periods where Toyota was not able to serve the global demand for the Prius. As Mr Hensley puts it, 'We were not able to produce the cars quickly enough.' He also stresses that the Prius clearly complements and supports Toyota's core business, as we explain below. He adds that the Prius continues to show itself to be a great investment for Toyota. Of course, its development and implementation were very expensive, but this investment increasingly has paid off.

Mr Hensley outlines an impressive list of business values that Toyota has gained from the sustainable innovation Prius. Firstly, one of the main reasons for the development of the Prius was the sustainability of the company itself. With the Prius, Toyota created a basis to uncouple itself from the fossil fuel dependency of the car industry. Anticipating the finite nature of fossil fuels, this is a necessary step to sustain the business itself. Secondly, the Prius has established Toyota's leadership in of low-CO_2 emission vehicles. This has tapped into an attractive customer group, which would not have considered buying a Toyota before this. He says this has opened up a new dimension for the company and had a positive knock-on effect for the rest of the core business. Thirdly, he mentions that the Prius created learning experiences, which helped to develop different areas in the company. It supported the engineering function by creating an invaluable understanding of how to combine different technologies. This was also useful know-how for systems integration, crucial for managing the various electronic devices combined in today's automobiles. In addition, the Prius experience forced Toyota to develop a competence to explain technology and its benefits to customers, which is essential for the translation of technological innovation into tangible revenues.

Mindset and drivers – opportunity thinking at Procter & Gamble

Procter & Gamble (P&G) had a revenue of US$83.503 billion in 2008 and manages more than 20 different billion-dollar brands. It is one of the leading multinational corporations when it comes to its core business activities. At the same time P&G is an impressive leader in corporate sustainability. The company has already generated more than $2 billion revenue from sustainable products in 2008. This is the first tangible outcome of the commitment P&G made in 2007 to produce $20 billion revenue from this product category by 2012. At the beginning of 2009, P&G decided to raise this goal to a massive $50 billion revenue from products with a notably improved environmental footprint. These impressive numbers are based on a fundamental shift in the mindset and drivers of sustainability. P&G actively searches for opportunities in sustainability.

Peter White, global head of sustainability at P&G, hardly talks about social and environmental responsibility since it does not reflect the way P&G

thinks about this topic. He tends instead to talk about business opportunities in sustainability. Sustainability at P&G is more about strategically building the company than merely protecting it. Consequently, there is no trade-off between acting sustainably and doing business. Mr White reminds us of the fact that the concept of sustainability is not just about acting socially and environmentally well, but also about excelling in the economic and business dimensions. The 'no trade-off' paradigm also holds true for the firm's attitude towards innovating new sustainable products. P&G realises sustainable innovation that gives consumers both an additional sustainability value and improved performance of the product. Mr White stresses the importance of sharing this very distinct mindset among all employees in all functions of the company. Only in this way can sustainability truly be built into the rhythm of the company. CSR at P&G is certainly a true complement to the traditional business activity. But Peter White says it is even more than that: it is part of the very DNA of doing business at P&G.

P&G has channelled this mindset into five concrete sustainability strategies. Each of these strategies not only fosters sustainability, but also has a business purpose, providing business opportunity. Strategy 1 is about sustainable products. The business purpose here is be to keep and win customers and revenues. Strategy 2 is eco-efficiency in operations. Mr White explains the business effect of eco-efficient operations by revealing the double meaning of the prefix 'eco' in the P&G dictionary. Eco-efficiency here means both ecological and economic efficiency. Acting ecologically efficient fosters an economic efficiency, which in turn tangibly saves money by improved usage of resources.

Strategy 3 deals with P&G's social responsibility, facilitating a social investment into the communities in which P&G operates. This investment pays off in various ways for the business. Benefits might be a better recruitment situation inside these communities, improved public relations or better employee motivation. Strategy 4 aims at engaging and equipping P&G's employees for the sustainability-related tasks. Mr White calls this the key to achieve the first three strategies and stresses the importance that, in performing their everyday duties, employees should achieve P&G's sustainability goals as a whole. Strategy 5 focuses on close stakeholder engagement. The business value of this strategy is to use stakeholders' ideas, know-how and criticism as an input for continuous improvement at P&G. German Saenz, the communication and sustainability manager for P&G in Latin America, explains that these global strategies cascade down into every function, business unit, geography and country. This results in a wide variety of different sub-strategies, each contributing a distinct set of value for P&G.

Location and interaction – sustainability for every occasion at the Royal Bank of Scotland Group[1]

The Royal Bank of Scotland Group (RBS) as one of the world's biggest financial institutions operates in 54 very different countries. Regional and cultural differences do not only pose challenges to the traditional banking business, but also to the management of corporate social responsibility and sustainability. RBS manages an amazing variety of different CSR and sustainability activities in very diverse locations. Examples throughout the year 2008 include for instance the leading role in establishing the world's largest solar power plant in Spain and the award for the best Islamic product in Malaysia. In the homeland of RBS, the United Kingdom, the focus is on financial education and the support of small and medium enterprises.

Analyzing these examples, it becomes clear how RBS adapts CSR and sustainability activities to the most different environments, locations and cultures. RBS presents a dominant and clearly shaped global sustainability strategy. Still, this global framework allows for highly localized sustainability activities. The process itself seems highly sensitive to local musts and needs. As will be shown in the following paragraph some CSR activities are more advantageous in one region than another.

RBS was lead arranger and financed the world's largest solar photovoltaic power plant in Spain which as a location for this specific activity is an advantageous choice. The European Union is highly supportive in the development of renewable energies, especially photovoltaic solar power. Southern Spain, being one of the regions with most sunshine hours per year on European Union ground, increases technical productivity improves the basis for profitability. RBS is in the vanguard of the promising new business field of Islamic finance and even won the award for the best Islamic with its Al-Sayf-structured Islamic deposit in Malaysia. Supporting the cause of providing financial products which are Shariah-based and compliant with Islamic standards finds a fertile breeding ground in Malaysia which has an Islamic majority and directly neighbours with Indonesia, which reflects more than 15% of the Muslim world population; an immense market for Islamic finance products. RBS strengthened its activities on United Kingdom ground especially in topics, which are strongly aligned with economic policy goals. The financial education program 'Money Sense', has been extended in 2008 and now also reaches out to adults. RBS also has massively strengthened its lending effort for the support of small and medium enterprises. Both activities seem strongly aligned with the local need for financial and economic stability in the financial-crisis-stricken United Kingdom. The decisive local factor in this example is the commitment resulting from the support which RBS received in order to cope with consequences of the world financial crisis by the government of the United Kingdom. This commitment can only be fulfilled on United Kingdom ground.

Stakeholder relationship – solid win-win for Coca-Cola and the WWF

The Coca-Cola Company (TCCC) and the World Wildlife Fund for Nature (WWF) are, at first sight, two very different organisations. The biggest common point might be that both are leaders in their respective fields. TCCC is one of the world's leading beverage companies, best known for its flagship brand Coca-Cola, while the WWF is the world's largest independent nature conservation organisation, which most people associate with its logo, the panda. Both these organisations, regardless of their differences, have joined forces on a global scale for the cause of water. TCCC not only productively co-operates with the WWF in a wide variety of projects related to water efficiency and freshwater conservation, but also funds the project with a budget of more than $23 million up to 2012. And as that figure suggests, there is something special about this partnership.

We spoke to both partners. Pablo Largacha is vice president of public affairs and communications at the Latin Center Business Unit of TCCC, and Katherine Neebe is senior programme officer, business and industry, at the World Wildlife Fund and the day-to-day manager of the partnership with TCCC. Both agree that this partnership is special and very beneficial to both sides. One of the main reasons for this is that both organisations have a profound mutual interest: water. Preserving the world's freshwater resources assures the key ingredient for the beverages Coca Cola produces, both in the production process and in the end-product. At the same time, water is the basic life-giving element of nature, which the WWF has set out to preserve. This mutual interest is the most important basis for the success of this unprecedented partnership.

Pablo Largacha gives us some insights from the business perspective, highlighting the corporate behaviour that fosters successful stakeholder engagement at TCCC. Firstly, he stresses the importance of strategically determining which stakeholder to engage with. The scattergun approach, trying to serve all stakeholders at the same time, dilutes efforts. Hence, a diligent stakeholder mapping and prioritisation process served to identify which of these TCCC wanted to work with in order to forward its global sustainability priorities. On top of these global priority stakeholders, he highlights the importance of more local stakeholder groups. Secondly, he stresses the importance and challenge of cultural change inside the company when working with stakeholders. This change has to embrace both thought and action. From his experience at TCCC, this process consists of the following steps. Companies first have to start searching, then reaching out and listening to stakeholders. Businesses then invite their stakeholders to the company and try to learn from them. The final step is to work with them and, at the most advanced level, to enter into partnership, such as that established with WWF. Thirdly, Mr Largacha stresses the importance of transparency. Especially for a company such as TCCC, which has been built up on a secret – that of the recipe for Coca-Cola itself – transparency is a delicate issue. Still, TCCC actively fosters access to the operations of the stakeholder's interest. The fourth and last recommendation is to behave proactively, listen, learn and change, before stakeholders become aggressive.

Asked about the value created for the partners, both interviewees pinpoint the trust that has grown up between them as the most important value. Such close co-operation between businesses and stakeholders helps to get rid of stereotypes, such as the 'bad company' with the sole interest of making money or the 'aggressive NGO' trying to destroy businesses. This trust-building in turn creates a better basis for working together productively, often exceeding the main subject of co-operation. Mr Largacha also stresses that the sustainability work of TCCC delivers an additional differentiation feature, which results in tangible brand preference and a competitive advantage. He has found that, especially among younger consumers, purchasing decisions are increasingly being made according to the ethical and sustainability behaviour of the company behind the product. Mr Largacha also mentions the value of learning and improvement in the business triggered by input from stakeholders. Ms Neebe adds that the partnership holds benefits for both the environment and business. When it comes to negotiations over water, TCCC and WWF have a joint bargaining position, which is much more powerful than each organisation acting alone.

Cause choice – the right cause for strategy and society at Cinépolis

Cinépolis is the fifth biggest cinema chain in the world. It operates more than 2,000 screens, mostly in Latin America. It has an extensive and multifaceted CSR programme, but bundles all of its activities into three main causes: visual health, education in the arts of cinema, and 'Let's all go to Cinépolis'. These causes are all very close to the core business and activity of Cinépolis, which is showing movies.

Lorena Guille-Laris, executive director of the Cinépolis Foundation gave us a detailed insight into the strategic cause choice made by Cinépolis. Its flagship cause, visual health, consists mainly of the activities in the campaign *'Del Amor Nace la Vista'* ('Love Gives Birth to Eyesight'). In 2008 the Cinépolis Foundation organised more than 3,000 operations restoring eyesight to blind people. Secondly, Cinépolis focuses on 'education in the arts of cinema', which covers a wide variety of movie-related activities. It promotes, for instance, the creation of short films on social topics such as human rights or drug addiction. Thirdly, Cinépolis creates the opportunity for people from economically challenged communities to go to the cinema. The campaign is called 'Let's all go to Cinépolis'. It is clear that these causes are closely tied to Cinépolis' business activity, showing movies. Ms Guille-Laris explains that this focus stems from the close alignment of the causes with Cinépolis' history as well as its social and business strategy. What results is a close focus on three main causes, all of them making a real difference for both society and environment.

Ms Guille-Laris explains that Cinépolis realises business value as a result of its CSR activities. She sees the CSR activity of Cinépolis as one of the main strategic advantages. Since the cinema market has a limited growth potential, the creation of differentiating features is vital. CSR at Cinépolis delivers such a differentiation feature, a result highlighted by the statistic that 70% of the firm's customers recognise its social responsibility. Ms Guille-Laris also points out that 75% of customers, when faced with the choice between identical products, tend to buy the one produced by a company that is perceived as socially responsible. At the same time, CSR delivers a great communication tool. Eighteen per cent of the media coverage on Cinépolis in 2008 was related to the social activity of the company. Ms Guille-Laris also highlights the strengthened relationships Cinépolis has with government agencies due to its CSR activity. A very important business value is also realised in the workforce of Cinépolis.

Ms Guille-Laris refers to advantages in recruitment and retention as well as increased motivation of employees as a result of Cinépolis' CSR activities.

The CSR 2.0 check

Which version is your CSR?

You have seen how the five CSR 2.0 corporate role models deploy 3D management for the creation of tangible business value and, ultimately, profit. It is time now to have a look at the CSR activity in your own company, your industry or the role of CSR in the economy of your country. You will find either the old-fashioned and expensive version of CSR 1.0 or the advanced and profit-creating CSR 2.0. We developed the CSR conduct questionnaire (Figure 20.2), consisting of 23 statements checking on the six dimensions of the CSR 2.0 business compass. Each statement gives two answer choices, one being CSR 2.0, the other CSR 1.0. Using the two columns on the right, you can interpret these results to determine in which of the six dimensions you are in CSR 2.0 and in which ones you are not.

When interpreting the results you might come to several conclusions. In the optimum case, you will find that you clearly cover the 2.0 version in all six dimensions. Congratulations, you are there already. It is possible that your business does have a very positive impact on society and the environment while making decent money from it. It is more likely, however, that you are caught somewhere in between 1.0 and 2.0. You might, for instance, be clearly 2.0 from the external perspective: you closely engage a strategic set of stakeholders, focus on a cause close to your core business and actively change your environment towards more sustainability. At the same time your internal perspective might be more oriented towards CSR 1.0: you see CSR as spending money, focusing on the business's responsibility while not realising the opportunities that are there, and having a shallow integration of CSR into your core business. This is like being CSR 1.5. Most likely, you are fulfilling your stakeholders' expectations in terms

I. Model		II. Questionnaire		III. Results					
				Statement		Dimension		Perspective	
Dimensions		CSR 1.0	CSR 2.0	1.0	2.0	1.0	2.0	1.0	2.0
Internal Perspective	I1: Business effect	CSR at my company delivers no or low value to my core business.	CSR at my company adds a high value to my core business.						
		CSR disturbs/corrodes the functions of my core business.	CSR supports and/or complements the functions of my core business.						
		CSR at my company is a mere expense. It will not yield tangible returns.	CSR at my company is an investment. It will yield tangible returns.						
	I2: Mindset & drivers	My company conducts CSR merely in order to avoid losses.	My company conducts CSR, not only to avoid losses, but also in order to generate profits.						
		CSR/Sustainability in my company is merely driven by a company external, third party interest.	CSR in my company is mainly driven by an innate, company internal interest.						
		My company sees CSR as a mere responsibility.	My company mainly sees CSR as an opportunity.						
	I3: Internal implementation	CSR activity is characterized by the promotion of social and environmental values but there is merely a tangible activity and impact.	My company's CSR activity translates my company's social and environmental values into tangible activity and impact.						
		CSR at my enterprise is loosely aligned or unaligned with the company's strategy.	CSR at my enterprise is closely aligned with the company's strategy.						
		CSR at my company is conducted by single/isolated business functions.	CSR at my company is implemented throughout all/most business functions.						
		Funding for CSR activities comes mainly from a centrally managed philanthropy budget.	Funding for CSR activities comes mainly from the business units it is conducted in.						
		My company and employees rather contribute by financial donations to the bettering of causes.	My company and employees contributed physically (e.g. employee volunteering, sustainable products) to selected causes.						
External Perspective	E1: Location & interaction	My company rather seeks to avoid CSR-related penalties and taxation.	My company also seeks for local CSR-related external support and input such as stakeholder feedback, subsidies or involvement.						
		My company does CSR in a "one fits all" environments and locations approach.	My company tailors CSR activities to the local circumstances and opportunities.						
		My company adopts merely mature CSR trends from its environment and location.	My company actively seeks to change its environment and location towards more sustainability.						
	E2: Stakeholder relationship	My company rather tries to contain stakeholder claims.	My company tends to engage actively and productively with stakeholders.						
		My company selectively reports the information we consider adequate for our stakeholders.	My company fosters transparency by stakeholder's access to internal information.						
		My company arbitrarily engages with various kinds of stakeholders.	My company systematically engages with stakeholders having strategic importance.						
		My company serves stakeholders' basic expectations.	My company exceeds stakeholder's basic expectations.						
	E3: Causes covered	The causes my company covers by CSR activities are rather distant from our core business or company theme.	The causes my company's CSR activity covers are very close and strategic to our core business or company theme.						
		My company tries to cover as many causes as possible.	My company tries to focus on one or very few causes.						
		When choosing a cause, my company rather considers the socio-environmental impact of the engagement for the causes.	Choosing a cause, my company considers both, the socio-environmental as well as the business impact of the engagement.						
IV. Scores									

Annotation: CSR in this context is to be understood as any business activity having an environmental and social impact (3 Dimensional Management). Hence, it would also include topics such as sustainability, business ethics, environmental management, philanthropy etc.

Figure 20.2 The CSR 2.0 questionnaire.

of your social responsibilities, but you are not able to earn money from practising CSR.

Corporate social responsibility thus becomes more profitable when more dimensions of the CSR business compass are conducted in the 2.0 style, since the dimensions form a mutually reinforcing system. The good news about this is that as soon as you start seriously moving one dimension towards CSR 2.0, the others are very likely to follow suit. If, for instance, you start tuning your 'mindset and drivers' (I2) towards 2.0, i.e. you start to see CSR as a possibility to create value for your business, this will ultimately also tune in the other dimensions on CSR 2.0. You will change your 'internal implementation' (I3) towards a deeper integration of CSR in your core business, which in turn creates the need to strategically manage your 'stakeholder relationships' (E2) and 'cause choice' (E3). In the dimension 'location, environment and interaction' (E1) you will start localising CSR activities in order to enable the strategic stakeholder and cause choice. The consequence of all these changes towards the 2.0 version will be a change in the 'business effect' (I1) CSR realises inside your enterprise: CSR will start to complement and support your core business. It will become a real investment, paying back in tangible business value. You will be able to earn money from doing good things, because you implemented the advanced version of CSR conduct: CSR 2.0 for profit.

When using the CSR business compass and questionnaire, you should not forget that your CSR programme is unlikely ever to be entirely 2.0. There will always be room for innovation and continuous improvement. For instance, you can use the CSR business compass for more in-depth checking not only of whole-company policies, but also every single CSR activity your business is conducting. The optimum application of the CSR business compass would be to conduct an initial check of all your 3D activities. You should not hesitate to change, or even dispense with, non-profitable CSR activities, while starting a creative process of establishing truly profitable CSR 2.0. After these changes, your company should implement a CSR 2.0 check on a regular basis to achieve a continuous improvement. In this way, you will be well on your way to setting a new standard for an even more advanced and profitable CSR 3.0.

Checked CSR 2.0 in all dimensions: Cemex

A role-model company that has already conducted the CSR 1.0–2.0 check with great success is the Mexico-based Cemex. It is the world's largest building materials supplier and third largest cement producer. To begin with, all CSR and sustainability activities at Cemex have to be self-sustaining in financial terms. With this prerequisite, the creation of business value, which is the centrepiece of the CSR business compass, is achieved almost automatically. At this point CSR truly ceases to be spending and begins to be about actively earning money. The converse argument is that, if Cemex is able to create business value from each of its CSR activities, it must be doing a lot of things correctly in terms of the CSR business compass.

Martha Herrera, in her capacity as director of social responsibility and community development, describes how Cemex conducts CSR 2.0 in all six dimensions. From an internal perspective, the 'business effect' (I1) of CSR at Cemex is value creation. CSR is seen as an investment which has to yield positive returns and hence adds value to its core business. 'Mindset and drivers' (I2) of CSR at Cemex come from a view of CSR not just as a responsibility but also as a business opportunity. A good example is the engagement of Cemex with the housing shortage in Mexico. The lack of shelter amongst the poor is something that requires urgent action, but it is also an opportunity for Cemex to gain access to an attractive niche market for its products. The internal implementation is characterised by delivering tangible activity and impact. Each of Cemex's four main stakeholder groups – employees, neighbourhoods, business partners and the natural environment – is connected to tangible indices facilitating a sound social and environmental performance record. While CSR is supported by a core department, it is actively conducted throughout all of Cemex's business units and functions. More than 3,000 employees offer not only their time but also their professional expertise to support worthy causes.

From an external perspective, throughout the process of 'cause choice' (E3) Cemex seeks out fields of activity that are strategically close to its core business. One of its three main causes is 'education for self-employment'. Here Cemex sets out to improve the level of education in the neighbourhoods of its business locations. Ms Herrera explains that this cause is strategic to Cemex's core business because the educational activities, while benefiting the learners, also provides the human resources that Cemex needs to grow, such as employees or suppliers. The 'stakeholder relationship' (E2) at Cemex is a clearly strategic management task. The four stakeholder groups have been identified as being crucial to the success of the core business. With regard to the last dimension, 'location, environment and interaction' (E1), Cemex neighbourhood and community programmes show how business can seek out local input and opportunities while tailoring their CSR activities to local needs. For instance, the organisation of community councils by Cemex in its business locations is an effective tool for tuning in to local circumstances, in order to detect needs and business opportunities or to receive valuable feedback.

Cemex is an impressive role model for truly implementing profitable CSR: CSR 2.0. One impressive statistic underlining this success story is that Cemex did not have to make any cutbacks to its social and environmental programmes during the economic crisis that began in 2008–09. CSR 2.0 is the CSR for times of crisis.

Conclusion and outlook

We hope you have been persuaded that CSR 2.0 is a straightforward, but detailed, tool for the profitable implementation of CSR. At the same time we hope we have contributed to a more integrative and practical understanding of CSR and neighbouring disciplines by introducing the concept of 3D management. Our biggest hope is that businesses actively start using these concepts for the good of all three dimensions. We are looking forward to see businesses implementing CSR 2.0 and making sound profit from it. We are looking forward even more to observing how this will provide a natural business incentive to engage in social and environmental causes to a greater degree. We strongly believe that this increased engagement is one of the keys to solving the severe social and environmental problems our planet is facing. The fascinating paradox here is that we can save the world by making a profit. [1]

Acknowledgements

The authors would like to thank the following for their invaluable support: Colin Hensley, General Manager, Corporate Affairs & Planning, Toyota Motor Europe; Edith Puerschel, Chief Integration Officer/Head of Brand & CSR Strategy, Deutsche Bank; Frank Ros, Assistant Vice President, The Coca-Cola Company; German Saenz, Corporate Communication & Sustainability Manager, P&G Latin America; Héctor Mauricio Escamilla Santana, Director-General, ITESM San Luis Potosi; Hilda Catalina Cruz, Vice Rector for Social Development, ITESM; Juan González Pérez, Director, Department for Ethics and Citizenship, ITESM San Luis Potosi; Katherine Neebe, Senior Program Officer, Business and Industry, World Wildlife Fund; Lorena Guillé-Laris, Executive Director, Cinépolis Foundation; Martha Herrera, Director of Social Responsibility and Community Development, Cemex; Michael Hoelz, Group Sustainability Officer, Deutsche Bank; Pablo Largacha, Vice President of Public Affairs and Communications, Latin Center Business Unit, The Coca-Cola Company; Peter White, Global Head of Sustainability, Procter & Gamble; and the research team comprising Alejandro Guerrero, Aranzazu Gomez, Carlos Mancilla, Fernando Diaz, Rogelio Munoz (all ITESM, Campus San Luis Potosi).

The complete interviews are available for download as podcast at: http:// csrmanagementfbo.ning.com/group/3DManagementPodcast.

Footnote

1 The text is based on the RBS sustainability report 2008.

21
CSR 2.0: the evolution and revolution of corporate social responsibility

Wayne Visser

Responsible Business: How to Manage a CSR Strategy Successfully
Edited by Manfred Pohl and Nick Tolhurst
Copyright © 2010 Manfred Pohl and Nick Tolhurst

In this chapter, the author describes the historical development of CSR and provides a glimpse of how it is likely to develop in future. He argues that CSR in its present form has only gone so far and outlines how the next step – CSR 2.0 – will become less Western-orientated and risk-averse, and evolve from niche 'nice-to-have' CSR into mass-market 'must-have' CSR, which will be incorporated into 'companies' DNA'.

The rise and fall of CSR

Corporate social responsibility (CSR) has been debated and practised in one form or another for more than 4,000 years. The ancient *Vedic* and *Sutra* texts of Hinduism and the *Jatakas* of Buddhism include ethical admonitions on usury (the charging of excessive interest), and Islam has long advocated the use of *zakat*, or a wealth tax (Visser & McIntosh 1998). The modern concept of CSR can be traced to the mid-to-late 1800s, with industrialists like John H. Patterson of National Cash Register seeding the industrial welfare movement, and philanthropists like John D. Rockefeller setting a charitable precedent that we see echoed more than 100 years later with the likes of Bill Gates (Carroll 2008).

Despite these early variations, CSR only entered the popular lexicon in the 1950s with R. Bowen's landmark book, *Social Responsibilities of the Businessman* (Bowen 1953). The concept was challenged and strengthened in the 1960s with the birth of the environmental movement, following Rachel Carson's critique of the chemicals industry in *Silent Spring* (Carson 1962), and that of the consumer movement arising out of Ralph Nader's social activism, most famously over General Motors's safety record (Nader 1965).

The 1970s saw the emergence of the first widely accepted definition of CSR – Archie Carroll's four-part concept of economic, legal, ethical and philanthropic responsibilities, later depicted as a CSR pyramid (Carroll 1979) – as well as the first CSR code, the Sullivan Principles. The 1980s brought the application of quality management to occupational health and safety and the introduction of CSR codes such as 'Responsible Care'.

In the 1990s, CSR was institutionalised with standards like ISO 14001 and SA8000, guidelines like the Global Reporting Initiative (GRI) and corporate governance codes like Cadbury and King. The 21st century has mostly seen more of the same, spawning a plethora of CSR guidelines, codes and standards (there are more than 100 listed in *The A to Z of Corporate Social Responsibility*), with industry sector and climate-change variations on the theme.

So why is a potted history of CSR important in a discussion about the future? First, it is to emphasise that CSR is a dynamic movement that has been evolving over decades, if not centuries. But second, and perhaps more importantly, it is to acknowledge that, despite this seemingly impressive steady march of progress, CSR has failed. Moreover, what we are witnessing is the decline of CSR, which will continue until its natural death, unless it is reborn and rejuvenated.

This is a bold claim, and as such it deserves substantiation. CSR has undoubtedly had many positive impacts, for communities and the environment. Yet, its success or failure should be judged in the context of the total impacts of business on society and the planet. Viewed in this way, on virtually every measure of social, ecological and ethical performance we have available, the negative impacts of business have been an unmitigated disaster, which CSR has completely failed to avert or even substantially moderate.

A few facts will suffice to make the point: our global ecological footprint has tripled since 1961; WWF's Living Planet Index shows a 29% species decline since 1970; and 60% of the world's ecosystems have been degraded, according to the Millennium Ecosystem Assessment. We do not fare much better on social issues: according to the United Nations Development Programme (UNDP), 2.5 billion people still live on less than $2 a day; one billion have no access to safe water; and 2.6 billion lack access to sanitation.

What about ethical issues? There's not much good news there either. In 2007, one in 10 people around the world had to pay a bribe to get services. Before Enron collapsed in fraudulent disgrace in 2001, *Fortune* magazine had voted it one of the '100 Best Companies to Work for in America' – in 2000. More worrying still, Enron had all the CSR codes, reports and practices you would expect from a socially responsible company. 'Houston, we have a problem!'

The failure of CSR

Why has CSR failed so spectacularly to address the very issues it claims to be most concerned about? This comes down to three factors – the 'triple curse' of modern CSR, if you like.

Curse 1: Incremental CSR

One of the great revolutions of the 1970s was total quality management, conceived by American statistician W. Edwards Deming, perfected by the Japanese and exported around the world as ISO 9001. At the very core of Deming's TQM model and the ISO standard is continual improvement, a principle that has now become ubiquitous in all management system approaches to performance. It is no surprise, therefore, that the most popular environmental management standard, ISO 14001, is also built on the same principle.

There is nothing wrong with continuous improvement *per se*. On the contrary, it has brought safety and reliability to the very products and services that we associate with a modern quality of life. But when we use it as the primary approach to tackling our social, environmental and ethical challenges, it fails on two critical counts: speed and scale. The incremental approach of CSR, while replete with evidence of micro-scale, gradual improvements, has completely and utterly failed to make any impact on the massive sustainability crises that we face, many of which are getting worse at a pace that far outstrips any futile CSR-led attempts at amelioration.

Curse 2: Peripheral CSR

Ask any CSR manager what their greatest frustration is and they will tell you: lack of top management commitment. This is 'code' for saying that CSR is, at best, a peripheral function in most companies. There may be a CSR manager, a CSR department even, a CSR report and a public commitment to any number of CSR codes and standards. But these do little to mask the underlying truth that shareholder-driven capitalism is rampant and its obsession with short-term financial measures of progress is contradictory in almost every way to the long-term, stakeholder approach needed for high-impact CSR. The reason Enron collapsed, and indeed why our current financial crisis was allowed to spiral out of control, was not because of a few rogue executives or creative accounting practices; it was because of a culture of greed embedded in the DNA of the company and the financial markets. Joel Baken (2004) goes so far as to suggest that companies are legally bound to act like psychopaths. Whether you agree or not (and despite the emerging research on 'responsible competitiveness'), it is hard to find any substantive examples in which the financial markets reward responsible behaviour.

Curse 3: Uneconomic CSR

If there was ever a monotonously repetitive, stuck record in CSR debates, it is the one about the so-called 'business case' for CSR. That is because CSR managers and consultants, and even the occasional saintly CEO, are desperate to find compelling evidence that 'doing good is good for business', i.e. CSR pays! And indeed, the lack of sympathetic research seems to be no impediment for these desperados endlessly incanting the motto of the business case, as if it were an entirely self-evident fact.

The rather more 'inconvenient truth' is that CSR sometimes pays, in specific circumstances, but more often does not. Of course, there are low-hanging fruit – like eco-efficiencies around waste and energy – but these only go so far. Most of the hard-core CSR changes that are needed to reverse the misery of poverty and the sixth mass extinction of species that is currently under way require strategic change and massive investment. They may very well be lucrative in the long term, economically rational over a generation or two, but we have already established that the financial markets don't work like that – at least, not yet.

CSR 1.0: burying the past

What would be far more productive than all this wishing and pretending that CSR is good and fluffy and cuddly and will help to solve the world's problems is to simply see it for what it is: an outdated, outmoded artifact that was once useful, but whose time has past. We need to let the 'old CSR' die gracefully and give it a dignified burial. By all means, let us give it the respect it deserves – a fitting eulogy about brave new frontiers of responsibility that it conquered in its heyday. But let us then look for the next generation of CSR – the newborn that will carry the torch forward. (At the launch of CSR International in March 2009, this is exactly what we did – we held a mock funeral with a coffin, out of which the new CSR baby was born. See www.csrinternational.org for a video of the ceremony.)

If we succeed in admitting the failure of CSR and burying the past, we may find ourselves on the cusp of a revolution, in much the same way as the internet transitioned from Web 1.0 to Web 2.0. The emergence of social media networks, user-generated content and open-source approaches is a fitting metaphor for the changes CSR will have to undergo if it is to redefine its contribution and make a serious impact on the social, environmental and ethical challenges the world faces.

For example, in the same way that Web 1.0 moved from a one-way, advertising-push approach to a more collaborative Google/Facebook mode, CSR 1.0 is starting to move beyond the outmoded approach of CSR as philanthropy or public relations (which has been widely criticised as 'greenwash') to a more interactive, stakeholder-driven model. Similarly, while Web 1.0 was dominated by standardised hardware and software, but now encourages co-creation and diversity, so too in CSR we are beginning to realise the limitations of the generic CSR codes and standards that have proliferated in the past 10 years.

Table 21.1 Similarities between Web 1.0/2.0 and CSR 1.0/2.0

Web 1.0	CSR 1.0
A flat world just beginning to connect itself and finding a new medium to push out information and plug advertising	A vehicle for companies to establish relationships with communities, channel philanthropic contributions and manage their image
Saw the rise to prominence of innovators like Netscape, but these were quickly out-muscled by giants like Microsoft with Internet Explorer	Included many start-up pioneers like Traidcraft, but has ultimately turned into a product for large multinationals such as Royal Dutch Shell
Focused largely on the standardised hardware and software of the PC as its delivery platform, rather than multi-level applications	Travelled down the road of 'one size fits all' standardisation, through codes, standards and guidelines to shape its offering
Web 2.0	**CSR 2.0**
Being defined by watch-words like 'collective intelligence', 'collaborative networks' and 'user participation'	Being defined by 'global commons', 'innovative partnerships' and 'stakeholder involvement'
Tools include social media, knowledge syndication and beta testing	Mechanisms include diverse stakeholder panels, real-time transparent reporting and new-wave social entrepreneurship
Is as much a state of being as a technical advance – it is a new philosophy or way of seeing the world differently	Recognising a shift in power from centralised to decentralised; a change in scale from few and big to many and small; and a change in application from single and exclusive to multiple and shared

The similarities between Web 1.0/2.0 and CSR 1.0/2.0 are illustrated in Table 21.1.

CSR 2.0: embracing the future

Let us explore in more detail this revolution that will, if successful, change the way we talk about and practise CSR and, ultimately, the way we do business. There are five principles that make up the DNA of CSR 2.0:

C   connectedness

S   scalability

R   responsiveness

2   duality

0   circularity

Principle 1: Connectedness (C)

In order to succeed in the CSR revolution, business has to break the hegemony of shareholders. It is as if companies are mere serfs in the kingdom of shareholder-value capitalism. They may appear to wield extraordinary power, but in reality they are subservient to invisible share-holders, bowed before the throne of financial markets and at the beck and call of City analysts. Most CEOs don't last more than three years and are slaves to stock price fluctuations during that time.

The only way to take the power back is to move from subservience to connectedness. Business has to start to institutionalise (and thereby legiti-mise) multi-stakeholder relationships. When the chemicals industry created their Responsible Care programme in 1985, in the wake of a spree of disasters like Seveso and Bhopal, it was a typical CSR 1.0 approach – unilateral, defensive and incremental. By contrast, the emergence of various multi-stakeholder initiatives in the 1990s, such as the Forest Stewardship Council and AccountAbility 1000, begins to give a glimpse of how the connectedness principle of CSR 2.0 may increasingly manifest.

In 1994, when McDonald's took two activists to court for criticising the company, their bullying tactics backfired and 'McLibel' (as the case came to be known in the popular media) turned into the longest trial in British legal history (313 days), creating a PR disaster for the company. By contrast, when Rio Tinto actively sought out a cross-sector partnership with the World Conservation Union to progressively tackle its biodiversity impacts, it showed a sensitivity to multi-stakeholder connectedness that was so patently lacking in McDonald's approach.

Principle 2: Scalability (S)

The CSR literature is liberally sprinkled with charming case studies of truly responsible and sustainable projects. The problem is that so few of them ever go to scale. It is almost as if, once the sound-bites and PR plaudits have been achieved, no further action is required. They become shining pilot projects and best-practice examples, tarnished only by the fact that they are endlessly repeated on the CSR conference circuits of the world, without any vision for how they might transform the core business of their progenitors.

The sustainability problems we face, be they climate change or poverty, are at such a massive scale, and are so urgent, that any CSR solutions that cannot match that scale and urgency are red herrings at best and evil diversions at worst. How long have we been tinkering away with ethical consumerism (organic, fairtrade and the like), with hardly any impact on the world's major corporations or supply chains? And yet, when Wal-Mart's former CEO, Lee Scott, had his post-Katrina Damascus experience and decided that all cotton will be organic and all fish MSC-certified, we started seeing CSR 2.0-type scalability.

There have always been charitable loans for the world's poor and destitute. But when Muhammad Yunus, in the aftermath of a devastating famine in Bangladesh, set up the Grameen Bank and it went from one $74 loan in 1974 to a $2.5 billion enterprise, spawning more than 3,000 similar micro-credit institutions in 50 countries and reaching over 133 million clients, he taught us a lesson in scalability. Alternatively, contrast Toyota's laudable but premium-priced hybrid Prius for the rich and eco-conscious with Tata's $2,500 Nano, a cheap and eco-friendly car for the masses. The one is an incremental solution with long-term potential; the other is scalable solution with immediate impact.

Principle 3: Responsiveness (R)

Business has a long track record of responsiveness to community needs – witness generations of philanthropy and heart-warming generosity following disasters like 9/11 or the Sichuan earthquake. But this is responsiveness on their own terms, responsiveness when giving is easy and cheque-writing does nothing to upset their commercial apple cart. However, the severity of the global problems we face demands that companies go much further. CSR 2.0 requires uncomfortable, transformative responsiveness, which questions whether the industry, or the business model itself, is part of the solution or part of the problem.

When it became clear that climate change posed a serious challenge to the sustainability of the fossil fuel industry, all the major oil companies formed the Global Climate Coalition, a lobby group explicitly designed to discredit and deny the science of climate change and the main international policy response, the Kyoto Protocol. In typical CSR 1.0 style, these same companies were simultaneously making hollow claims about their CSR credentials. By contrast, the Prince of Wales's Corporate Leaders Group on Climate Change has, since 2005, been lobbying for bolder UK, EU and international legislation on climate change, accepting that carbon emission reductions of between 50 and 85% will be needed by 2050.

CSR 2.0 responsiveness also means greater transparency, not only through reporting mechanisms like the Global Reporting Initiative and Carbon Disclosure Project, but also by sharing critical intellectual resources. The Eco-Patent Commons, set up by the World Business Council for Sustainable Development to make technology patents available, without royalty, to help reduce waste, pollution, global warming and energy demands, is one such step in the right direction. Another is the donor exchange platforms that have begun to proliferate, allowing individual and corporate donors to connect directly with beneficiaries via the web, thereby tapping 'the long tail of CSR' (this is a reference to *The Long Tail*, by Chris Anderson, as it might apply to CSR).

Principle 4: Duality (2)

Much of the debate on CSR in the past has dwelt in a polarised world of 'either/or' – either your company is responsible or it isn't; either you support genetically modified organisms or you don't; either you make life-saving drugs available for free or you don't. This fails to recognise that most CSR issues manifest as dilemmas, rather than easy choices. In a complex, interconnected CSR 2.0 world, companies (and their critics) will have to become far more sophisticated in understanding local contexts and the appropriate local solutions they demand, without forsaking universal principles.

For example, a few years ago, BHP Billiton was vexed by their relatively poor performance on the (then) Business in the Environment (BiE) Index, run by UK charity Business in the Community. Further analysis showed that the company had been marked down for their high energy use and relative energy inefficiency. Fair enough – or was it? Most of BHP Billiton's operations were, at that time, based in southern Africa, home to some of the world's cheapest electricity. No wonder this was not a high priority. What was a priority, however, was controlling malaria in the community, where they had made a huge positive impact. But the BiE Index didn't have any rating questions on malaria, so this was ignored. Instead, it demonstrated a typical, Western-driven, one-size-fits-all CSR 1.0 approach (The index has subsequently been reformed and now runs as a more integrated Corporate Responsibility Index – see www.bitc.org.uk)

Carroll's CSR pyramid has already been mentioned, but in a sugar farming co-operative in Guatemala, they have their own CSR pyramid – economic responsibility is still the platform, but rather than legal, ethical and philanthropic dimensions, their pyramid includes responsibility to the family (of employees), the community and policy engagement. Clearly, both Carroll's pyramid and the Guatemala pyramid are helpful in their own appropriate context. Hence, CSR 2.0 replaces 'either/or' with 'both/and' thinking – both SA8000 and the Chinese national labour standard have their role to play; both premium branded and cheap generic drugs have a place in the solution to global health issues. CSR 2.0 is a search for the Chinese concept of a harmonious society, which implies a dynamic yet productive tension of opposites – a *Tai Chi* of CSR, balancing *yin* and *yang*.

Principle 5: Circularity (0)

The reason CSR 1.0 has failed is not through lack of good intent, nor even through lack of effort. The old CSR has failed because our global economic system is based on a fundamentally flawed design. For all the miraculous energy unleashed by Adam Smith's 'invisible hand' of the free market, our modern capitalist system is faulty at its very core. Simply put, it is conceived as an abstract system without limits. As far back as the 1960s, pioneering economist Kenneth Boulding called this a 'cowboy economy', where endless frontiers imply no limits on resource consumption or waste disposal. By contrast, he argued, we need to design a 'spaceship economy', where there is no 'away'; everything is engineered to constantly recycle.

In the 1990s, in *The Ecology of Commerce*, Paul Hawken translated these ideas into three basic rules for sustainability: waste equals food; nature runs off current solar income; and nature depends on diversity. He also proposed replacing our product-sales economy with a service-lease model, famously using the example of Interface 'Evergreen' carpets that are leased and constantly replaced and recycled. William McDonough and Michael Braungart (2002) extended this thinking in their 'cradle to cradle' industrial model. Cradle to cradle is not only about closing the loop on production, but about designing for 'good', rather than the CSR 1.0 modus operandi of 'less bad'.

Hence, CSR 2.0 circularity would create buildings that, like trees, produce more energy than they consume and purify their own waste water; or factories that produce drinking water as effluent; or products that decompose and become food and nutrients; or materials that can feed into industrial cycles as high-quality raw materials for new products. Circularity needn't only apply to the environment. Business should be constantly feeding and replenishing its social and human capital, not only through education and training, but also by nourishing community and employee well-being. CSR 2.0 raises the importance of meaning in work and life to equal status alongside ecological integrity and financial viability.

Shapeshifting: from CSR 1.0 to CSR 2.0

Even revolutions involve a transition, so what might we expect to see as markers along the transformational road? Table 21.2 summarises some of the shifts in principles between the CSR 1.0 and CSR 2.0. It can be seen that paternalistic relationships between companies and the community based on philanthropy give way to more equal partnerships. Defensive, minimalist responses to social and environmental issues are replaced with proactive strategies and investment in growing responsibility markets, such as clean technology. Reputation-conscious PR approaches to CSR are no longer credible and so companies are judged on actual social, environmental and ethical performance (are things getting better on the ground in absolute, cumulative terms?).

Although CSR specialists still have a role to play, each dimension of CSR 2.0 performance is embedded and integrated into the core operations of companies. Standardised approaches remain useful as guides to

Table 21.2 Shifting CSR principles

CSR 1.0	CSR 2.0
Paternalistic	Collaborative
Risk-based	Reward-based
Image-driven	Performance-driven
Specialised	Integrated
Standardised	Diversified
Marginal	Scalable
Western	Global

Table 21.3 Shifting CSR practices

CSR 1.0	CSR 2.0
Premium markets	Base of the pyramid markets
Charity projects	Social enterprise
CSR indexes	CSR ratings
CSR departments	CSR incentives
Ethical consumerism	Choice editing
Product liability	Service agreements
CSR reporting cycles	CSR data streams
Stakeholder groups	Social networks
Process standards	Performance standards

consensus, but CSR finds diversified expression and implementation at very local levels. CSR solutions, including responsible products and services, go from niche 'nice to haves' to mass-market 'must haves'. And the whole concept of CSR loses its Western conceptual and operational dominance, giving way to a more culturally diverse and internationally applied concept. How might these shifting principles manifest as CSR practices? Table 21.3 summarises some key changes to the way in which CSR will be visibly operationalised.

CSR will no longer manifest as luxury products and services (as with current green and fairtrade options), but as affordable solutions for those who most need quality-of-life improvements. Investment in self-sustaining social enterprises will be favoured over cheque-book charity. CSR indices, which rank the same large companies over and over (often revealing contradictions between indices) will make way for CSR rating systems, which turn social, environmental, ethical and economic performance into corporate scores (A+, B–, etc., not dissimilar to credit ratings), which analysts and others can usefully employ to compare and integrate into their decision-making.

Reliance on CSR departments will disappear or disperse, as performance across responsibility and sustainability dimensions are increasingly built into corporate performance appraisal and market incentive systems. Self-selecting ethical consumers will become irrelevant, as CSR 2.0 companies begin to choice-edit, i.e. cease offering implicitly 'less ethical' product ranges, thus allowing guilt-free shopping. Post-use liability for products will become obsolete, as the service-lease and take-back economy goes mainstream. Annual CSR reporting will be replaced by online, real-time CSR performance data flows. Feeding into these live communications will be Web 2.0 connected social networks, instead of periodic meetings of rather cumbersome stakeholder panels. And typical CSR 1.0 management systems standards like ISO 14001 will be less credible than new performance standards, such as those emerging in climate change, which set absolute limits and thresholds.

CSR 2.0: the new DNA of business

All of these visions of the future imply such a radical shift from the current model of CSR that they beg the question: do we need a new model of CSR? Certainly, Carroll's enduring CSR pyramid, with its Western cultural assumptions, static design and wholesale omission of environmental issues, must be regarded as no longer fit for purpose. Even the emphasis on 'social' in corporate social responsibility implies a rather limited view of the agenda. So what might a new model look like?

The CSR 2.0 model proposes that we keep the acronym, but rebalance the scales, so to speak. Hence, CSR comes to stand for 'corporate sustainability and responsibility'. This change acknowledges that 'sustainability' (with roots in the environmental movement) and 'responsibility' (with roots in the social activist movement) are really the two main games in town. A cursory look at companies' non-financial reports will rapidly confirm this – they are mostly either corporate sustainability or corporate responsibility reports.

However, CSR 2.0 also proposes a new interpretation on these terms. Like two intertwined strands of DNA, sustainability and responsibility can be

Figure 21.1 Corporate sustainability and responsibility (the new CSR).

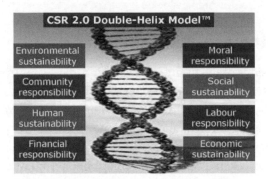

Figure 21.2 The DNA of CSR 2.0 (double-helix model).

thought of as different, yet complementary, elements of CSR. Hence, as illustrated in Figure 21.1, sustainability can be conceived as the destination – the challenges, vision, strategy and goals, i.e. what we are aiming for – while responsibility is more about the journey – solutions, responses, management and actions, i.e. how we get there.

The DNA of CSR 2.0 (Figure 21.2) can be conceived as spiralling, interconnected, non-hierarchical levels, representing economic, human, social and environmental systems, each with a twinned sustainability/responsibility manifestation: economic sustainability and financial responsibility; human sustainability and labour responsibility; social sustainability and community responsibility; and environmental sustainability and moral responsibility.

Conclusion: the purpose of business

Ultimately, CSR 2.0 comes down to one thing: clarification and reorientation of the purpose of business. It is completely incorrect to believe that the purpose of business is to be profitable or to serve shareholders. These are simply means to an end. Ultimately, the purpose of business is to serve society, through the provision of safe, high-quality products and services that enhance our well-being, without eroding our ecological and community life-support systems. As David Packard, co-founder of Hewlett-Packard, wisely put it:

> Why are we here? Many people assume, wrongly, that a company exists solely to make money. People get together and exist as a company so that they are able to accomplish something collectively that they could not accomplish separately – they make a contribution to society.

Making a positive contribution to society is the essence of CSR 2.0 – not just as a marginal afterthought, but as a way of doing business. This is not about bailing out the Titanic with a teaspoon – which is the current effect of CSR 1.0 – but turning the whole ship around. CSR 2.0 is about designing and adopting an inherently sustainable and responsible business model, supported by a reformed financial and economic system that makes creating a better world the easiest, most natural and rewarding thing to do. CSR is dead! Long live CSR!

References

Baken, J. (2004) *The Corporation: The Pathological Pursuit of Profit and Power*, Constable, Vancouver.

Bowen, H.R. (1953) *Social Responsibilities of the Businessman*, Harper & Row, New York.

Carroll, A.B. (1979) A three-dimensional conceptual model of corporate social performance, *Academy of Management Review*, **4**: 497–505.

Carroll, A.B. (2008) A history of corporate social responsibility. In: Crane, A., McWilliams, A., Matten, D., Moon, J. and Siegel, D.S. (eds), *The Oxford Handbook of Corporate Social Responsibility*, OUP, Oxford.

Carson, R. (1962) *Silent Spring*, Houghton Mifflin, New York.

Nader, R. (1965) *Unsafe At Any Speed: The Designed-In Dangers of the American Automobile*, Grossman Publishers, New York.

McDonough, W. and Braungart, M. (2002) *Cradle to Cradle: Remaking the Way We Make Things*, North Point Press.

Visser, W. and McIntosh, A. (1998) A short review of the historical critique of usury, *Accounting, Business & Financial History*, **8**(2): 175–189.

Websites

CSR International – www.csrinternational.org

Wayne Visser – www.waynevisser.com

Further reading

AccountAbility (2008) *AA1000 AccountAbility Principles Standard*, AccountAbility.

AccountAbility (2008) *AA1000 Assurance Standard*, AccountAbility.

Acre Resources, Acona and Ethical Performance (2009) *The CSR Salary Survey*. Acre Resources, Acona and Ethical Performance.

Blowfield, M. and Frynas, J.G. (2005) Setting new agendas: critical perspectives on corporate social responsibility in the developing world, *International Affairs*, **81**(3): 499–513.

Blumberg, M. and Scheubel, V. (2007) *Hand in Hand: Corporate Volunteering als Instrument der Organisationsentwicklung in Deutschland*, Bremen: Brands & Values GmbH.

Broekhoff, D. (2007) *Linking Markets for GHG Reductions: Can It Be Done?* International Network for Environmental Compliance and Enforcement. Online: http://www.inece.org/emissions/dublin/Broekhoff.pdf.

Business for Social Responsibility (2007) *Getting Carbon Offsets Right: A Business Brief on Engaging Offset Providers*. Online: http://www.bsr.org/reports/BSR_Getting-Carbon-Offsets-Right.pdf.

Capoor, K. and Ambrosi, P. (2007) *State and Trends of the Carbon Market 2007*, World Bank, Washington, DC.

Carbon Life (2009). *Carbon Offsetting Explained*. Online: http://www.carbonlifeltd.com/carbonoffsettingexplained.html.

Chivers, D. (2007) *The Companies Act 2006: Directors' Duties Guidance*, The Corporate Responsibility (CORE) Coalition.

Corporate Register (2008) *Assure View. The CSR Assurance Statement Report*, Corporate Register.

Crane, A. and Matten, D. (2003). *Business Ethics*, Oxford University Press.

Diehl, B. and Conrad, C. (2008) Corporate volunteering – chance für das Talentmanagement, *Wirtschaftspsychologie Aktuell*, **3**: 57–60.

Graafland, J. and Smid, H. (2004) Reputation, corporate social responsibility and market regulation, *Tijdschrift voor Economie en Management*, **XLIX**(2): 271–308.

Gray, K. (2009) *ROI: Companies See Financial Benefit in CSR Programs*. Online: http://www.shrm.org/hrdisciplines/ethics/articles/Pages/ROICompaniesSeeFinancial BenefitinCSRPrograms.aspx.

Gunther, M. (2008) *Cooking up Carbon Credits*, Fortune Magazine.

Hamilton, K., Bayon, R., Turner, G. and Higgins, D. (2007) *State of the Voluntary Carbon Markets 2007: Picking Up Steam*. Online: http://ecosystemmarketplace.com/documents/ acrobat/StateoftheVoluntaryCarbonMarket18July_Final.pdf.

Henningfeld, J., Pohl, M. and Tolhurst, N. (eds) (2006) *The ICCA Handbook on Corporate Social Responsibility*, John Wiley & Sons, Chichester, UK.

Hohnen, P. (2007) *Corporate Social Responsibility; An Implementation Guide for Business*, in Potts, J. (ed.), Winnipeg: International Institute for Sustainable Development (IISD).

International Auditing and Assurance Standards Board (2005) *ISAE3000, International Standard on Assurance Engagements 3000*, International Auditing and Assurance Standards Board.

Intergovernmental Panel on Climate Change (2007) *Climate Change 2007: Synthesis Report*. Online: www.ipcc.ch/pdf/assessment-report/ar4/syr/ar4_syr.pdf.

Jamali, D. (2007) The case for strategic corporate social responsibility in developing countries, *Business and Society Review*, **112**: 1–27.

Koestoer, Y.T. (2007) *Corporate Social Responsibility in Indonesia*. Online: http://www.asean-foundation.org/seminar/gcsg/papers/Yanti%20Koestoer%20%20Paper%202007.pdf.

Lewis, R.E. and Heckman, R.J. (2006) Talent management: A critical review, *Human Resource Management Review*, **16**: 139–154.

Lockwood, N.R. (2006) Talent management: driver for organizational success, *SHRM Research Quarterly*, June: 1–11.

Lyon, T. and Maxwell, J. (2007) *Corporate Social Responsibility and the Environment: A Theoretical Perspective*, Kelley School of Business, Indiana.

Matura, B.O. (2004) *Profit Maximization and Business Social Responsibility Objectives in Business Management. Shareholder Value and the Common Good*, Don Bosco Printing Press, Nairobi.

Mendoza, A.M.E. and Torralba, C.T. (2004) *The Challenge of Business: Going beyond Wealth Maximization and Profit Maximization. Shareholder Value and the Common Good*, Don Bosco Printing Press, Nairobi.

Okafor, E., Hassan, A. and Doyin-Hassan, A. (2008) Environmental issues and corporate social responsibility: the Nigeria experience, *Journal of Human Ecology*, **23**(2): 101–107.

Opondo, M. (2005) *Emerging Corporate Social Responsibility in Kenya's Cut Flower Industry*. Online: http://www.unisa.ac.za/contents/colleges/col_econ_man_science/ccc/docs/Opondo.pdf.

Panse, S. (2006) *Ubuntu – African Philosophy*. Online: http://www.buzzle.com/editorials/7-22-2006-103206.asp.

Perry, B. and Gregory, L. (2009) The European panorama: directors' economic and social responsibilities, *International Company and Commercial Law Review*, **25**.

Pinter, A. (2008) Corporate volunteering als Instrument zur strategischen Implementierung von Corporate Social Responsibility. In: Müller, M. and Schaltegger, S. (eds), *Corporate Social Responsibility Trend oder Modeerscheinung?* Oekom Verlag.

Schöffmann, D. (ed.) (2003) *Wenn alle Gewinnen – Bürgerschaftliches Engagement von Unternehmen*, Herausgeber: Körber-Stiftung.

Scott, W.R. (1992) *Organisations: Rational, Natural and Open System*, Prentice Hall, Englewood Cliffs, NJ, USA.

Sheikh, P.A., Gorte, R.W. and Sidener, J. (2008) *Climate Change and International Deforestation: Legislative Analysis*, Congressional Research Service (CRS) Reports and Issue Briefs, Congressional Research Service.

Sussman, F.G. and Randall Freed, J. (2008) *Adapting to Climate Change: A Business Approach*, The Pew Center on Global Climate Change.

Sturdivant, F.D. (1985) *Business and Society: A Managerial Approach*, 3rd edn, Richard D Irwin Inc., Homewood, IL, USA.

SustainAbility (2004) *Gearing Up: From Corporate Responsibility to Good Governance and Scaleable Solutions*, Sustainability, London.

The Netherlands Environmental Assessment Agency (2009) Press release: *Global CO_2 Emissions: annual increase halved in 2008*.

The Department of Energy and Climate Change (DECC) (2009) *Carbon Offsetting Explained: The UK Government's Quality Assurance Scheme for Carbon Offsetting*. Available: http://offsetting.decc.gov.uk/cms/offsetting-explained-4/.

United Nations Framework Convention on Climate Change (UNFCC) (1997) *Kyoto Protocol to the United Nations Framework Convention on Climate Change*, UNFCC.

United Nations Population Fund (UNFPA) (2001) *The State of World Population 2001*, UNFPA.

United Nations Industrial Development Organization (UNIDO) (2002) *Corporate Social Responsibility: Implications to Small and Medium Scale Enterprises in Developing Countries*, UNIDO, Vienna.

Valentino B (2007) *MBA Toolkit For CSR: Supply Chain Management And Corporate Social Responsibility*. Online: http://www.chinacsr.com/en/2007/12/12/1938-mba-toolkit-for-csr-supply-chain-management-and-corporate-social-responsibility/.

Verdantix (2008) *Green Quadrant: How to Select a CSR Assurance Provider*, Verdantix.

Visser, W. (2005) *Corporate Social Responsibility in Developing Countries*. Online: www.waynevisser.com.

Visser, W. (2008) *CSR in Developing Countries: Distinctive Characteristics*. Online: http://csrinternational.blogspot.com/2008/10/csr-in-developing-countries.html.

Visser, W., Matten, D., Pohl, M. and Tolhurst, N. (2007). *The A to Z of Corporate Social Responsibility: The Complete Reference of Concepts, Codes and Organisations*, John Wiley & Sons, Chichester, UK.

World Business Council for Sustainable Development (1999) *Corporate Social Responsibility. Meeting Changing Expectations*. Online: http://www.wbcsd.org/DocRoot/hbdf19Txhm k3kDxBQDWW/CSRmeeting.pdf.

Websites

The Clean Development Mechanism (CDM) – http://cdm.unfccc.int/index.html.

The CarbonNeutral Company – www.carbonneutral.com.

Carbon Footprint Ltd – www.carbonfootprint.com.

Carbon Catalog – www.carboncatalog.org.

PowerTree Carbon Company – www.powertreecarboncompany.com.

The World Future Council – www.worldfuturecouncil.org/startseite.html.

Index

Index compiled by Terry Halliday